Docker in Action

Docker in Action

JEFF NICKOLOFF

MANNING

SHELTER ISLAND

For online information and ordering of this and other Manning books, please visit
www.manning.com. The publisher offers discounts on this book when ordered in quantity.
For more information, please contact

> Special Sales Department
> Manning Publications Co.
> 20 Baldwin Road
> PO Box 761
> Shelter Island, NY 11964
> Email: orders@manning.com

Manning Publications Co.
20 Baldwin Road
PO Box 761
Shelter Island, NY 11964

Development editor:	Cynthia Kane
Technical development editor:	Robert Wenner
Technical proofreader:	Niek Palm
Copyeditor:	Linda Recktenwald
Proofreader:	Corbin Collins
Typesetter:	Marija Tudor
Cover designer:	Marija Tudor

ISBN: 9781633430235
Printed in the United States of America
1 2 3 4 5 6 7 8 9 10 – EBM – 21 20 19 18 17 16

contents

foreword

I heard about Docker for the first time in a YouTube video that was posted to Hacker News from PyCon 2013. In his five-minute lightning talk entitled "The Future of Linux Containers," the creator of Docker, Solomon Hykes, was unveiling the future of how we ship and run software to the public—not just in Linux, but on nearly all platforms and architectures. Although he was abruptly silenced at the five-minute mark, it was clear to me that this technique of running Linux applications in sandboxed environments, with its user-friendly command-line tool and unique concepts such as image layering, was going to change a lot of things.

Docker vastly changed many software development and operations paradigms all at once. The ways we architect, develop, ship, and run software before and after Docker are vastly different. Although Docker does not prescribe a certain recipe, it forces people to think in terms of microservices and immutable infrastructure.

Once Docker was more widely adopted, and as people started to investigate the low-level technologies utilized by Docker, it became clearer that the secret to Docker's success was not the technology itself, but the human-friendly interface, APIs, and ecosystem around the project.

Many big companies such as Google, Microsoft, and IBM have gathered around the Docker project and worked together to make it even better rather than creating a competitor to it. In fact, companies like Microsoft, Joyent, Intel, and VMware have swapped out Docker's Linux containers implementation but kept the novel Docker command-line interface for their own container offerings. In only two years, many new companies have sprouted up to enhance the developer experience and fill in the blanks of the Docker ecosystem—the sign of a healthy and enthusiastic community around Docker.

For my own part, I began helping Microsoft adopt and contribute to Docker by publishing Microsoft's first official Docker image for cross-platform ASP.NET. My next contribution was porting the Docker command-line interface to Windows. This project helped many Windows developers become familiar with Docker and laid the foundation for Microsoft's long journey of contributing to the Docker project. The Windows porting project also skyrocketed me to the top Docker contributor spot for more than two months. Later on, we contributed many other bits and pieces to make sure Docker became a first-class citizen on Microsoft's Azure cloud offering. Our next big step is Windows Containers, a new feature in Windows Server 2016, which is fully integrated with Docker.

It is exciting to know that we're still at the start of the containers revolution. The scene moves incredibly fast, as new technologies and open source tools emerge daily. Everything we take for granted today can and will change in the next few months. This is an area where innovators and the greatest minds of our industry are collaborating to build tools of mass innovation and make the problem of shipping and running software at scale one less thing to worry about for the rest of the software industry.

Through his many online articles about Docker and microservices, Jeff Nickoloff has shown himself to be the champion of the nascent Docker community. His well-written, thorough explanations of some very technical topics have allowed developers to quickly learn and use the Docker ecosystem for all its benefits, and, equally important, he notes its drawbacks. In this book, he goes from zero to Docker, shows practices of deploying Docker in production, and demonstrates many features of Docker with comprehensive descriptions and comparisons of various ways of achieving the same task.

While reading this book, not only will you learn how to use Docker effectively, you'll also grasp how it works, how each detailed feature of Docker is meant to be used, and the best practices concocted for using Docker in production. I personally had many "Oh, that's what this feature is for" moments while reading this book. Although writing a book about a technology that moves at an incredible pace is very much like trying to paint a picture of a car moving at 60 mph, Jeff has done a fantastic job at both covering cutting-edge features in Docker and laying a solid foundation throughout the book. This foundation builds an appreciation and understanding for the philosophy of containers and microservices that is unlikely to change, no matter what Docker looks like in the coming months and years.

I hope you find this book as enjoyable and educational as I did.

AHMET ALP BALKAN
OPEN SOURCE SOFTWARE ENGINEER AT MICROSOFT,
DOCKER CONTRIBUTOR

preface

In 2011, I started working at Amazon.com. In that first week my life was changed as I learned how to use their internal build, dependency modeling, and deployment tooling. This was the kind of automated management I had always known was possible but had never seen. I was coming from a team that would deploy quarterly and take 10 hours to do so. At Amazon I was watching rolling deployments push changes I had made earlier that day to hundreds of machines spread all over the globe. If big tech firms had an engineering advantage over the rest of the corporate landscape, this was it.

Early in 2013, I wanted to work with Graphite (a metrics collection and graphing suite). One day I sat down to install the software and start integrating a personal project. At this point I had several years of experience working with open source applications, but few were as dependent on such large swaths of the Python ecosystem. The installation instructions were long and murky. Over the next several hours, I discovered many undocumented installation steps. These were things that might have been more obvious to a person with deeper Python ecosystem knowledge. After pouring over several installation guides, reading through configuration files, and fighting an epic battle through the deepest parts of dependency hell, I threw in the towel.

Those had been some of the least inspiring hours of my life. I wanted nothing to do with the project. To make matters worse, I had altered my environment in a way that was incompatible with other software that I use regularly. Reverting those changes took an embarrassingly long time.

I distinctly remember sitting at my desk one day in May that year. I was between tasks when I decided to check Hacker News for new ways to grow my skillset. Articles about a technology called Docker had made the front page a few times that week. That evening I decided to check it out. I hit the site and had the software installed within a few minutes. I was running Ubuntu on my desktop at home, and Docker only had two dependencies: LXC and the Linux kernel itself.

Like everyone else, I kicked the tires with a "Hello, World" example, but learned little. Next I fired up Memcached. It was downloaded and running in under a minute. Then I started WordPress, which came bundled with its own MySQL server. I pulled a couple different Java images, and then Python images. Then my mind flashed back to that terrible day with Graphite. I popped over to the Docker Index (this was before Docker Hub) and did a quick search.

The results came back, and there it was. Some random user had created a Graphite image. I pulled it down and created a new container. It was running. A simple but fully configured Graphite server was running on my machine. I had accomplished in less than a minute of download time what I had failed to do with several hours a few months earlier. Docker was able to demonstrate value with the simplest of examples and minimum effort. I was sold.

Over the next week, I tried the patience of a close friend by struggling to direct our conversations toward Docker and containers. I explained how package management was nice, but enforcing file system isolation as a default solved several management problems. I rattled on about resource efficiency and provisioning latency. I repeated this conversation with several other colleagues and fumbled through the container story. Everyone had the same set of tired questions, "Oh, it's like virtualization?" and "Why do I need this if I have virtual machines?" The more questions people asked, the more I wanted to know. Based on the popularity of the project, this is a story shared by many.

I began including sessions about Docker when I spoke publicly. In 2013 and 2014, only a few people had heard of Docker, and even fewer had actually tried the software. For the most part, the crowds consisted of a few skeptical system administrator types and a substantial number of excited developers. People reacted in a multitude of ways. Some were pure rejectionists who clearly preferred the status quo. Others could see problems that they experienced daily solved in a matter of moments. Those people reacted with an excitement similar to mine.

In the summer of 2014, an associate publisher with Manning called me to talk about Docker. After a bit more than an hour on the phone he asked me if there was enough content there for a book. I suggested that there was enough for a few books. He asked me if I was interested in writing it, and I became more excited than I had been for some time. That fall I left Amazon.com and started work on *Docker in Action*.

Today, I'm sitting in front of the finished manuscript. My goal in writing this book was to create something that would help people of mixed backgrounds get up to speed on Docker as quickly as possible, but in such a way that they understand the underlying mechanisms. The hope is that with that knowledge, readers can understand how Docker has been applied to certain problems, and how they might apply it in their own use-cases.

acknowledgments

I believe that I've spent enough of my life doing easy things. Before I began this book, I knew that writing it would require a high degree of discipline and an unending stream of motivation. I was not disappointed.

First I'd like to acknowledge Manning Publications for the opportunity to publish this work. I'd like to thank Ahmet Alp Baken for writing a foreword to the book, as well as Niek Palm for giving the whole manuscript a technical proofread. Many others reviewed the manuscript and offered comments at various stages of development, including Robert Wenner, Jean-Pol Landrain, John Guthrie, Benoît Benedetti, Thomas Peklak, Jeremy Gailor, Fernando Fraga Rodrigues, Gregor Zurowski, Peter Sellars, Mike Shepard, Peter Krey, Fernando Kobayashi, and Edward Kuns.

In this and most other difficult ventures, success is dependent on the collective contributions of a support network. I wouldn't be here today without contributions from the following:

- Portia Dean, for her partnership and support over the last year. Portia, you are my partner, my righteous and stubborn center. Without you I would have lost my mind somewhere in this maze of a year. I've loved the adventure and can't wait for what comes next.
- My parents, Kathy and Jeff Nickoloff, Sr., for supporting my technical curiosity from a young age and cultivating my strong will.
- Neil Fritz, for hacking out projects with me over the last 15 years and always being open to getting Slices Pizza.
- Andy Will and the strong engineers of PHX2, for welcoming me to Amazon and always raising our technical bar. Working with them was an education in itself.
- Nick Ciubotariu, for fighting the good fight and raising the bar for technical leadership.

- Cartel Coffee Lab, I spent more time in your HQ than I did my own house this year. You have one of the best roasts in the world. People in San Francisco are missing out.

Finally, I want to acknowledge my like-minded friends around the world who've shared in some part of this journey through learning, sharing, challenging, or just listening. #nogui

about this book

Docker in Action's purpose is to introduce developers, system administrators, and other computer users of a mixed skillset to the Docker project and Linux container concepts. Both Docker and Linux are open source projects with a wealth of online documentation, but getting started with either can be a daunting task.

Docker is one of the fastest-growing open source projects ever, and the ecosystem that has grown around it is evolving at a similar pace. For these reasons, this book focuses on the Docker toolset exclusively. This restriction of scope should both help the material age well and help readers understand how to apply Docker features to their specific use-cases. Readers will be prepared to tackle bigger problems and explore the ecosystem once they develop a solid grasp of the fundamentals covered in this book.

Roadmap

This book is split into three parts.

Part 1 introduces Docker and container features. Reading it will help you understand how to install and uninstall software distributed with Docker. You'll learn how to run, manage, and link different kinds of software in different container configurations. Part 1 covers the basic skillset that every Docker user will need.

Part 2 is focused on packaging and distributing software with Docker. It covers the underlying mechanics of Docker images, nuances in file sizes, and a survey of different packaging and distribution methods. This part wraps up with a deep dive into the Docker Distribution project.

Part 3 explores multi-container projects and multi-host environments. This includes coverage of the Docker Compose, Machine, and Swarm projects. These chapters walk you through building and deploying multiple real world examples that should closely resemble large-scale server software you'd find in the wild.

Code conventions and downloads

This book is about a multi-purpose tool, and so there is very little "code" included in the book. In its place are hundreds of shell commands and configuration files. These are typically provided in POSIX-compliant syntax. Notes for Windows users are provided where Docker exposes some Windows-specific features. Care was taken to break up commands into multiple lines in order to improve readability or clarify annotations. Referenced repositories are available on Docker Hub (https://hub.docker.com/u/dockerinaction/) with sources hosted on GitHub (https://github.com/dockerinaction). No prior knowledge of Docker Hub or GitHub is required to run the examples.

This book uses several open source projects to both demonstrate various features of Docker and help the reader shift software-management paradigms. No single software "stack" or family is highlighted other than Docker itself. Working through the examples, the reader will use tools such as WordPress, Elasticsearch, Postgres, shell scripts, Netcat, Flask, JavaScript, NGINX, and Java. The sole commonality is a dependency on the Linux kernel.

About the author

Jeff Nickoloff builds large-scale services, writes about technology, and helps people achieve their product goals. He has done these things at Amazon.com, Limelight Networks, and Arizona State University. After leaving Amazon in 2014, he founded a consulting company and focused on delivering tools, training, and best practices for Fortune 100 companies and startups alike. If you'd like to chat or work together, you can find him at http://allingeek.com, or on Twitter as @allingeek.

Author Online

Purchase of *Docker in Action* includes free access to a private web forum run by Manning Publications where you can make comments about the book, ask technical questions, and receive help from the author and from other users. To access the forum and subscribe to it, point your web browser to www.manning.com/books/docker-in-action. This page provides information on how to get on the forum once you're registered, what kind of help is available, and the rules of conduct on the forum.

Manning's commitment to our readers is to provide a venue where a meaningful dialog between individual readers and between readers and the author can take place. It is not a commitment to any specific amount of participation on the part of the author, whose contribution to the Author Online remains voluntary (and unpaid). We suggest you try asking the author some challenging questions lest his interest stray! The Author Online forum and the archives of previous discussions will be accessible from the publisher's website as long as the book is in print.

about the cover illustration

The figure on the cover of *Docker in Action* is captioned "The Angler." The illustration is taken from a nineteenth-century collection of works by many artists, edited by Louis Curmer and published in Paris in 1841. The title of the collection is *Les Français peints par eux-mêmes,* which translates as *The French People Painted by Themselves.* Each illustration is finely drawn and colored by hand and the rich variety of drawings in the collection reminds us vividly of how culturally apart the world's regions, towns, villages, and neighborhoods were just 200 years ago. Isolated from each other, people spoke different dialects and languages. In the streets or in the countryside, it was easy to identify where they lived and what their trade or station in life was just by their dress.

Dress codes have changed since then and the diversity by region, so rich at the time, has faded away. It is now hard to tell apart the inhabitants of different continents, let alone different towns or regions. Perhaps we have traded cultural diversity for a more varied personal life—certainly for a more varied and fast-paced technological life.

At a time when it is hard to tell one computer book from another, Manning celebrates the inventiveness and initiative of the computer business with book covers based on the rich diversity of regional life of two centuries ago, brought back to life by pictures from collections such as this one.

## Part 1

Keeping a Tidy Computer

Isolation is a core concept to so many computing patterns, resource management strategies, and general accounting practices that it is difficult to even begin compiling a list. Someone who learns how Linux containers provide isolation for running programs and how to use Docker to control that isolation can accomplish amazing feats of reuse, resource efficiency, and system simplification.

A thorough understanding of the material in this part is a solid foundation for every reader to take on the rapidly growing Docker and container ecosystem. Like the Docker tool set itself, the pieces covered here provide building blocks to solving larger problems. For that reason, I suggest that you try to resist the urge to skip ahead. It may take some time to get to the specific question that is on your mind, but I'm confident that you'll have more than a few revelations along the way.

Welcome to Docker 1

This chapter covers

- What Docker is
- An introduction to containers
- How Docker addresses software problems that most people tolerate
- When, where, and why you should use Docker
- Example: "Hello, World"

If you're anything like me, you prefer to do only what is necessary to accomplish an unpleasant or mundane task. It's likely that you'd prefer tools that are simple to use to great effect over those that are complex or time-consuming. If I'm right, then I think you'll be interested in learning about Docker.

Suppose you like to try out new Linux software but are worried about running something malicious. Running that software with Docker is a great first step in protecting your computer because Docker helps even the most basic software users take advantage of powerful security tools.

If you're a system administrator, making Docker the cornerstone of your software management toolset will save time and let you focus on high-value activities because Docker minimizes the time that you'll spend doing mundane tasks.

3

If you write software, distributing your software with Docker will make it easier for your users to install and run it. Writing your software in a Docker-wrapped development environment will save you time configuring or sharing that environment, because from the perspective of your software, every environment is the same.

Suppose you own or manage large-scale systems or data centers. Creating build, test, and deployment pipelines is simplified using Docker because moving any software through such a pipeline is identical to moving any other software through.

Launched in March 2013, Docker works with your operating system to package, ship, and run software. You can think of Docker as a software logistics provider that will save you time and let you focus on high-value activities. You can use Docker with network applications like web servers, databases, and mail servers and with terminal applications like text editors, compilers, network analysis tools, and scripts; in some cases it's even used to run GUI applications like web browsers and productivity software.

> **NOT JUST LINUX**   Docker is Linux software but works well on most operating systems.

Docker isn't a programming language, and it isn't a framework for building software. Docker is a tool that helps solve common problems like installing, removing, upgrading, distributing, trusting, and managing software. It's open source Linux software, which means that anyone can contribute to it, and it has benefited from a variety of perspectives. It's common for companies to sponsor the development of open source projects. In this case, Docker Inc. is the primary sponsor. You can find out more about Docker Inc. at https://docker.com/company/.

1.1   What is Docker?

Docker is a command-line program, a background daemon, and a set of remote services that take a logistical approach to solving common software problems and simplifying your experience installing, running, publishing, and removing software. It accomplishes this using a UNIX technology called containers.

1.1.1   Containers

Historically, UNIX-style operating systems have used the term *jail* to describe a modified runtime environment for a program that prevents that program from accessing protected resources. Since 2005, after the release of Sun's Solaris 10 and Solaris Containers, *container* has become the preferred term for such a runtime environment. The goal has expanded from preventing access to protected resources to isolating a process from all resources except where explicitly allowed.

Using containers has been a best practice for a long time. But manually building containers can be challenging and easy to do incorrectly. This challenge has put them out of reach for some, and misconfigured containers have lulled others into a false sense of security. We need a solution to this problem, and Docker helps. Any software run with Docker is run inside a container. Docker uses existing container engines to provide consistent containers built according to best practices. This puts stronger security within reach for everyone.

With Docker, users get containers at a much lower cost. As Docker and its container engines improve, you get the latest and greatest jail features. Instead of keeping up with the rapidly evolving and highly technical world of building strong application jails, you can let Docker handle the bulk of that for you. This will save you a lot of time and money and bring peace of mind.

1.1.2 Containers are not virtualization

Without Docker, businesses typically use hardware virtualization (also known as virtual machines) to provide isolation. Virtual machines provide virtual hardware on which an operating system and other programs can be installed. They take a long time (often minutes) to create and require significant resource overhead because they run a whole copy of an operating system in addition to the software you want to use.

Unlike virtual machines, Docker containers don't use hardware virtualization. Programs running inside Docker containers interface directly with the host's Linux kernel. Because there's no additional layer between the program running inside the container and the computer's operating system, no resources are wasted by running redundant software or simulating virtual hardware. This is an important distinction. Docker is not a virtualization technology. Instead, it helps you use the container technology already built into your operating system.

1.1.3 Running software in containers for isolation

As noted earlier, containers have existed for decades. Docker uses Linux namespaces and cgroups, which have been part of Linux since 2007. Docker doesn't provide the container technology, but it specifically makes it simpler to use. To understand what containers look like on a system, let's first establish a baseline. Figure 1.1 shows a basic example running on a simplified computer system architecture.

Notice that the command-line interface, or CLI, runs in what is called user space memory just like other programs that run on top of the operating system. Ideally,

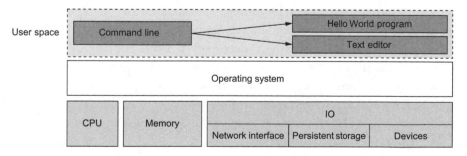

Figure 1.1 A basic computer stack running two programs that were started from the command line

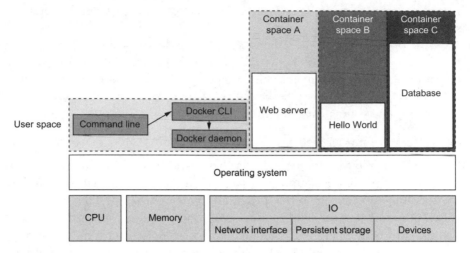

Figure 1.2   Docker running three containers on a basic Linux computer system

programs running in user space can't modify kernel space memory. Broadly speaking, the operating system is the interface between all user programs and the hardware that the computer is running on.

You can see in figure 1.2 that running Docker means running two programs in user space. The first is the Docker daemon. If installed properly, this process should always be running. The second is the Docker CLI. This is the Docker program that users interact with. If you want to start, stop, or install software, you'll issue a command using the Docker program.

Figure 1.2 also shows three running containers. Each is running as a child process of the Docker daemon, wrapped with a container, and the delegate process is running in its own memory subspace of the user space. Programs running inside a container can access only their own memory and resources as scoped by the container.

The containers that Docker builds are isolated with respect to eight aspects. Part 1 of this book covers each of these aspects through an exploration of Docker container features. The specific aspects are as follows:

- *PID namespace*—Process identifiers and capabilities
- *UTS namespace*—Host and domain name
- *MNT namespace*—File system access and structure
- *IPC namespace*—Process communication over shared memory
- *NET namespace*—Network access and structure
- *USR namespace*—User names and identifiers
- chroot()—Controls the location of the file system root
- *cgroups*—Resource protection

Linux namespaces and cgroups take care of containers at runtime. Docker uses another set of technologies to provide containers for files that act like shipping containers.

1.1.4   *Shipping containers*

You can think of a Docker container as a physical shipping container. It's a box where you store and run an application and all of its dependencies. Just as cranes, trucks, trains, and ships can easily work with shipping containers, so can Docker run, copy, and distribute containers with ease. Docker completes the traditional container metaphor by including a way to package and distribute software. The component that fills the shipping container role is called an *image.*

A Docker image is a bundled snapshot of all the files that should be available to a program running inside a container. You can create as many containers from an image as you want. But when you do, containers that were started from the same image don't share changes to their file system. When you distribute software with Docker, you distribute these images, and the receiving computers create containers from them. Images are the shippable units in the Docker ecosystem.

Docker provides a set of infrastructure components that simplify distributing Docker images. These components are *registries* and *indexes.* You can use publicly available infrastructure provided by Docker Inc., other hosting companies, or your own registries and indexes.

1.2   *What problems does Docker solve?*

Using software is complex. Before installation you have to consider what operating system you're using, the resources the software requires, what other software is already installed, and what other software it depends on. You need to decide where it should be installed. Then you need to know how to install it. It's surprising how drastically installation processes vary today. The list of considerations is long and unforgiving. Installing software is at best inconsistent and overcomplicated.

Most computers have more than one application installed and running. And most applications have dependencies on other software. What happens when two or more applications you want to use don't play well together? Disaster. Things are only made more complicated when two or more applications share dependencies:

- What happens if one application needs an upgraded dependency but the other does not?
- What happens when you remove an application? Is it really gone?
- Can you remove old dependencies?
- Can you remember all the changes you had to make to install the software you now want to remove?

The simple truth is that the more software you use, the more difficult it is to manage. Even if you can spend the time and energy required to figure out installing and running applications, how confident can you be about your security? Open and closed source programs release security updates continually, and being aware of all of the issues is often impossible. The more software you run, the greater the risk that it's vulnerable to attack.

All of these issues can be solved with careful accounting, management of resources, and logistics, but those are mundane and unpleasant things to deal with. Your time would be better spent using the software that you're trying to install, upgrade, or publish. The people who built Docker recognized that, and thanks to their hard work you can breeze through the solutions with minimal effort in almost no time at all.

It's possible that most of these issues seem acceptable today. Maybe they feel trivial because you're used to them. After reading how Docker makes these issues approachable, you may notice a shift in your opinion.

1.2.1 *Getting organized*

Without Docker, a computer can end up looking like a junk drawer. Applications have all sorts of dependencies. Some applications depend on specific system libraries for common things like sound, networking, graphics, and so on. Others depend on standard libraries for the language they're written in.

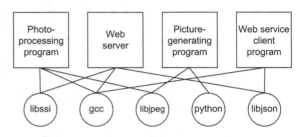

Figure 1.3   **Dependency relationships of example program**

Some depend on other applications, such as how a Java program depends on the Java Virtual Machine or a web application might depend on a database. It's common for a running program to require exclusive access to some scarce resource such as a network connection or a file.

Today, without Docker, applications are spread all over the file system and end up creating a messy web of interactions. Figure 1.3 illustrates how example applications depend on example libraries without Docker.

Docker keeps things organized by isolating everything with containers and images. Figure 1.4 illustrates these same applications and their dependencies running inside

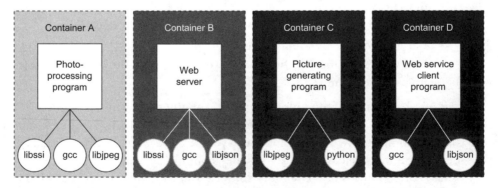

Figure 1.4   **Example programs running inside containers with copies of their dependencies**

containers. With the links broken and each application neatly contained, understanding the system is an approachable task.

1.2.2 *Improving portability*

Another software problem is that an application's dependencies typically include a specific operating system. Portability between operating systems is a major problem for software users. Although it's possible to have compatibility between Linux software and Mac OS X, using that same software on Windows can be more difficult. Doing so can require building whole ported versions of the software. Even that is only possible if suitable replacement dependencies exist for Windows. This represents a major effort for the maintainers of the application and is frequently skipped. Unfortunately for users, a whole wealth of powerful software is too difficult or impossible to use on their system.

At present, Docker runs natively on Linux and comes with a single virtual machine for OS X and Windows environments. This convergence on Linux means that software running in Docker containers need only be written once against a consistent set of dependencies. You might have just thought to yourself, "Wait a minute. You just finished telling me that Docker is better than virtual machines." That's correct, but they are complementary technologies. Using a virtual machine to contain a single program is wasteful. This is especially so when you're running several virtual machines on the same computer. On OS X and Windows, Docker uses a single, small virtual machine to run all the containers. By taking this approach, the overhead of running a virtual machine is fixed while the number of containers can scale up.

This new portability helps users in a few ways. First, it unlocks a whole world of software that was previously inaccessible. Second, it's now feasible to run the same software—exactly the same software—on any system. That means your desktop, your development environment, your company's server, and your company's cloud can all run the same programs. Running consistent environments is important. Doing so helps minimize any learning curve associated with adopting new technologies. It helps software developers better understand the systems that will be running their programs. It means fewer surprises. Third, when software maintainers can focus on writing their programs for a single platform and one set of dependencies, it's a huge time-saver for them and a great win for their customers.

Without Docker or virtual machines, portability is commonly achieved at an individual program level by basing the software on some common tool. For example, Java lets programmers write a single program that will mostly work on several operating systems because the programs rely on a program called a Java Virtual Machine (JVM). Although this is an adequate approach while writing software, other people, at other companies, wrote most of the software we use. For example, if there is a popular web server that I want to use, but it was not written in Java or another similarly portable language, I doubt that the authors would take time to rewrite it for me. In addition to this shortcoming, language interpreters and software libraries are the very things that create dependency problems. Docker improves the portability of every program regardless of the language it was written in, the operating system it was designed for, or the state of the environment where it's running.

1.2.3   *Protecting your computer*

Most of what I've mentioned so far have been problems from the perspective of working with software and the benefits of doing so from outside a container. But containers also protect us from the software running inside a container. There are all sorts of ways that a program might misbehave or present a security risk:

- A program might have been written specifically by an attacker.
- Well-meaning developers could write a program with harmful bugs.
- A program could accidentally do the bidding of an attacker through bugs in its input handling.

Any way you cut it, running software puts the security of your computer at risk. Because running software is the whole point of having a computer, it's prudent to apply the practical risk mitigations.

Like physical jail cells, anything inside a container can only access things that are inside it as well. There are exceptions to this rule but only when explicitly created by the user. Containers limit the scope of impact that a program can have on other running programs, the data it can access, and system resources. Figure 1.5 illustrates the difference between running software outside and inside a container.

What this means for you or your business is that the scope of any security threat associated with running a particular application is limited to the scope of the application itself. Creating strong application containers is complicated and a critical component of any defense in-depth strategy. It is far too commonly skipped or implemented in a half-hearted manner.

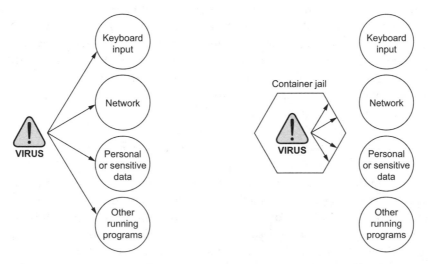

Figure 1.5   Left: a malicious program with direct access to sensitive resources. Right: a malicious program inside a container.

1.3   *Why is Docker important?*

Docker provides what is called an *abstraction*. Abstractions allow you to work with complicated things in simplified terms. So, in the case of Docker, instead of focusing on all the complexities and specifics associated with installing an application, all we need consider is what software we'd like to install. Like a crane loading a shipping container onto a ship, the process of installing any software with Docker is identical to any other. The shape or size of the thing inside the shipping container may vary, but the way that the crane picks up the container will always be the same. All the tooling is reusable for any shipping container.

This is also the case for application removal. When you want to remove software, you simply tell Docker which software to remove. No lingering artifacts will remain because they were all carefully contained and accounted for. Your computer will be as clean as it was before you installed the software.

The container abstraction and the tools Docker provides for working with containers will change the system administration and software development landscape. Docker is important because it makes containers available to everyone. Using it saves time, money, and energy.

The second reason Docker is important is that there is significant push in the software community to adopt containers and Docker. This push is so strong that companies like Amazon, Microsoft, and Google have all worked together to contribute to its development and adopt it in their own cloud offerings. These companies, which are typically at odds, have come together to support an open source project instead of developing and releasing their own solutions.

The third reason Docker is important is that it has accomplished for the computer what app stores did for mobile devices. It has made software installation, compartmentalization, and removal very simple. Better yet, Docker does it in a cross-platform and open way. Imagine if all of the major smartphones shared the same app store. That would be a pretty big deal. It's possible with this technology in place that the lines between operating systems may finally start to blur, and third-party offerings will be less of a factor in choosing an operating system.

Fourth, we're finally starting to see better adoption of some of the more advanced isolation features of operating systems. This may seem minor, but quite a few people are trying to make computers more secure through isolation at the operating system level. It's been a shame that their hard work has taken so long to see mass adoption. Containers have existed for decades in one form or another. It's great that Docker helps us take advantage of those features without all the complexity.

1.4   *Where and when to use Docker*

Docker can be used on most computers at work and at home. Practically, how far should this be taken?

Docker *can* run almost anywhere, but that doesn't mean you'll want to do so. For example, currently Docker can only run applications that can run on a Linux operating system. This means that if you want to run an OS X or Windows native application, you can't yet do so through Docker.

So, by narrowing the conversation to software that typically runs on a Linux server or desktop, a solid case can be made for running almost any application inside a container. This includes server applications like web servers, mail servers, databases, proxies, and the like. Desktop software like web browsers, word processors, email clients, or other tools are also a great fit. Even trusted programs are as dangerous to run as a program you downloaded from the Internet if they interact with user-provided data or network data. Running these in a container and as a user with reduced privileges will help protect your system from attack.

Beyond the added in-depth benefit of defense, using Docker for day-to-day tasks helps keep your computer clean. Keeping a clean computer will prevent you from running into shared resource issues and ease software installation and removal. That same ease of installation, removal, and distribution simplifies management of computer fleets and could radically change the way companies think about maintenance.

The most important thing to remember is when containers are inappropriate. Containers won't help much with the security of programs that have to run with full access to the machine. At the time of this writing, doing so is possible but complicated. Containers are not a total solution for security issues, but they can be used to prevent many types of attacks. Remember, you shouldn't use software from untrusted sources. This is especially true if that software requires administrative privileges. That means it's a bad idea to blindly run customer-provided containers in a collocated environment.

1.5   *Example: "Hello, World"*

I like to get people started with an example. In keeping with tradition, we'll use "Hello, World." Before you begin, download and install Docker for your system. Detailed instructions are kept up-to-date for every available system at https://docs.docker.com/installation/. OS X and Windows users will install the full Docker suite of applications using the Docker Toolbox. Once you have Docker installed and an active internet connection, head to your command prompt and type the following:

```
docker run dockerinaction/hello_world
```

> **TIP** Docker runs as the root user on your system. On some systems you'll need to execute the docker command line using sudo. Failing to do so will result in a permissions error message. You can eliminate this requirement by creating a "docker" group, setting that group as the owner of the docker socket, and adding your user to that group. Consult the Docker online documentation for your distribution for detailed instructions, or try it both ways and stick with the option that works for you. For consistency, this book will omit the sudo prefix.

After you do so, Docker will spring to life. It will start downloading various components and eventually print out "hello world." If you run it again, it will just print out

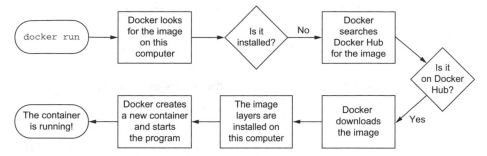

Figure 1.6 What happens after running `docker run`

"hello world." Several things are happening in this example, and the command itself has a few distinct parts.

First, you use the `docker run` command to start a new container. This single command triggers a sequence (shown in figure 1.6) that installs, runs, and stops a program inside a container.

Second, the program that you tell it to run in a container is `dockerinaction/ hello_world`. This is called the repository (or image) name. For now, you can think of the repository name as the name of the program you want to install or run.

> **NOTE** This repository and several others were created specifically to support the examples in this book. By the end of part 2 you should feel comfortable examining these open source examples. Any suggestions you have on how they might be improved are always welcome.

The first time you give the command, Docker has to figure out if `dockerinaction/ hello_world` is already installed. If it's unable to locate it on your computer (because it's the first thing you do with Docker), Docker makes a call to Docker Hub. Docker Hub is a public registry provided by Docker Inc. Docker Hub replies to Docker running on your computer where `dockerinaction/hello_world` can be found, and Docker starts the download.

Once installed, Docker creates a new container and runs a single command. In this case, the command is simple:

```
echo "hello world"
```

After the command prints "hello world" to the terminal, it exits, and the container is automatically stopped. Understand that the running state of a container is directly tied to the state of a single running program inside the container. If a program is running, the container is running. If the program is stopped, the container is stopped. Restarting a container runs the program again.

When you give the command a second time, Docker will check again to see if `dockerinaction/hello_world` is installed. This time it finds it and can build a new

Figure 1.7   Running `docker run` **a second time. Because the image is already installed, Docker can start the new container right away.**

container and execute it right away. I want to emphasize an important detail. When you use `docker run` the second time, it creates a second container from the same repository (figure 1.7 illustrates this). This means that if you repeatedly use `docker run` and create a bunch of containers, you'll need to get a list of the containers you've created and maybe at some point destroy them. Working with containers is as straightforward as creating them, and both topics are covered in chapter 2.

Congratulations! You're now an official Docker user. Take a moment to reflect on how straightforward that was.

1.6   *Summary*

This chapter has been a brief introduction to Docker and the problems it helps system administrators, developers, and other software users solve. In this chapter you learned that:

- Docker takes a logistical approach to solving common software problems and simplifies your experience with installing, running, publishing, and removing software. It's a command-line program, a background daemon, and a set of remote services. It's integrated with community tools provided by Docker Inc.
- The container abstraction is at the core of its logistical approach.
- Working with containers instead of software creates a consistent interface and enables the development of more sophisticated tools.
- Containers help keep your computers tidy because software inside containers can't interact with anything outside those containers, and no shared dependencies can be formed.
- Because Docker is available and supported on Linux, OS X, and Windows, most software packaged in Docker images can be used on any computer.
- Docker doesn't provide container technology; it hides the complexity of working directly with the container software.

Running software in containers

This chapter covers

- Running interactive and daemon terminal programs with containers
- Containers and the PID namespace
- Container configuration and output
- Running multiple programs in a container
- Injecting configuration into containers
- Durable containers and the container life cycle
- Cleaning up

Before the end of this chapter you'll understand all the basics for working with containers and how Docker helps solve clutter and conflict problems. You're going to work through examples that introduce Docker features as you might encounter them in daily use.

2.1 Getting help with the Docker command line

You'll use the `docker` command-line program throughout the rest of this book. To get you started with that, I want to show you how to get information about commands from the docker program itself. This way you'll understand how to use the exact version of Docker on your computer. Open a terminal, or command prompt, and run the following command:

```
docker help
```

Running docker help will display information about the basic syntax for using the docker command-line program as well as a complete list of commands for your version of the program. Give it a try and take a moment to admire all the neat things you can do.

docker help gives you only high-level information about what commands are available. To get detailed information about a specific command, include the command in the <COMMAND> argument. For example, you might enter the following command to find out how to copy files from a location inside a container to a location on the host machine:

```
docker help cp
```

That will display a usage pattern for docker cp, a general description of what the command does, and a detailed breakdown of its arguments. I'm confident that you'll have a great time working through the commands introduced in the rest of this book now that you know how to find help if you need it.

2.2 *Controlling containers: building a website monitor*

Most examples in this book will use real software. Practical examples will help introduce Docker features and illustrate how you will use them in daily activities. In this first example, you're going to install a web server called NGINX. Web servers are programs that make website files and programs accessible to web browsers over a network. You're not going to build a website, but you are going to install and start a web server with Docker. If you follow the instructions in this example, the web server will be available only to other programs on your computer.

Suppose a new client walks into your office and makes you an outrageous offer to build them a new website. They want a website that's closely monitored. This particular client wants to run their own operations, so they'll want the solution you provide to email their team when the server is down. They've also heard about this popular web server software called NGINX and have specifically requested that you use it. Having read about the merits of working with Docker, you've decided to use it for this project. Figure 2.1 shows your planned architecture for the project.

This example uses three containers. The first will run NGINX; the second will run a program called a mailer. Both of these will run as detached containers. *Detached* means that the container will run in the background, without being attached to any input or output stream. A third program, called an agent, will run in an interactive container. Both the mailer and agent are small scripts created for this example. In this section you'll learn how to do the following:

- Create detached and interactive containers
- List containers on your system

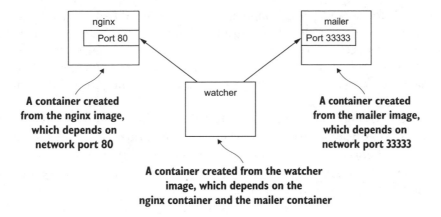

Figure 2.1 The three containers that you'll build in this example

- View container logs
- Stop and restart containers
- Reattach a terminal to a container
- Detach from an attached container

Without further delay, let's get started filling your client's order.

2.2.1 Creating and starting a new container

When installing software with Docker, we say that we're installing an *image*. There are different ways to install an image and several sources for images. Images are covered in depth in chapter 3. In this example we're going to download and install an image for NGINX from Docker Hub. Remember, Docker Hub is the public registry provided by Docker Inc. The NGINX image is from what Docker Inc. calls a trusted repository. Generally, the person or foundation that publishes the software controls the trusted repositories for that software. Running the following command will download, install, and start a container running NGINX:

```
docker run --detach \
    --name web nginx:latest              Note the detach flag
```

When you run this command, Docker will install `nginx:latest` from the NGINX repository hosted on Docker Hub (covered in chapter 3) and run the software. After Docker has installed and started running NGINX, one line of seemingly random characters will be written to the terminal. It will look something like this:

```
7cb5d2b9a7eab87f07182b5bf58936c9947890995b1b94f412912fa822a9ecb5
```

That blob of characters is the unique identifier of the container that was just created to run NGINX. Every time you run `docker run` and create a new container, that container will get a similar unique identifier. It's common for users to capture this output with a variable for use with other commands. You don't need to do so for the purposes of this example. After the identifier is displayed, it might not seem like anything has happened. That's because you used the `--detach` option and started the program in the background. This means that the program started but isn't attached to your terminal. It makes sense to start NGINX this way because we're going to run a few different programs.

Running detached containers is a perfect fit for programs that sit quietly in the background. That type of program is called a *daemon*. A daemon generally interacts with other programs or humans over a network or some other communication tool. When you launch a daemon or other program in a container that you want to run in the background, remember to use either the `--detach` flag or its short form, `-d`.

Another daemon that your client needs is a mailer. A mailer waits for connections from a caller and then sends an email. The following command will install and run a mailer that will work for this example:

```
docker run -d \
    --name mailer \        ◄─┐  Start detached
```

This command uses the short form of the `--detach` flag to start a new container named mailer in the background. At this point you've run two commands and delivered two-thirds of the system that your client wants. The last component, called the agent, is a good fit for an interactive container.

2.2.2 *Running interactive containers*

Programs that interact with users tend to feel more interactive. A terminal-based text editor is a great example. The `docker` command-line tool is a perfect example of an interactive terminal program. These types of programs might take input from the user or display output on the terminal. Running interactive programs in Docker requires that you bind parts of your terminal to the input or output of a running container.

To get started working with interactive containers, run the following command:

```
docker run --interactive --tty \    ◄─┐  Create a virtual terminal
    --link web:web \                   │  and bind stdin
    --name web_test \
    busybox:latest /bin/sh
```

The command uses two flags on the `run` command: `--interactive` (or `-i`) and `--tty` (or `-t`). First, the `--interactive` option tells Docker to keep the standard input stream (stdin) open for the container even if no terminal is attached. Second, the `--tty` option tells Docker to allocate a virtual terminal for the container, which will allow you to pass signals to the container. This is usually what you want from an interactive command-line program. You'll usually use both of these when you're running an interactive program like a shell in an interactive container.

Just as important as the interactive flags, when you started this container you specified the program to run inside the container. In this case you ran a shell program called sh. You can run any program that's available inside the container.

The command in the interactive container example creates a container, starts a UNIX shell, and is linked to the container that's running NGINX (linking is covered in chapter 5). From this shell you can run a command to verify that your web server is running correctly:

```
wget -O - http://web:80/
```

This uses a program called wget to make an HTTP request to the web server (the NGINX server you started earlier in a container) and then display the contents of the web page on your terminal. Among the other lines, there should be a message like "Welcome to NGINX!" If you see that message, then everything is working correctly and you can go ahead and shut down this interactive container by typing exit. This will terminate the shell program and stop the container.

It's possible to create an interactive container, manually start a process inside that container, and then detach your terminal. You can do so by holding down the Crtl (or Control) key and pressing P and then Q. This will work only when you've used the --tty option.

To finish the work for your client, you need to start an agent. This is a monitoring agent that will test the web server as you did in the last example and send a message with the mailer if the web server stops. This command will start the agent in an interactive container using the short-form flags:

```
docker run -it \                      ◄──┐  Create a virtual terminal
    --name agent \                        │  and bind stdin
    --link web:insideweb \
    --link mailer:insidemailer \
    dockerinaction/ch2_agent
```

When running, the container will test the web container every second and print a message like the following:

```
System up.
```

Now that you've seen what it does, detach your terminal from the container. Specifically, when you start the container and it begins writing "System up," hold the Ctrl (or Control) key and then press P and then Q. After doing so you'll be returned to the shell for your host computer. Do not stop the program; otherwise, the monitor will stop checking the web server.

Although you'll usually use detached or daemon containers for software that you deploy to servers on your network, interactive containers are very useful for running software on your desktop or for manual work on a server. At this point you've started all three applications in containers that your client needs. Before you can confidently claim completion, you should test the system.

2.2.3 *Listing, stopping, restarting, and viewing output of containers*

The first thing you should do to test your current setup is check which containers are currently running by using the docker ps command:

```
docker ps
```

Running the command will display the following information about each running container:

- The container ID
- The image used
- The command executed in the container
- The time since the container was created
- The duration that the container has been running
- The network ports exposed by the container
- The name of the container

At this point you should have three running containers with names: web, mailer, and agent. If any is missing but you've followed the example thus far, it may have been mistakenly stopped. This isn't a problem because Docker has a command to restart a container. The next three commands will restart each container using the container name. Choose the appropriate ones to restart the containers that were missing from the list of running containers.

```
docker restart web
docker restart mailer
docker restart agent
```

Now that all three containers are running, you need to test that the system is operating correctly. The best way to do that is to examine the logs for each container. Start with the web container:

```
docker logs web
```

That should display a long log with several lines that contain this substring:

```
"GET / HTTP/1.0" 200
```

This means that the web server is running and that the agent is testing the site. Each time the agent tests the site, one of these lines will be written to the log. The docker logs command can be helpful for these cases but is dangerous to rely on. Anything that the program writes to the stdout or stderr output streams will be recorded in this log. The problem with this pattern is that the log is never rotated or truncated, so the data written to the log for a container will remain and grow as long as the container exists. That long-term persistence can be a problem for long-lived processes. A better way to work with log data uses volumes and is discussed in chapter 4.

You can tell that the agent is monitoring the web server by examining the logs for web alone. For completeness you should examine the log output for mailer and agent as well:

```
docker logs mailer
docker logs agent
```

The logs for mailer should look something like this:

```
CH2 Example Mailer has started.
```

The logs for agent should contain several lines like the one you watched it write when you started the container:

```
System up.
```

> **TIP** The docker logs command has a flag, --follow or -f, that will display the logs and then continue watching and updating the display with changes to the log as they occur. When you've finished, press Ctrl (or Command) and the C key to interrupt the logs command.

Now that you've validated that the containers are running and that the agent can reach the web server, you should test that the agent will notice when the web container stops. When that happens, the agent should trigger a call to the mailer, and the event should be recorded in the logs for both agent and mailer. The docker stop command tells the program with PID #1 in the container to halt. Use it in the following commands to test the system:

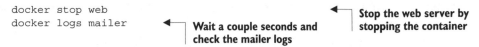

```
docker stop web
docker logs mailer
```
Wait a couple seconds and check the mailer logs

Stop the web server by stopping the container

Look for a line at the end of the mailer logs that reads like:

```
"Sending email: To: admin@work  Message: The service is down!"
```

That line means the agent successfully detected that the NGINX server in the container named web had stopped. Congratulations! Your client will be happy, and you've built your first real system with containers and Docker.

Learning the basic Docker features is one thing, but understanding why they're useful and how to use them in building more comprehensive systems is another task entirely. The best place to start learning that is with the process identifier namespace provided by Linux.

2.3 Solved problems and the PID namespace

Every running program—or process—on a Linux machine has a unique number called a process identifier (PID). A PID namespace is the set of possible numbers that identify processes. Linux provides facilities to create multiple PID namespaces. Each namespace has a complete set of possible PIDs. This means that each PID namespace will contain its own PID 1, 2, 3, and so on. From the perspective of a process in one namespace, PID 1 might refer to an init system process like runit or supervisord. In a different namespace, PID 1 might refer to a command shell like bash. Creating a PID namespace for each container is a critical feature of Docker. Run the following to see it in action:

```
docker run -d --name namespaceA \
    busybox:latest /bin/sh -c "sleep 30000"
docker run -d --name namespaceB \
    busybox:latest /bin/sh -c "nc -l -p 0.0.0.0:80"

docker exec namespaceA ps          ◄──❶
docker exec namespaceB ps              ◄──❷
```

Command ❶ above should generate a process list similar to the following:

```
PID    USER      COMMAND
  1    root      /bin/sh -c sleep 30000
  5    root      sleep 30000
  6    root      ps
```

Command ❷ above should generate a slightly different process list:

```
PID    USER      COMMAND
  1    root      /bin/sh -c nc -l -p 0.0.0.0:80
  7    root      nc -l -p 0.0.0.0:80
  8    root      ps
```

In this example you use the docker exec command to run additional processes in a running container. In this case the command you use is called ps, which shows all the running processes and their PID. From the output it's clear to see that each container has a process with PID 1.

Without a PID namespace, the processes running inside a container would share the same ID space as those in other containers or on the host. A container would be able to determine what other processes were running on the host machine. Worse, namespaces transform many authorization decisions into domain decisions. That means processes in one container might be able to control processes in other containers. Docker would be much less useful without the PID namespace. The Linux features that Docker uses, such as namespaces, help you solve whole classes of software problems.

Like most Docker isolation features, you can optionally create containers without their own PID namespace. You can try this yourself by setting the --pid flag on docker create or docker run and setting the value to host. Try it yourself with a container running BusyBox Linux and the ps Linux command:

```
docker run --pid host busybox:latest ps      ◄──┐  Should list all processes
                                                  └  running on the computer
```

Consider the previous web-monitoring example. Suppose you were not using Docker and were just running NGINX directly on your computer. Now suppose you forgot that you had already started NGINX for another project. When you start NGINX again, the second process won't be able to access the resources it needs because the first process already has them. This is a basic software conflict example. You can see it in action by trying to run two copies of NGINX in the same container:

```
docker run -d --name webConflict nginx:latest        The output should
docker logs webConflict                              be empty
docker exec webConflict nginx -g 'daemon off;'       Start a second nginx process
                                                     in the same container
```

The last command should display output like:

```
2015/03/29 22:04:35 [emerg] 10#0: bind() to 0.0.0.0:80 failed (98:
Address already in use)
nginx: [emerg] bind() to 0.0.0.0:80 failed (98: Address already in use)
...
```

The second process fails to start properly and reports that the address it needs is already in use. This is called a port conflict, and it's a common issue in real-world systems where several processes are running on the same computer or multiple people contribute to the same environment. It's a great example of a conflict problem that Docker simplifies and solves. Run each in a different container, like this:

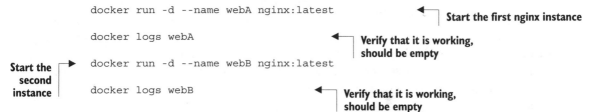

```
docker run -d --name webA nginx:latest        Start the first nginx instance

docker logs webA                              Verify that it is working,
                                              should be empty
docker run -d --name webB nginx:latest

docker logs webB                              Verify that it is working,
                                              should be empty
```

Start the second instance

To generalize ways that programs might conflict with each other, let's consider a parking lot metaphor. A paid parking lot has a few basic features: a payment system, a few reserved parking spaces, and numbered spaces.

Tying these features back to a computer system, a payment system represents some shared resource with a specific interface. A payment system might accept cash or credit cards or both. People who carry only cash won't be able to use a garage with a payment system that accepts only credit cards, and people without money to pay the fee won't be able to park in the garage at all.

Similarly, programs that have a dependency on some shared component such as a specific version of a programming language library won't be able to run on computers that either have a different version of that library or lack that library completely. Just like if two people who each use a different payment method want to park in the same garage that accepts only one method, conflict arises when you want to use two programs that require different versions of a library.

Reserved spaces in this metaphor represent scarce resources. Imagine that the parking garage attendant assigns the same reserved space to two cars. As long as only one driver wanted to use the garage at a time, there would be no issue. But if both wanted to use the space simultaneously, the first one in would win and the second wouldn't be able to park. As you'll see in the conflict example in section 2.7, this is the same type of conflict that happens when two programs try to bind to the same network port.

Lastly, consider what would happen if someone changed the space numbers in the parking lot while cars were parked. When owners return and try to locate their vehicles, they may be unable to do so. Although this is clearly a silly example, it's a great metaphor for what happens to programs when shared environment variables change. Programs often use environment variables or registry entries to locate other resources that they need. These resources might be libraries or other programs. When programs conflict with each other, they might modify these variables in incompatible ways.

Here are some common conflict problems:

- Two programs want to bind to the same network port.
- Two programs use the same temporary filename, and file locks are preventing that.
- Two programs want to use different versions of some globally installed library.
- Two copies of the same program want to use the same PID file.
- A second program you installed modified an environment variable that another program uses. Now the first program breaks.

All these conflicts arise when one or more programs have a common dependency but can't agree to share or have different needs. Like in the earlier port conflict example, Docker solves software conflicts with such tools as Linux namespaces, file system roots, and virtualized network components. All these tools are used to provide isolation to each container.

2.4   *Eliminating metaconflicts: building a website farm*

In the last section you saw how Docker helps you avoid software conflicts with process isolation. But if you're not careful, you can end up building systems that create *metaconflicts,* or conflicts between containers in the Docker layer.

Consider another example where a client has asked you to build a system where you can host a variable number of websites for their customers. They'd also like to employ the same monitoring technology that you built earlier in this chapter. Simply expanding the system you built earlier would be the simplest way to get this job done without customizing the configuration for NGINX. In this example you'll build a system with several containers running web servers and a monitoring agent (agent) for each web server. The system will look like the architecture described in figure 2.2.

One's first instinct might be to simply start more web containers. That's not as simple as it sounds. Identifying containers gets complicated as the number of containers increases.

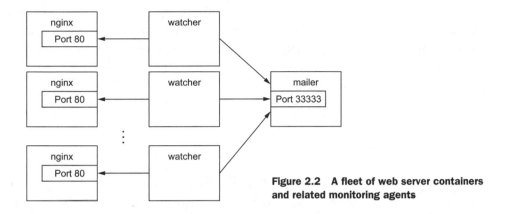

Figure 2.2 **A fleet of web server containers and related monitoring agents**

2.4.1 *Flexible container identification*

The best way to find out why simply creating more copies of the NGINX container you used in the last example is a bad idea is to try it for yourself:

```
docker run -d --name webid nginx
docker run -d --name webid nginx
```

◄ Create a container named "webid"

◄ Create another container named "webid"

The second command here will fail with a conflict error:

```
FATA[0000] Error response from daemon: Conflict. The name "webid" is
already in use by container 2b5958ba6a00. You have to delete (or rename)
that container to be able to reuse that name.
```

Using fixed container names like *web* is useful for experimentation and documentation, but in a system with multiple containers, using fixed names like that can create conflicts. By default Docker assigns a unique (human-friendly) name to each container it creates. The --name flag simply overrides that process with a known value. If a situation arises where the name of a container needs to change, you can always rename the container with the docker rename command:

```
docker rename webid webid-old
docker run -d --name webid nginx
```

◄ Rename the current web container to "webid-old"

◄ Create another container named "webid"

Renaming containers can help alleviate one-off naming conflicts but does little to help avoid the problem in the first place. In addition to the name, Docker assigns a unique identifier that was mentioned in the first example. These are hex-encoded 1024-bit numbers and look something like this:

```
7cb5d2b9a7eab87f07182b5bf58936c9947890995b1b94f412912fa822a9ecb5
```

When containers are started in detached mode, their identifier will be printed to the terminal. You can use these identifiers in place of the container name with any command that needs to identify a specific container. For example, you could use the previous ID with a stop or exec command:

```
docker exec \
    7cb5d2b9a7eab87f07182b5bf58936c9947890995b1b94f412912fa822a9ecb5 \
ps

docker stop \
    7cb5d2b9a7eab87f07182b5bf58936c9947890995b1b94f412912fa822a9ecb5
```

The high probability of uniqueness of the IDs that are generated means that it is unlikely that there will ever be a collision with this ID. To a lesser degree it is also unlikely that there would even be a collision of the first 12 characters of this ID on the same computer. So in most Docker interfaces, you'll see container IDs truncated to their first 12 characters. This makes generated IDs a bit more user friendly. You can use them wherever a container identifier is required. So the previous two commands could be written like this:

```
docker exec 7cb5d2b9a7ea ps
docker stop 7cb5d2b9a7ea
```

Neither of these IDs is particularly well suited for human use. But they work very well with scripts and automation techniques. Docker has several means of acquiring the ID of a container to make automation possible. In these cases the full or truncated numeric ID will be used.

The first way to get the numeric ID of a container is to simply start or create a new one and assign the result of the command to a shell variable. As you saw earlier, when a new container is started in detached mode, the container ID will be written to the terminal (stdout). You'd be unable to use this with interactive containers if this were the only way to get the container ID at creation time. Luckily you can use another command to create a container without starting it. The docker create command is very similar to docker run, the primary difference being that the container is created in a stopped state:

```
docker create nginx
```

The result should be a line like:

```
b26a631e536d3caae348e9fd36e7661254a11511eb2274fb55f9f7c788721b0d
```

If you're using a Linux command shell like sh or bash, you can simply assign that result to a shell variable and use it again later:

```
CID=$(docker create nginx:latest)      ◀—┐ This will work on POSIX-
echo $CID                                └ compliant shells
```

Shell variables create a new opportunity for conflict, but the scope of that conflict is limited to the terminal session or current processing environment that the script was launched in. Those conflicts should be easily avoidable because one use or program is managing that environment. The problem with this approach is that it won't help if multiple users or automated processes need to share that information. In those cases you can use a container ID (CID) file.

Both the docker run and docker create commands provide another flag to write the ID of a new container to a known file:

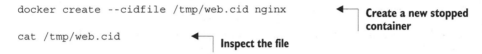

```
docker create --cidfile /tmp/web.cid nginx        ◀── Create a new stopped
                                                      container

cat /tmp/web.cid         ◀── Inspect the file
```

Like the use of shell variables, this feature increases the opportunity for conflict. The name of the CID file (provided after --cidfile) must be known or have some known structure. Just like manual container naming, this approach uses known names in a global (Docker-wide) namespace. The good news is that Docker won't create a new container using the provided CID file if that file already exists. The command will fail just as it does when you create two containers with the same name.

One reason to use CID files instead of names is that CID files can be shared with containers easily and renamed for that container. This uses a Docker feature called volumes, which is covered in chapter 4.

> **TIP** One strategy for dealing with CID file-naming collisions is to partition the namespace by using known or predictable path conventions. For example, in this scenario you might use a path that contains all web containers under a known directory and further partition that directory by the customer ID. This would result in a path like /containers/web/customer1/web.cid or /containers/web/customer8/web.cid.

In other cases, you can use other commands like docker ps to get the ID of a container. For example, if you want to get the truncated ID of the last created container, you can use this:

```
CID=$(docker ps --latest --quiet)         ◀── This will work on POSIX-
echo $CID                                     compliant shells

CID=$(docker ps -l -q)      ◀── Run again with the
echo $CID                       short-form flags
```

> **TIP** If you want to get the full container ID, you can use the --no-trunc option on the docker ps command.

Automation cases are covered by the features you've seen so far. But even though truncation helps, these container IDs are rarely easy to read or remember. For this reason, Docker also generates human-readable names for each container.

The naming convention uses a personal adjective, an underscore, and the last name of an influential scientist, engineer, inventor, or other such thought leader. Examples of generated names are compassionate_swartz, hungry_goodall, and distracted_turing. These seem to hit a sweet spot for readability and memory. When you're working with the docker tool directly, you can always use docker ps to look up the human-friendly names.

Container identification can be tricky, but you can manage the issue by using the ID and name-generation features of Docker.

2.4.2   *Container state and dependencies*

With this new knowledge, the new system might looks something like this:

```
MAILER_CID=$(docker run -d dockerinaction/ch2_mailer)      Make sure mailer from
WEB_CID=$(docker create nginx)                             first example is running

AGENT_CID=$(docker create --link $WEB_CID:insideweb \
    --link $MAILER_CID:insidemailer \
    dockerinaction/ch2_agent)
```

This snippet could be used to seed a new script that launches a new NGINX and agent instance for each of your client's customers. You can use docker ps to see that they've been created:

```
docker ps
```

The reason neither the NGINX nor the agent was included with the output has to do with container state. Docker containers will always be in one of four states and transition via command according to the diagram in figure 2.3.

Neither of the new containers you started appears in the list of containers because docker ps shows only running containers by default. Those containers were specifically created with docker create and never started (the exited state). To see all the containers (including those in the exited state), use the -a option:

```
docker ps -a
```

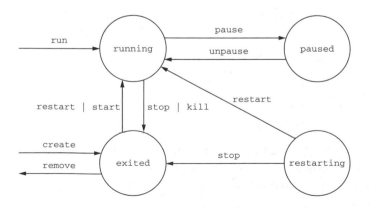

Figure 2.3   The state transition diagram for Docker containers as reported by the status column

Now that you've verified that both of the containers were created, you need to start them. For that you can use the docker start command:

```
docker start $AGENT_CID
docker start $WEB_CID
```

Running those commands will result in an error. The containers need to be started in reverse order of their dependency chain. Because you tried to start the agent container before the web container, Docker reported a message like this one:

```
Error response from daemon: Cannot start container
    03e65e3c6ee34e714665a8dc4e33fb19257d11402b151380ed4c0a5e38779d0a: Cannot
    link to a non running container: /clever_wright AS /modest_hopper/
    insideweb
FATA[0000] Error: failed to start one or more containers
```

In this example, the agent container has a dependency on the web container. You need to start the web container first:

```
docker start $WEB_CID
docker start $AGENT_CID
```

This makes sense when you consider the mechanics at work. The link mechanism injects IP addresses into dependent containers, and containers that aren't running don't have IP addresses. If you tried to start a container that has a dependency on a container that isn't running, Docker wouldn't have an IP address to inject. Container linking is covered in chapter 5, but it's useful to demonstrate this important point in starting containers.

Whether you're using docker run or docker create, the resulting containers need to be started in the reverse order of their dependency chain. This means that circular dependencies are impossible to build using Docker container relationships.

At this point you can put everything together into one concise script that looks like the following:

```
MAILER_CID=$(docker run -d dockerinaction/ch2_mailer)

WEB_CID=$(docker run -d nginx)

AGENT_CID=$(docker run -d \
    --link $WEB_CID:insideweb \
    --link $MAILER_CID:insidemailer \
    dockerinaction/ch2_agent)
```

Now you're confident that this script can be run without exception each time your client needs to provision a new site. Your client has come back and thanked you for the web and monitoring work you've completed so far, but things have changed.

They've decided to focus on building their websites with WordPress (a popular open source content-management and blogging program). Luckily, WordPress is published through Docker Hub in a repository named wordpress:4. All you'll need to deliver is a set of commands to provision a new WordPress website that has the same monitoring and alerting features that you've already delivered.

The interesting thing about content-management systems and other stateful systems is that the data they work with makes each running program specialized. Adam's WordPress blog is different from Betty's WordPress blog, even if they're running the same software. Only the content is different. Even if the content is the same, they're different because they're running on different sites.

If you build systems or software that know too much about their environment—like addresses or fixed locations of dependency services—it's difficult to change that environment or reuse the software. You need to deliver a system that minimizes environment dependence before the contract is complete.

2.5   *Building environment-agnostic systems*

Much of the work associated with installing software or maintaining a fleet of computers lies in dealing with specializations of the computing environment. These specializations come as global-scoped dependencies (like known host file system locations), hard-coded deployment architectures (environment checks in code or configuration), or data locality (data stored on a particular computer outside the deployment architecture). Knowing this, if your goal is to build low-maintenance systems, you should strive to minimize these things.

Docker has three specific features to help build environment-agnostic systems:

- Read-only file systems
- Environment variable injection
- Volumes

Working with volumes is a big subject and the topic of chapter 4. In order to learn the first two features, consider a requirements change for the example situation used in the rest of this chapter.

WordPress uses a database program called MySQL to store most of its data, so it's a good idea to start with making sure that a container running WordPress has a read-only file system.

2.5.1   *Read-only file systems*

Using read-only file systems accomplishes two positive things. First, you can have confidence that the container won't be specialized from changes to the files it contains. Second, you have increased confidence that an attacker can't compromise files in the container.

To get started working on your client's system, create and start a container from the WordPress image using the `--read-only` flag:

```
docker run -d --name wp --read-only wordpress:4
```

When this is finished, check that the container is running. You can do so using any of the methods introduced previously, or you can inspect the container metadata directly. The following command will print true if the container named wp is running and false otherwise.

```
docker inspect --format "{{.State.Running}}" wp
```

The docker inspect command will display all the metadata (a JSON document) that Docker maintains for a container. The format option transforms that metadata, and in this case it filters everything except for the field indicating the running state of the container. This command should simply output false.

In this case, the container isn't running. To determine why, examine the logs for the container:

```
docker logs wp
```

That should output something like:

```
error: missing WORDPRESS_DB_HOST and MYSQL_PORT_3306_TCP environment
variables
Did you forget to --link some_mysql_container:mysql or set an external db
with -e WORDPRESS_DB_HOST=hostname:port?
```

It appears that WordPress has a dependency on a MySQL database. A database is a program that stores data in such a way that it's retrievable and searchable later. The good news is that you can install MySQL using Docker just like WordPress:

```
docker run -d --name wpdb \
    -e MYSQL_ROOT_PASSWORD=ch2demo \
    mysql:5
```

Once that is started, create a different WordPress container that's linked to this new database container (linking is covered in depth in chapter 5):

```
docker run -d --name wp2 \
    --link wpdb:mysql \              ← Use a unique name
    -p 80 --read-only \   ← Create a link
    wordpress:4              to the database
```

Check one more time that WordPress is running correctly:

```
docker inspect --format "{{.State.Running}}" wp2
```

You can tell that WordPress failed to start again. Examine the logs to determine the cause:

```
docker logs wp2
```

There should be a line in the logs that is similar to the following:

```
... Read-only file system: AH00023: Couldn't create the rewrite-map mutex
(file /var/lock/apache2/rewrite-map.1)
```

You can tell that WordPress failed to start again, but this time the problem is that it's trying to write a lock file to a specific location. This is a required part of the startup process and is not a specialization. It's appropriate to make an exception to the read-only file system in this case. You need to use a volume to make that exception. Use the following to start WordPress without any issues:

```
# Start the container with specific volumes for read only exceptions
docker run -d --name wp3 --link wpdb:mysql -p 80 \
    -v /run/lock/apache2/ \                        Create specific volumes
    -v /run/apache2/ \                             for writeable space
    --read-only wordpress:4
```

An updated version of the script you've been working on should look like this:

```
SQL_CID=$(docker create -e MYSQL_ROOT_PASSWORD=ch2demo mysql:5)

docker start $SQL_CID

MAILER_CID=$(docker create dockerinaction/ch2_mailer)
docker start $MAILER_CID

WP_CID=$(docker create --link $SQL_CID:mysql -p 80 \
    -v /run/lock/apache2/ -v /run/apache2/ \
    --read-only wordpress:4)

docker start $WP_CID

AGENT_CID=$(docker create --link $WP_CID:insideweb \
    --link $MAILER_CID:insidemailer \
    dockerinaction/ch2_agent)

docker start $AGENT_CID
```

Congratulations, at this point you should have a running WordPress container! By using a read-only file system and linking WordPress to another container running a database, you can be sure that the container running the WordPress image will never change. This means that if there is ever something wrong with the computer running a client's WordPress blog, you should be able to start up another copy of that container elsewhere with no problems.

But there are two problems with this design. First, the database is running in a container on the same computer as the WordPress container. Second, WordPress is using several default values for important settings like database name, administrative user, administrative password, database salt, and so on. To deal with this problem, you could create several versions of the WordPress software, each with a special configuration for the client. Doing so would turn your simple provisioning script into a monster that creates images and writes files. A better way to inject that configuration would be through the use of environment variables.

2.5.2 *Environment variable injection*

Environment variables are key-value pairs that are made available to programs through their execution context. They let you change a program's configuration without modifying any files or changing the command used to start the program.

Docker uses environment variables to communicate information about dependent containers, the host name of the container, and other convenient information for programs running in containers. Docker also provides a mechanism for a user to inject environment variables into a new container. Programs that know to expect important information through environment variables can be configured at container-creation time. Luckily for you and your client, WordPress is one such program.

Before diving into WordPress specifics, try injecting and viewing environment variables on your own. The UNIX command env displays all the environment variables in the current execution context (your terminal). To see environment variable injection in action, use the following command:

```
docker run --env MY_ENVIRONMENT_VAR="this is a test" \
    busybox:latest \
    env
```

Inject an environment variable →

Execute the env command inside the container ←

The --env flag—or -e for short—can be used to inject any environment variable. If the variable is already set by the image or Docker, then the value will be overridden. This way programs running inside containers can rely on the variables always being set. WordPress observes the following environment variables:

- WORDPRESS_DB_HOST
- WORDPRESS_DB_USER
- WORDPRESS_DB_PASSWORD
- WORDPRESS_DB_NAME
- WORDPRESS_AUTH_KEY
- WORDPRESS_SECURE_AUTH_KEY
- WORDPRESS_LOGGED_IN_KEY
- WORDPRESS_NONCE_KEY
- WORDPRESS_AUTH_SALT
- WORDPRESS_SECURE_AUTH_SALT
- WORDPRESS_LOGGED_IN_SALT
- WORDPRESS_NONCE_SALT

TIP This example neglects the KEY and SALT variables, but any real production system should absolutely set these values.

To get started, you should address the problem that the database is running in a container on the same computer as the WordPress container. Rather than using linking to satisfy WordPress's database dependency, inject a value for the WORDPRESS_DB_HOST variable:

```
docker create --env WORDPRESS_DB_HOST=<my database hostname> wordpress:4
```

This example would create (not start) a container for WordPress that will try to connect to a MySQL database at whatever you specify at <my database hostname>.

Because the remote database isn't likely using any default user name or password, you'll have to inject values for those settings as well. Suppose the database administrator is a cat lover and hates strong passwords:

```
docker create \
    --env WORDPRESS_DB_HOST=<my database hostname> \
    --env WORDPRESS_DB_USER=site_admin \
    --env WORDPRESS_DB_PASSWORD=MeowMix42 \
    wordpress:4
```

Using environment variable injection this way will help you separate the physical ties between a WordPress container and a MySQL container. Even in the case where you want to host the database and your customer WordPress sites all on the same machine, you'll still need to fix the second problem mentioned earlier. All the sites are using the same default database name. You'll need to use environment variable injection to set the database name for each independent site:

```
docker create --link wpdb:mysql \
    -e WORDPRESS_DB_NAME=client_a_wp wordpress:4          ◄─┐  For client A

docker create --link wpdb:mysql \
    -e WORDPRESS_DB_NAME=client_b_wp wordpress:4          ◄─┘  For client B
```

Now that you've solved these problems, you can revise the provisioning script. First, set the computer to run only a single MySQL container:

```
DB_CID=$(docker run -d -e MYSQL_ROOT_PASSWORD=ch2demo mysql:5)

MAILER_CID=$(docker run -d dockerinaction/ch2_mailer)
```

Then the site provisioning script would be this:

```
if [ ! -n "$CLIENT_ID" ]; then          ◄─┐  Assume $CLIENT_ID variable
    echo "Client ID not set"               │  is set as input to script
    exit 1
fi

WP_CID=$(docker create \
    --link $DB_CID:mysql \                 ◄─┐  Create link using DB_CID
    --name wp_$CLIENT_ID \
    -p 80 \
    -v /run/lock/apache2/ -v /run/apache2/ \
    -e WORDPRESS_DB_NAME=$CLIENT_ID \
    --read-only wordpress:4)

docker start $WP_CID

AGENT_CID=$(docker create \
    --name agent_$CLIENT_ID \
    --link $WP_CID:insideweb \
    --link $MAILER_CID:insidemailer \
    dockerinaction/ch2_agent)

docker start $AGENT_CID
```

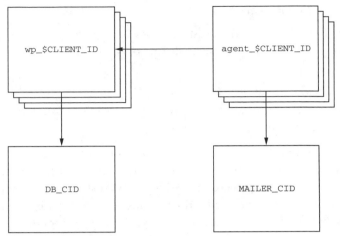

Figure 2.4 Each WordPress and agent container uses the same database and mailer.

This new script will start an instance of WordPress and the monitoring agent for each customer and connect those containers to each other as well as a single mailer program and MySQL database. The WordPress containers can be destroyed, restarted, and upgraded without any worry about loss of data. Figure 2.4 shows this architecture.

The client should be pleased with what is being delivered. But one thing might be bothering you. In earlier testing you found that the monitoring agent correctly notified the mailer when the site was unavailable, but restarting the site and agent required manual work. It would be better if the system tried to automatically recover when a failure was detected. Docker provides restart policies to help deal with that, but you might want something more robust.

2.6 *Building durable containers*

There are cases where software fails in rare conditions that are temporary in nature. Although it's important to be made aware when these conditions arise, it's usually at least as important to restore the service as quickly as possible. The monitoring system that you built in this chapter is a fine start for keeping system owners aware of problems with a system, but it does nothing to help restore service.

When all the processes in a container have exited, that container will enter the exited state. Remember, a Docker container can be in one of four states:

- Running
- Paused
- Restarting
- Exited (also used if the container has never been started)

A basic strategy for recovering from temporary failures is automatically restarting a process when it exits or fails. Docker provides a few options for monitoring and restarting containers.

2.6.1 *Automatically restarting containers*

Docker provides this functionality with a restart policy. Using the `--restart` flag at container-creation time, you can tell Docker to do any of the following:

- Never restart (default)
- Attempt to restart when a failure is detected
- Attempt for some predetermined time to restart when a failure is detected
- Always restart the container regardless of the condition

Docker doesn't always attempt to immediately restart a container. If it did, that would cause more problems than it solved. Imagine a container that does nothing but print the time and exit. If that container was configured to always restart and Docker always immediately restarted it, the system would do nothing but restart that container. Instead, Docker uses an exponential backoff strategy for timing restart attempts.

A backoff strategy determines how much time should pass between successive restart attempts. An exponential backoff strategy will do something like double the previous time spent waiting on each successive attempt. For example, if the first time the container needs to be restarted Docker waits 1 second, then on the second attempt it would wait 2 seconds, 4 seconds on the third attempt, 8 on the fourth, and so on. Exponential backoff strategies with low initial wait times are a common service-restoration technique. You can see Docker employ this strategy yourself by building a container that always restarts and simply prints the time:

```
docker run -d --name backoff-detector --restart always busybox date
```

Then after a few seconds use the trailing logs feature to watch it back off and restart:

```
docker logs -f backoff-detector
```

The logs will show all the times it has already been restarted and will wait until the next time it is restarted, print the current time, and then exit. Adding this single flag to the monitoring system and the WordPress containers you've been working on would solve the recovery issue.

The only reason you might not want to adopt this directly is that during backoff periods, the container isn't running. Containers waiting to be restarted are in the restarting state. To demonstrate, try to run another process in the backoff-detector container:

```
docker exec backoff-detector echo Just a Test
```

Running that command should result in an error message:

```
Cannot run exec command ... in container ...: No active container exists
with ID ...
```

That means you can't do anything that requires the container to be in a running state, like execute additional commands in the container. That could be a problem if you need to run diagnostic programs in a broken container. A more complete strategy is to use containers that run init or supervisor processes.

2.6.2   *Keeping containers running with supervisor and startup processes*

A supervisor process, or init process, is a program that's used to launch and maintain the state of other programs. On a Linux system, PID #1 is an init process. It starts all the other system processes and restarts them in the event that they fail unexpectedly. It's a common practice to use a similar pattern inside containers to start and manage processes.

Using a supervisor process inside your container will keep the container running in the event that the target process—a web server, for example—fails and is restarted. There are several programs that might be used inside a container. The most popular include init, systemd, runit, upstart, and supervisord. Publishing software that uses these programs is covered in chapter 8. For now, take a look at a container that uses supervisord.

A company named Tutum provides software that produces a full LAMP (Linux, Apache, MySQL PHP) stack inside a single container. Containers created this way use supervisord to make sure that all the related processes are kept running. Start an example container:

```
docker run -d -p 80:80 --name lamp-test tutum/lamp
```

You can see what processes are running inside this container by using the docker top command:

```
docker top lamp-test
```

The top subcommand will show the host PID for each of the processes in the container. You'll see supervisord, mysql, and apache included in the list of running programs. Now that the container is running, you can test the supervisord restart functionality by manually stopping one of the processes inside the container.

The problem is that to kill a process inside of a container from within that container, you need to know the PID in the container's PID namespace. To get that list, run the following exec subcommand:

```
docker exec lamp-test ps
```

The process list generated will have listed apache2 in the CMD column:

```
PID TTY          TIME CMD
  1 ?        00:00:00 supervisord
433 ?        00:00:00 mysqld_safe
835 ?        00:00:00 apache2
842 ?        00:00:00 ps
```

The values in the PID column will be different when you run the command. Find the PID on the row for apache2 and then insert that for <PID> in the following command:

```
docker exec lamp-test kill <PID>
```

Running this command will run the Linux kill program inside the lamp-test container and tell the apache2 process to shut down. When apache2 stops, the supervisord process will log the event and restart the process. The container logs will clearly show these events:

```
...
... exited: apache2 (exit status 0; expected)
... spawned: 'apache2' with pid 820
... success: apache2 entered RUNNING state, process has stayed up for >
       than 1 seconds (startsecs)
```

A common alternative to the use of init or supervisor programs is using a startup script that at least checks the preconditions for successfully starting the contained software. These are sometimes used as the default command for the container. For example, the WordPress containers that you've created start by running a script to validate and set default environment variables before starting the WordPress process. You can view this script by overriding the default command and using a command to view the contents of the startup script:

```
docker run wordpress:4 cat /entrypoint.sh
```

Running that command will result in an error messages like:

```
error: missing WORDPRESS_DB_HOST and MYSQL_PORT_3306_TCP environment
variables
...
```

This failed because even though you set the command to run as `cat /entrypoint.sh`, Docker containers run something called an entrypoint before executing the command. Entrypoints are perfect places to put code that validates the preconditions of a container. Although this is discussed in depth in part 2 of this book, you need to know how to override or specifically set the entrypoint of a container on the command line. Try running the last command again but this time using the `--entrypoint` flag to specify the program to run and using the command section to pass arguments:

```
docker run --entrypoint="cat" \
    wordpress:4 /entrypoint.sh
```

Use "cat" as the entrypoint

Pass /entrypoint.sh as the argument to cat

If you run through the displayed script, you'll see how it validates the environment variables against the dependencies of the software and sets default values. Once the script has validated that WordPress can execute, it will start the requested or default command.

Startup scripts are an important part of building durable containers and can always be combined with Docker restart policies to take advantage of the strengths of each. Because both the MySQL and WordPress containers already use startup scripts, it's appropriate to simply set the restart policy for each in an updated version of the example script.

With that final modification, you've built a complete WordPress site-provisioning system and learned the basics of container management with Docker. It has taken considerable experimentation. Your computer is likely littered with several containers that you no longer need. To reclaim the resources that those containers are using, you need to stop them and remove them from your system.

2.7 *Cleaning up*

Ease of cleanup is one of the strongest reasons to use containers and Docker. The isolation that containers provide simplifies any steps that you'd have to take to stop processes and remove files. With Docker, the whole cleanup process is reduced to one of a few simple commands. In any cleanup task, you must first identify the container that you want to stop and/or remove. Remember, to list all of the containers on your computer, use the `docker ps` command:

```
docker ps -a
```

Because the containers you created for the examples in this chapter won't be used again, you should be able to safely stop and remove all the listed containers. Make sure you pay attention to the containers you're cleaning up if there are any that you created for your own activities.

All containers use hard drive space to store logs, container metadata, and files that have been written to the container file system. All containers also consume resources in the global namespace like container names and host port mappings. In most cases, containers that will no longer be used should be removed.

To remove a container from your computer, use the `docker rm` command. For example, to delete the stopped container named wp you'd run:

```
docker rm wp
```

You should go through all the containers in the list you generated by running `docker ps -a` and remove all containers that are in the exited state. If you try to remove a container that's running, paused, or restarting, Docker will display a message like the following:

```
Error response from daemon: Conflict, You cannot remove a running container.
    Stop the container before attempting removal or use -f
FATA[0000] Error: failed to remove one or more containers
```

The processes running in a container should be stopped before the files in the container are removed. You can do this with the `docker stop` command or by using the `-f` flag on `docker rm`. The key difference is that when you stop a process using the `-f` flag, Docker sends a `SIG_KILL` signal, which immediately terminates the receiving process. In contrast, using `docker stop` will send a `SIG_HUP` signal. Recipients of `SIG_HUP` have time to perform finalization and cleanup tasks. The `SIG_KILL` signal makes for no such allowances and can result in file corruption or poor network experiences. You can issue a `SIG_KILL` directly to a container using the `docker kill` command. But you should use `docker kill` or `docker rm -f` only if you must stop the container in less than the standard 30-second maximum stop time.

In the future, if you're experimenting with short-lived containers, you can avoid the cleanup burden by specifying `--rm` on the command. Doing so will automatically remove the container as soon as it enters the exited state. For example, the following command will write a message to the screen in a new BusyBox container, and the container will be removed as soon as it exits:

```
docker run --rm --name auto-exit-test busybox:latest echo Hello World
docker ps -a
```

In this case, you could use either `docker stop` or `docker rm` to properly clean up, or it would be appropriate to use the single-step `docker rm -f` command. You should also use the `-v` flag for reasons that will be covered in chapter 4. The docker CLI makes it is easy to compose a quick cleanup command:

```
docker rm -vf $(docker ps -a -q)
```

This concludes the basics of running software in containers. Each chapter in the remainder of part 1 will focus on a specific aspect of working with containers. The next chapter focuses on installing and uninstalling images, how images relate to containers, and working with container file systems.

2.8   Summary

The primary focus of the Docker project is to enable users to run software in containers. This chapter shows how you can use Docker for that purpose. The ideas and features covered include the following:

- Containers can be run with virtual terminals attached to the user's shell or in detached mode.
- By default, every Docker container has its own PID namespace, isolating process information for each container.
- Docker identifies every container by its generated container ID, abbreviated container ID, or its human-friendly name.
- All containers are in any one of four distinct states: running, paused, restarting, or exited.
- The `docker exec` command can be used to run additional processes inside a running container.
- A user can pass input or provide additional configuration to a process in a container by specifying environment variables at container-creation time.
- Using the `--read-only` flag at container-creation time will mount the container file system as read-only and prevent specialization of the container.
- A container restart policy, set with the `--restart` flag at container-creation time, will help your systems automatically recover in the event of a failure.
- Docker makes cleaning up containers with the `docker rm` command as simple as creating them.

Software installation
simplified

Chapters 1 and 2 introduce all-new concepts and abstractions provided by Docker. This chapter dives deeper into container file systems and software installation. It breaks down software installation into three steps, as illustrated in figure 3.1.

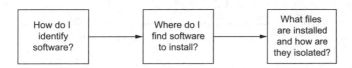

Figure 3.1   Flow of topics covered in this chapter

The first step in installing any software is identifying the software you want to install. You know that software is distributed using images, but you need to know how to tell Docker exactly which image you want to install. I've already mentioned that repositories hold images, but in this chapter I show how repositories and tags are used to identify images in order to install the software you want.

This chapter goes into detail on the three main ways to install Docker images:

- Docker Hub and other registries
- Using image files with `docker save` and `docker load`
- Building images with Dockerfiles

In the course of reading this material you'll learn how Docker isolates installed software and you'll be exposed to a new term, *layer*. Layers are an important concept when dealing with images and have an important impact on software users. This chapter closes with a section about how images work. That knowledge will help you evaluate the image quality and establish a baseline skillset for part 2 of this book.

3.1 *Identifying software*

Suppose you want to install a program called TotallyAwesomeBlog 2.0. How would you tell Docker what you wanted to install? You would need a way to name the program, specify the version that you want to use, and specify the source that you want to install it from. Learning how to identify specific software is the first step in software installation, as illustrated in figure 3.2.

Figure 3.2 Step 1—Software identification

You've learned that Docker creates containers from images. An image is a file. It holds files that will be available to containers created from it and metadata about the image. This metadata contains information about relationships between images, the command history for an image, exposed ports, volume definitions, and more.

Images have identifiers, so they could be used as a name and version for the software, but in practice it's rare to actually work with raw image identifiers. They are long, unique sequences of letters and numbers. Each time a change is made to an image, the image identifier changes. Image identifiers are difficult to work with because they're unpredictable. Instead, users work with repositories.

3.1.1 *What is a repository?*

A *repository* is a named bucket of images. The name is similar to a URL. A repository's name is made up of the name of the host where the image is located, the user account that owns the image, and a short name. For example, later in this chapter you will install an image from the repository named quay.io/dockerinaction/ ch3_hello_registry.

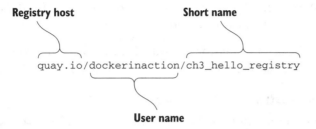

Just as there can be several versions of software, a repository can hold several images. Each of the images in a repository is identified uniquely with tags. If I were to release a new version of quay.io/dockerinaction/ch3_hello_registry, I might tag it "v2" while tagging the old version with "v1." If you wanted to download the old version, you could specifically identify that image by its v1 tag.

In chapter 2 you installed an image from the NGINX repository on Docker Hub that was identified with the "latest" tag. A repository name and tag form a composite key, or a unique reference made up of a combination of non-unique components. In that example, the image was identified by nginx:latest. Although identifiers built in this fashion may occasionally be longer than raw image identifiers, they're predictable and communicate the intention of the image.

3.1.2 *Using tags*

Tags are both an important way to uniquely identify an image and a convenient way to create useful aliases. Whereas a tag can only be applied to a single image in a repository, a single image can have several tags. This allows repository owners to create useful versioning or feature tags.

For example, the Java repository on Docker Hub maintains the following tags: 7, 7-jdk, 7u71, 7u71-jdk, openjdk-7, and openjdk-7u71. All these tags are applied to the same image. But as the current minor version of Java 7 increases, and they release 7u72, the 7u71 tag will likely go away and be replaced with 7u72. If you care about what minor version of Java 7 you're running, you have to keep up with those tag changes. If you just want to make sure you're always running the most recent version of Java 7, just use the image tagged with 7. It will always be assigned to the newest minor revision of Java 7. These tags give users great flexibility.

It's also common to see different tags for images with different software configurations. For example, I've released two images for an open source program called freegeoip. It's a web application that can be used to get the rough geographical location associated with a network address. One image is configured to use the default configuration for the software. It's meant to run by itself with a direct link to the world. The second is configured to run behind a web load balancer. Each image has a distinct tag that allows the user to easily identify the image with the features required.

TIP   When you're looking for software to install, always pay careful attention to the tags offered in a repository. If you're not sure which one you need, you can download all the tagged images in a repository by simply omitting the tag qualifier when you pull from the repository. I occasionally do this by accident, and it can be annoying. But it's easy to clean up.

This is all there is to identifying software for use with Docker. With this knowledge, you're ready to start looking for and installing software with Docker.

3.2   *Finding and installing software*

You can identify software by a repository name, but how do you find the repositories that you want to install? Discovering trustworthy software is complex, and it is the second step in learning how to install software with Docker, as shown in figure 3.3.

Figure 3.3   Step 2—Locating repositories

To find repositories, you could either keep guessing until you get lucky or use an index. Indexes are search engines that catalog repositories. There are several public Docker indexes, but by default Docker is integrated with an index named Docker Hub.

Docker Hub is a registry and index with a website run by Docker Inc. It's the default registry and index used by Docker. When you issue a `docker pull` or `docker run` command without specifying an alternative registry, Docker will default to looking for the repository on Docker Hub. Docker Hub makes Docker more useful out of the box.

Docker Inc. has made efforts to ensure that Docker is an open ecosystem. It publishes a public image to run your own registry, and the `docker` command-line tool can be easily configured to use alternative registries. Later in this chapter I cover alternative image installation and distribution tools included with Docker. But first, the next section covers how to use Docker Hub so you can get the most from the default toolset.

3.2.1   *Docker Hub from the command line*

Almost anything worth doing with Docker can be done from the command line. This includes searching Docker Hub for repositories.

The `docker` command line will search the Docker Hub index for you and display the results, including details like the number of times each repository has been starred, a flag to indicate that a particular repository is official (the OFFICIAL column), and a flag to indicate if the repository is what they call a trusted image (the TRUSTED column). The Docker Hub website allows registered users to star a repository in a similar fashion to other community development sites like GitHub. A repository's star count can act as a proxy metric for image quality and popularity or trust by the community. Docker Hub also provides a set of official repositories that are maintained by Docker Inc. or the current software maintainers. These are often called *libraries*.

There are two ways that an image author can publish their images on Docker Hub:

- *Use the command line to push images that they built independently and on their own systems.* Images pushed this way are considered by some to be less trustworthy because it's not clear how exactly they were built.
- *Make a Dockerfile publicly available and use Docker Hub's continuous build system.* Dockerfiles are scripts for building images. Images created from these automated builds are preferred because the Dockerfile is available for examination prior to installing the image. Images published in this second way will be marked as trusted.

Working with private Docker Hub registries or pushing into registries that you control on Docker Hub does require that you authenticate. In this case, you can use the `docker login` command to log in to Docker Hub. Once you've logged in, you'll be able to pull from private repositories, push to any repository that you control, and tag images in your repositories. Chapter 7 covers pushing and tagging images.

Running `docker login` will prompt you for your Docker Hub credentials. Once you've provided them, your command-line client will be authenticated, and you'll be able to access your private repositories. When you've finished working with your account, you can log out with the `docker logout` command.

If you want to find software to install, you'll need to know where to begin your search. The next example demonstrates how to search for repositories using the `docker search` command. This command may take a few seconds, but it has a timeout built in, so it will eventually return. When you run this command, it will only search the index; nothing will be installed.

Suppose Bob, a software developer, decided that the project he was working on needed a database. He had heard about a popular program named Postgres. He wondered if it was available on Docker Hub, so he ran the following command:

```
docker search postgres
```

After a few seconds several results were returned. At the top of the list he identified a very popular repository with hundreds of stars. He also liked that it was an official repository, which meant that the Docker Hub maintainers had carefully selected the owners of the repository. He used `docker pull` to install the image and moved on with his project.

This is a simple example of how to search for repositories using the `docker` command line. The command will search Docker Hub for any repositories with the term `postgres`. Because Docker Hub is a free public service, users tend to build up lots of public but personal copies. Docker Hub lets users star a repository, similar to a Facebook Like. This is a reasonable proxy indicator for image quality, but you should be careful not to use it as an indicator of trustworthy code.

Imagine if someone builds up a repository with several hundred stars by providing some high-quality open source software. One day a malicious hacker gains control of their repository and publishes an image to the repository that contains a virus. Although containers might be effective for containing malicious code, that notion does not hold true for malicious images. If an attacker controls how an image is built or has targeted an attack specifically to break out of a weakened image, an image can cause serious harm. For this reason, images that are built using publicly available scripts are considered much more trustworthy. In the search results from running `docker search`, you can tell that an image was built from a public script by looking for an [OK] in the column label AUTOMATED.

Now you've seen how to find software on Docker Hub without leaving your terminal. Although you can do most things from the terminal, there are some things that you can do only through the website.

3.2.2   *Docker Hub from the website*

If you have yet to stumble upon it while browsing docker.com, you should take a moment to check out https://hub.docker.com. Docker Hub lets you search for repositories, organizations, or specific users. User and organization profile pages list the repositories that the account maintains, recent activity on the account, and the repositories that the account has starred. On repository pages you can see the following:

- General information about the image provided by the image publisher
- A list of the tags available in the repository
- The date the repository was created
- The number of times it has been downloaded
- Comments from registered users

Docker Hub is free to join, and you'll need an account later in this book. When you're signed in, you can star and comment on repositories. You can create and manage your own repositories. We will do that in part 2. For now, just get a feel for the site and what it has to offer.

Activity: a Docker Hub scavenger hunt

It's good to practice finding software on Docker Hub using the skills you learned in chapter 2. This activity is designed to encourage you to use Docker Hub and practice creating containers. You will also be introduced to three new options on the `docker run` command.

In this activity you're going to create containers from two images that are available through Docker Hub. The first is available from the dockerinaction/ch3_ex2_hunt repository. In that image you'll find a small program that prompts you for a password. You can only find the password by finding and running a container from the second mystery repository on Docker Hub. To use the programs in these images, you'll need to attach your terminal to the containers so that the input and output of your terminal are connected directly to the running container. The following command demonstrates how to do that and run a container that will be removed automatically when stopped:

```
docker run -it --rm dockerinaction/ch3_ex2_hunt
```

When you run this command, the scavenger hunt program will prompt you for the password. If you know the answer already, go ahead and enter it now. If not, just enter anything and it will give you a hint. At this point you should have all the tools you need to complete the activity. Figure 3.4 illustrates what you need to do from this point.

Still stuck? I can give you one more hint. The mystery repository is one that was created for this book. Maybe you should try searching for this book's Docker Hub repositories. Remember, repositories are named with a username/repository pattern.

When you get the answer, pat yourself on the back and remove the images using the `docker rmi` command. Concretely, the commands you run should look something like these:

```
docker rmi dockerinaction/ch3_ex2_hunt
docker rmi <mystery repository>
```

If you were following the examples and using the `--rm` option on your `docker run` commands, you should have no containers to clean up. You've learned a lot in this example. You've found a new image on Docker Hub and used the `docker run` command in a new way. There's a lot to know about running interactive containers. The next section covers that in greater detail.

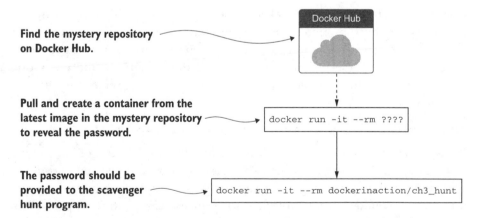

Find the mystery repository on Docker Hub.

Pull and create a container from the latest image in the mystery repository to reveal the password.

```
docker run -it --rm ????
```

The password should be provided to the scavenger hunt program.

```
docker run -it --rm dockerinaction/ch3_hunt
```

Figure 3.4 The steps required to complete the Docker Hub scavenger hunt. Find the mystery repository on Docker Hub. Install the latest image from that repository and run it interactively to get the password.

Docker Hub is by no means the only source for software. Depending on the goals and perspective of software publishers, Docker Hub may not be an appropriate distribution point. Closed source or proprietary projects may not want to risk publishing their software through a third party. There are three other ways to install software:

- You can use alternative repository registries or run your own registry.
- You can manually load images from a file.
- You can download a project from some other source and build an image using a provided Dockerfile.

All three of these options are viable for private projects or corporate infrastructure. The next few subsections cover how to install software from each alternative source.

3.2.3 *Using alternative registries*

As mentioned earlier, Docker makes the registry software available for anyone to run. Hosting companies have integrated it into their offerings, and companies have begun running their own internal registries. I'm not going to cover running a registry until chapter 8, but it's important that you learn how to use them early.

Using an alternative registry is simple. It requires no additional configuration. All you need is the address of the registry. The following command will download another "Hello World" type example from an alternative registry:

```
docker pull quay.io/dockerinaction/ch3_hello_registry:latest
```

The registry address is part of the full repository specification covered in section 3.1. The full pattern is as follows:

```
[REGISTRYHOST/][USERNAME/]NAME[:TAG]
```

Docker knows how to talk to Docker registries, so the only difference is that you specify the registry host. In some cases, working with registries will require an authentication step. If you encounter a situation where this is the case, consult the documentation or the group that configured the registry to find out more. When you're finished with the hello-registry image you installed, remove it with the following command:

```
docker rmi quay.io/dockerinaction/ch3_hello_registry
```

Registries are powerful. They enable a user to relinquish control of image storage and transportation. But running your own registry can be complicated and may create a potential single point of failure for your deployment infrastructure. If running a custom registry sounds a bit complicated for your use case, and third-party distribution tools are out of the question, you might consider loading images directly from a file.

3.2.4 *Images as files*

Docker provides a command to load images into Docker from a file. With this tool, you can load images that you acquired through other channels. Maybe your company has chosen to distribute images through a central file server or some type of version-control system. Maybe the image is small enough that your friend just sent it to you over email or shared it via flash drive. However you came upon the file, you can load it into Docker with the `docker load` command.

You'll need an image file to load before I can show you the `docker load` command. Because it's unlikely that you have an image file lying around, I'll show you how to save one from a loaded image. For the purposes of this example, you'll pull `busybox:latest`. That image is small and easy to work with. To save that image to a file, use the `docker save` command. Figure 3.5 demonstrates `docker save` by creating a file from BusyBox.

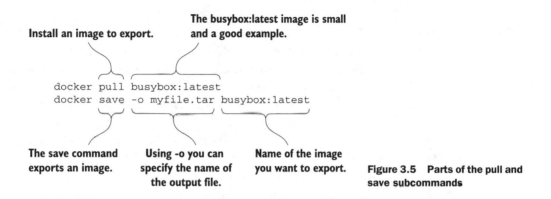

Figure 3.5 Parts of the pull and save subcommands

I used the .tar filename suffix in this example because the `docker save` command creates TAR archive files. You can use any filename you want. If you omit the `-o` flag, the resulting file will be streamed to the terminal.

> **TIP** Other ecosystems that use TAR archives for packing define custom file extensions. For example, Java uses .jar, .war, and .ear. In cases like these, using custom file extensions can help hint at the purpose and content of the archive. Although there are no defaults set by Docker and no official guidance on the matter, you may find using a custom extension useful if you work with these files often.

After running the `save` command, the `docker` program will terminate unceremoniously. Check that it worked by listing the contents of your current working directory. If the specified file is there, use this command to remove the image from Docker:

```
docker rmi busybox
```

After removing the image, load it again from the file you created using the `docker load` command. Like `docker save`, if you run `docker load` without the `-i` command, Docker will use the standard input stream instead of reading the archive from a file:

```
docker load -i myfile.tar
```

Once you've run the `docker load` command, the image should be loaded. You can verify this by running the `docker images` command again. If everything worked correctly, BusyBox should be included in the list.

Working with images as files is as easy as working with registries, but you miss out on all the nice distribution facilities that registries provide. If you want to build your own distribution tools, or you already have something else in place, it should be trivial to integrate with Docker using these commands.

Another popular project distribution pattern uses bundles of files with installation scripts. This approach is popular with open source projects that use public version-control repositories for distribution. In these cases you work with a file, but the file is not an image; it is a Dockerfile.

3.2.5 *Installing from a Dockerfile*

A Dockerfile is a script that describes steps for Docker to take to build a new image. These files are distributed along with software that the author wants to be put into an image. In this case, you're not technically installing an image. Instead, you're following instructions to build an image. Working with Dockerfiles is covered in depth in chapter 7.

Distributing a Dockerfile is similar to distributing image files. You're left to your own distribution mechanisms. A common pattern is to distribute a Dockerfile with software from common version-control systems like Git or Mercurial. If you have Git installed, you can try this by running an example from a public repository:

```
git clone https://github.com/dockerinaction/ch3_dockerfile.git
docker build -t dia_ch3/dockerfile:latest ch3_dockerfile
```

In this example you copy the project from a public source repository onto your computer and then build and install a Docker image using the Dockerfile included with that project. The value provided to the `-t` option of `docker build` is the repository where you want to install the image. Building images from Dockerfiles is a light way to move projects around that fits into existing workflows. There are two disadvantages to taking this approach. First, depending on the specifics of the project, the build process might take some time. Second, dependencies may drift between the time when the Dockerfile was authored and when an image is built on a user's computer. These issues make distributing build files less than an ideal experience for a user. But it remains popular in spite of these drawbacks.

When you're finished with this example, make sure to clean up your workspace:

```
docker rmi dia_ch3/dockerfile
rm -rf ch3_dockerfile
```

After reading this section you should have a complete picture of your options to install software with Docker. But when you install software, you should have an idea about what changes are being made to your computer.

3.3 Installation files and isolation

Understanding how images are identified, discovered, and installed is a minimum proficiency for a Docker user. If you understand what files are actually installed and how those files are built and isolated at runtime, you'll be able to answer more difficult questions that come up with experience, such as these:

- What image properties factor into download and installation speeds?
- What are all these unnamed images that are listed when I use the `docker images` command?
- Why does output from the `docker pull` command include messages about pulling dependent layers?
- Where are the files that I wrote to my container's file system?

Learning this material is the third and final step to understanding software installation with Docker, as illustrated in figure 3.6.

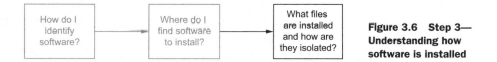

Figure 3.6 Step 3—Understanding how software is installed

So far, when I've written about installing software, I've used the term *image*. This was to infer that the software you were going to use was in a single image and that an image was contained within a single file. Although this may occasionally be accurate, most of the time what I've been calling an image is actually a collection of image layers. A *layer* is an image that's related to at least one other image. It is easier to understand layers when you see them in action.

3.3.1 Image layers in action

In this example you're going to install the two images. Both depend on Java 6. The applications themselves are simple Hello World–style programs. What I want you to keep an eye on is what Docker does when you install each. You should notice how long it takes to install the first compared to the second and read what it's printing to the terminal. When an image is being installed, you can watch Docker determine which dependencies it needs to download and then see the progress of the individual image layer downloads. Java is great for this example because the layers are quite large, and that will give you a moment to really see Docker in action.

The two images you're going to install are dockerinaction/ch3_myapp and dockerinaction/ch3_myotherapp. You should just use the `docker pull` command because you only need to see the images install, not start a container from them. Here are the commands you should run:

```
docker pull dockerinaction/ch3_myapp
docker pull dockerinaction/ch3_myotherapp
```

Did you see it? Unless your network connection is far better than mine, or you had already installed Java 6 as a dependency of some other image, the download for dockerinaction/ch3_myapp should have been much slower than dockerinaction/ ch3_myotherapp.

When you installed ch3_myapp, Docker determined that it needed to install the openjdk-6 image because it's the direct dependency (parent layer) of the requested image. When Docker went to install that dependency, it discovered the dependencies of that layer and downloaded those first. Once all the dependencies of a layer are installed, that layer is installed. Finally, openjdk-6 was installed, and then the tiny ch3_myapp layer was installed.

When you issued the command to install ch3_myotherapp, Docker identified that openjdk-6 was already installed and immediately installed the image for ch3_myotherapp. This was simpler, and because less than one megabyte of data was transferred, it was faster. But again, to the user it was an identical process.

From the user perspective this ability is nice to have, but you wouldn't want to have to try to optimize for it. Just take the benefits where they happen to work out. From the perspective of a software or image author, this ability should play a major factor in your image design. I cover that more in chapter 7.

If you run `docker images` now, you'll see the following repositories listed:

- dockerinaction/ch3_myapp
- dockerinaction/ch3_myotherapp
- java:6

By default, the `docker images` command will only show you repositories. Similar to other commands, if you specify the `-a` flag, the list will include every installed interme- diate image or layer. Running `docker images -a` will show a list that includes several repositories listed as `<none>`. The only way to refer to these is to use the value in the `IMAGE ID` column.

In this example you installed two images directly, but a third parent repository was installed as well. You'll need to clean up all three. You can do so more easily if you use the condensed `docker rmi` syntax:

```
docker rmi \
    dockerinaction/ch3_myapp \
    dockerinaction/ch3_myotherapp \
    java:6
```

The `docker rmi` command allows you to specify a space-separated list of images to be removed. This comes in handy when you need to remove a small set of images after an example. I'll be using this when appropriate throughout the rest of the examples in this book.

3.3.2 *Layer relationships*

Images maintain parent/child relationships. In these relationships they build from their parents and form layers. The files available to a container are the union of all of the layers in the lineage of the image the container was created from. Images can have relationships with any other image, including images in different repositories with different owners. The two images in section 3.3.1 use a Java 6 image as their parent. Figure 3.7 illustrates the full image ancestry of both images.

The layers shown in figure 3.7 are a sample of the java:6 image at the time of this writing. An image is named when its author tags and publishes it. A user can create aliases, as you

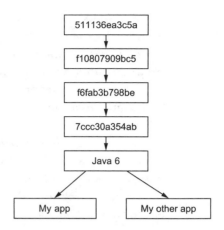

Figure 3.7   The full lineage of the two Docker images used in section 3.3.1

did in chapter 2 using the docker tag command. Until an image is tagged, the only way to refer to it is to use its unique identifier (UID) that was generated when the image was built. In figure 3.7, the parents of the common Java 6 image are labeled using the first 12 digits of their UID. These layers contain common libraries and dependencies of the Java 6 software. Docker truncates the UID from 65 (base 16) digits to 12 for the benefit of its human users. Internally and through API access, Docker uses the full 65. It's important to be aware of this when you've installed images along with similar unnamed images. I wouldn't want you to think something bad happened or some malicious software had made it into your computer when you see these images included when you use the docker images command.

The Java images are sizable. At the time of this writing, the openjdk-6 image is 348 MB, and the openjdk-7 image is 590 MB. You get some space savings when you use the runtime-only images, but even openjre-6 is 200 MB. Again, Java was chosen here because its images are particularly large for a common dependency.

3.3.3 *Container file system abstraction and isolation*

Programs running inside containers know nothing about image layers. From inside a container, the file system operates as though it's not running in a container or operating on an image. From the perspective of the container, it has exclusive copies of the files provided by the image. This is made possible with something called a union file system. Docker uses a variety of union file systems and will select the best fit for your system. The details of how the union file system works are beyond what you need to know to use Docker effectively.

A union file system is part of a critical set of tools that combine to create effective file system isolation. The other tools are MNT namespaces and the chroot system call.

The file system is used to create mount points on your host's file system that abstract the use of layers. The layers created are what are bundled into Docker image layers. Likewise, when a Docker image is installed, its layers are unpacked and appropriately configured for use by the specific file system provider chosen for your system.

The Linux kernel provides a namespace for the MNT system. When Docker creates a container, that new container will have its own MNT namespace, and a new mount point will be created for the container to the image.

Lastly, chroot is used to make the root of the image file system the root in the container's context. This prevents anything running inside the container from referencing any other part of the host file system.

Using chroot and MNT namespaces is common for container technologies. By adding a union file system to the recipe, Docker containers have several benefits.

3.3.4   *Benefits of this toolset and file system structure*

The first and perhaps most important benefit of this approach is that common layers need to be installed only once. If you install any number of images and they all depend on some common layer, that common layer and all of its parent layers will need to be downloaded or installed only once. This means you might be able to install several specializations of a program without storing redundant files on your computer or downloading redundant layers. By contrast, most virtual machine technologies will store the same files as many times as you have redundant virtual machines on a computer.

Second, layers provide a coarse tool for managing dependencies and separating concerns. This is especially handy for software authors, and chapter 7 talks more about this. From a user perspective, this benefit will help you quickly identify what software you're running by examining which images and layers you're using.

Lastly, it's easy to create software specializations when you can layer minor changes on top of some basic image. That's another subject covered in detail in chapter 7. Providing specialized images helps users get exactly what they need from software with minimal customization. This is one of the best reasons to use Docker.

3.3.5   *Weaknesses of union file systems*

Docker will choose the best file system for the system it's running on, but no implementation is perfect for every workload. In fact, there are some specific use cases when you should pause and consider using another Docker feature.

Different file systems have different rules about file attributes, sizes, names, and characters. Union file systems are in a position where they often need to translate between the rules of different file systems. In the best cases they're able to provide acceptable translations. In the worst cases features are omitted. For example, neither btrfs nor OverlayFS provides support for the extended attributes that make SELinux work.

Union file systems use a pattern called copy-on-write, and that makes implementing memory-mapped files (the mmap() system call) difficult. Some union file systems provide implementations that work under the right conditions, but it may be a better idea to avoid memory-mapping files from an image.

The backing file system is another pluggable feature of Docker. You can determine which file system your installation is using with the `info` subcommand. If you want to specifically tell Docker which file system to use, do so with the `--storage-driver` or `-s` option when you start the Docker daemon. Most issues that arise with writing to the union file system can be addressed without changing the storage provider. These can be solved with volumes, the subject of chapter 4.

3.4 Summary

The task of installing and managing software on a computer presents a unique set of challenges. This chapter explains how you can use Docker to address them. The core ideas and features covered by this chapter are as follows:

- Human Docker users use repository names to communicate which software they would like Docker to install.
- Docker Hub is the default Docker registry. You can find software on Docker Hub through either the website or the `docker` command-line program.
- The `docker` command-line program makes it simple to install software that's distributed through alternative registries or in other forms.
- The image repository specification includes a registry host field.
- The `docker load` and `docker save` commands can be used to load and save images from TAR archives.
- Distributing a Dockerfile with a project simplifies image builds on user machines.
- Images are usually related to other images in parent/child relationships. These relationships form layers. When we say that we have installed an image, we are saying that we have installed a target image and each image layer in its lineage.
- Structuring images with layers enables layer reuse and saves bandwidth during distribution and storage space on your computer.

Persistent storage and
shared state with volumes

4

This chapter covers

- An introduction to volumes
- The two types of volumes
- How to share data between the host and a container
- How to share data between containers
- The volume life cycle
- Data management and control patterns with volumes

At this point in the book, you've installed and run a few programs. You've seen a few toy examples but haven't run anything that resembles the real world. The difference between the examples in the first three chapters and the real world is that in the real world, programs work with data. This chapter introduces Docker volumes and strategies that you'll use to manage data with containers.

Consider what it might look like to run a database program inside a container. You could package the software with the image, and when you start the container it might initialize an empty database. When programs connect to the database and enter data, where is that data stored? Is it in a file inside the container? What happens to that data when you stop the container or remove it? How would you move your data if you wanted to upgrade the database program?

Consider another situation where you're running a couple of different web applications inside different containers. Where would you write log files so that they will outlive the container? How would you get access to those logs to troubleshoot a problem? How can other programs such as log digest tools get access to those files? The answer to all these questions involves the use of volumes.

4.1 Introducing volumes

A host or container's directory tree is created by a set of mount points that describe how to piece together one or more file systems. A *volume* is a mount point on the container's directory tree where a portion of the host directory tree has been mounted. Most people are only minimally familiar with file systems and mount points and rarely customize them. People have a more difficult time with volumes than with any other Docker topic. That lack of familiarity with mount points is a contributing factor.

Without volumes, container users are limited to working with the union file system that provides image mounts. Figure 4.1 shows a program running in a container and writing to files. The first file is written to the root file system. The operating system directs root file system changes to the top layer of the mounted union file system. The second file is written to a volume that has been mounted on the container's directory tree at /data. That change is made directly on the host's file system through the volume.

Although the union file system works for building and sharing images, it's less than ideal for working with persistent or shared data. Volumes fill those use cases and play a critical role in containerized system design.

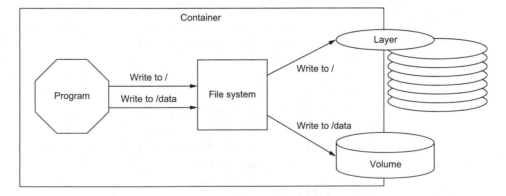

Figure 4.1   A container with a mounted volume and writeable top layer of the union file system

4.1.1   *Volumes provide container-independent data management*

Semantically, a volume is a tool for segmenting and sharing data that has a scope or life cycle that's independent of a single container. That makes volumes an important part of any containerized system design that shares or writes files. Examples of data that differs in scope or access from a container include the following:

- Database software versus database data
- Web application versus log data
- Data processing application versus input and output data
- Web server versus static content
- Products versus support tools

Volumes enable separation of concerns and create modularity for architectural components. That modularity helps you understand, build, support, and reuse parts of larger systems more easily.

Think about it this way: images are appropriate for packaging and distributing relatively static files like programs; volumes hold dynamic data or specializations. This distinction makes images reusable and data simple to share. This separation of relatively static and dynamic file space allows application or image authors to implement advanced patterns such as polymorphic and composable tools.

A *polymorphic* tool is one that maintains a consistent interface but might have several implementations that do different things. Consider an application such as a general application server. Apache Tomcat, for example, is an application that provides an HTTP interface on a network and dispatches any requests it receives to pluggable programs. Tomcat has polymorphic behavior. Using volumes, you can inject behavior into containers without modifying an image. Alternatively, consider a database program like MongoDB or MySQL. The value of a database is defined by the data it contains. A database program always presents the same interface but takes on a wholly different value depending on the data that can be injected with a volume. The polymorphic container pattern is the subject of section 4.5.3.

More fundamentally, volumes enable the separation of application and host concerns. At some point an image will be loaded onto a host and a container created from it. Docker knows little about the host where it's running and can only make assertions about what files should be available to a container. That means Docker alone has no way to take advantage of host-specific facilities like mounted network storage or mixed spinning and solid-state hard drives. But a user with knowledge of the host can use volumes to map directories in a container to appropriate storage on that host.

Now that you're familiar with what volumes are and why they're important, you can get started with them in a real-world example.

4.1.2   *Using volumes with a NoSQL database*

The Apache Cassandra project provides a column database with built-in clustering, eventual consistency, and linear write scalability. It's a popular choice in modern system designs, and an official image is available on Docker Hub. Cassandra is like other databases in that it stores its data in files on disk. In this section you'll use the official Cassandra image to create a single-node Cassandra cluster, create a keyspace, delete the container, and then recover that keyspace on a new node in another container.

Get started by creating a single container that defines a volume. This is called a volume container. Volume containers are one of the advanced patterns discussed later in this chapter:

```
docker run -d \
    --volume /var/lib/cassandra/data \      ◀─┐ Specify volume mount point
    --name cass-shared \                       │ inside the container
    alpine echo Data Container
```

The volume container will immediately stop. That is appropriate for the purposes of this example. Don't remove it yet. You're going to use the volume it created when you create a new container running Cassandra:

```
docker run -d \
    --volumes-from cass-shared \      ◀─┐ Inherit volume
    --name cass1 \                       │ definitions
    cassandra:2.2
```

After Docker pulls the cassandra:2.2 image from Docker Hub, it creates a new container and copies the volume definitions from the volume container. After that, both containers have a volume mounted at /var/lib/cassandra/data that points to the same location on the host's directory tree. Next, start a container from the cassandra:2.2 image, but run a Cassandra client tool and connect to your running server:

```
docker run -it --rm \
    --link cass1:cass \
    cassandra:2.2 cqlsh cass
```

Now you can inspect or modify your Cassandra database from the CQLSH command line. First, look for a keyspace named docker_hello_world:

```
select *
from system.schema_keyspaces
where keyspace_name = 'docker_hello_world';
```

Cassandra should return an empty list. This means the database hasn't been modified by the example. Next, create that keyspace with the following command:

```
create keyspace docker_hello_world
with replication = {
    'class' : 'SimpleStrategy',
    'replication_factor': 1
};
```

Now that you've modified the database, you should be able to issue the same query again to see the results and verify that your changes were accepted. The following command is the same as the one you ran earlier:

```
select *
from system.schema_keyspaces
where keyspace_name = 'docker_hello_world';
```

This time Cassandra should return a single entry with the properties you specified when you created the keyspace. If you're satisfied that you've connected to and modified your Cassandra node, quit the CQLSH program to stop the client container:

```
# Leave and stop the current container
quit
```

The client container was created with the --rm flag and was automatically removed when the command stopped. Continue cleaning up the first part of this example by stopping and removing the Cassandra node you created:

```
docker stop cass1
docker rm -vf cass1
```

Both the Cassandra client and server you created will be deleted after running those commands. If the modifications you made are persisted, the only place they could remain is the volume container. If that is true, then the scope of that data has expanded to include two containers, and its life cycle has extended beyond the container where the data originated.

You can test this by repeating these steps. Create a new Cassandra node, attach a client, and query for the keyspace. Figure 4.2 illustrates the system and what you will have built.

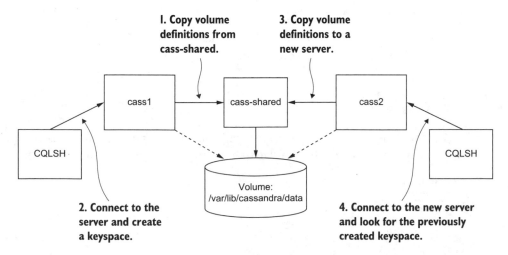

Figure 4.2   Key steps in creating and recovering data persisted to a volume with Cassandra

The next three commands will test recovery of the data:

```
docker run -d \
    --volumes-from cass-shared \
    --name cass2 \
    cassandra:2.2

docker run -it --rm \
    --link cass2:cass \
    cassandra:2.2 \
    cqlsh cass

select *
from system.schema_keyspaces
where keyspace_name = 'docker_hello_world';
```

The last command in this set returns a single entry, and it matches the keyspace you created in the previous container. This confirms the previous claims and demonstrates how volumes might be used to create durable systems. Before moving on, quit the CQLSH program and clean up your workspace. Make sure to remove that volume container as well:

```
quit

docker rm -vf cass2 cass-shared
```

This example demonstrates one way to use volumes without going into how they work, the patterns in use, or how to manage volume life cycle. The remainder of this chapter dives deeper into each facet of volumes, starting with the different types available.

4.2 Volume types

There are two types of volume. Every volume is a mount point on the container directory tree to a location on the host directory tree, but the types differ in where that location is on the host. The first type of volume is a bind mount. Bind mount volumes use any user-specified directory or file on the host operating system. The second type is a managed volume. Managed volumes use locations that are created by the Docker daemon in space controlled by the daemon, called Docker managed space. The volume types are illustrated in figure 4.3.

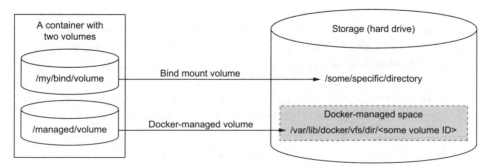

Figure 4.3 Docker provides both bind mount and managed volumes.

Each type of volume has advantages and disadvantages. Depending on your specific use case, you may need to use one or be unable to use the other. This section explores each type in depth.

4.2.1 Bind mount volumes

A bind mount volume is a volume that points to a user-specified location on the host file system. Bind mount volumes are useful when the host provides some file or directory that needs to be mounted into the container directory tree at a specific point, as shown in figure 4.4.

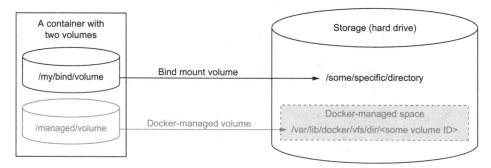

Figure 4.4   A host directory as a bind mount volume

Bind mount volumes are useful if you want to share data with other processes running outside a container, such as components of the host system itself. They also work if you want to share data that lives on your host at some known location with a specific program that runs in a container.

For example, suppose you're working on a document or web page on your local computer and want to share your work with a friend. One way to do so would be to use Docker to launch a web server and serve content that you've copied into the web server image. Although that would work and might even be a best practice for production environments, it's cumbersome to rebuild the image every time you want to share an updated version of the document.

Instead, you could use Docker to launch the web server and bind mount the location of your document into the new container at the web server's document root. You can try this for yourself. Create a new directory in your home directory called example-docs. Now create a file named index.html in that directory. Add a nice message for your friend to the file. The following command will start an Apache HTTP server where your new directory is bind mounted to the server's document root:

```
docker run -d --name bmweb \
    -v ~/example-docs:/usr/local/apache2/htdocs \
```

```
-p 80:80 \
httpd:latest
```

With this container running, you should be able to point your web browser at the IP address where your Docker engine is running and see the file you created.

In this example you used the -v option and a location map to create the bind mount volume. The map is delimited with a colon (as is common with Linux-style command-line tools). The map key (the path before the colon) is the absolute path of a location on the host file system, and the value (the path after the colon) is the location where it should be mounted inside the container. You must specify locations with absolute paths.

This example touches on an important attribute or feature of volumes. When you mount a volume on a container file system, it replaces the content that the image provides at that location. In this example, the httpd:latest image provides some default HTML content at /usr/local/apache2/htdocs/, but when you mounted a volume at that location, the content provided by the image was overridden by the content on the host. This behavior is the basis for the polymorphic container pattern discussed later in the chapter.

Expanding on this use case, suppose you want to make sure that the Apache HTTP web server can't change the contents of this volume. Even the most trusted software can contain vulnerabilities, and it's best to minimize the impact of an attack on your website. Fortunately, Docker provides a mechanism to mount volumes as read-only. You can do this by appending :ro to the volume map specification. In the example, you should change the run command to something like the following:

```
docker rm -vf bmweb

docker run --name bmweb_ro \
    --volume ~/example-docs:/usr/local/apache2/htdocs/:ro \
    -p 80:80 \
    httpd:latest
```

By mounting the volume as read-only, you can prevent any process inside the container from modifying the content of the volume. You can see this in action by running a quick test:

```
docker run --rm \
    -v ~/example-docs:/testspace:ro \
    alpine \
    /bin/sh -c 'echo test > /testspace/test'
```

This command starts a container with a similar read-only bind mount as the web server. It runs a command that tries to add the word *test* to a file named test in the volume. The command fails because the volume is mounted as read-only.

Finally, note that if you specify a host directory that doesn't exist, Docker will create it for you. Although this can come in handy, relying on this functionality isn't the best idea. It's better to have more control over the ownership and permissions set on a directory.

```
ls ~/example-docs/absent                                          ◄──── Verify that "absent"
                                                                         does not exist
docker run --rm -v ~/example-docs/absent:/absent alpine:latest \
    /bin/sh -c 'mount | grep absent'              ◄──── Examine the volume
                                                         mount definition
ls ~/example-docs/absent
```

Examine the created directory → points to `ls ~/example-docs/absent`

Bind mount volumes aren't limited to directories, though that's how they're frequently used. You can use bind mount volumes to mount individual files. This provides the flexibility to create or link resources at a level that avoids conflict with other resources. Consider when you want to mount a specific file into a directory that contains other files. Concretely, suppose you only wanted to serve a single additional file alongside the web content that shipped with some image. If you use a bind mount of a whole directory over that location, the other files will be lost. By using a specific file as a volume, you can override or inject individual files.

The important thing to note in this case is that the file must exist on the host before you create the container. Otherwise, Docker will assume that you wanted to use a directory, create it on the host, and mount it at the desired location (even if that location is occupied by a file).

The first problem with bind mount volumes is that they tie otherwise portable container descriptions to the file system of a specific host. If a container description depends on content at a specific location on the host file system, then that description isn't portable to hosts where the content is unavailable or available in some other location.

The next big problem is that they create an opportunity for conflict with other containers. It would be a bad idea to start multiple instances of Cassandra that all use the same host location as a volume. In that case, each of the instances would compete for the same set of files. Without other tools such as file locks, that would likely result in corruption of the database.

Bind mount volumes are appropriate tools for workstations or machines with specialized concerns. It's better to avoid these kinds of specific bindings in generalized platforms or hardware pools. You can take advantage of volumes in a host-agnostic and portable way with Docker-managed volumes.

4.2.2 *Docker-managed volumes*

Managed volumes are different from bind mount volumes because the Docker daemon creates managed volumes in a portion of the host's file system that's owned by Docker, as shown in figure 4.5. Using managed volumes is a method of decoupling volumes from specialized locations on the file system.

Managed volumes are created when you use the -v option (or --volume) on docker run but only specify the mount point in the container directory tree. You

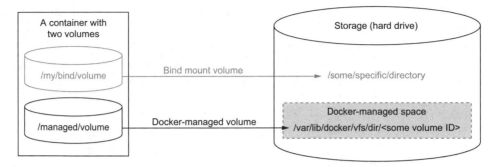

Figure 4.5 A directory in Docker-managed space mounted as a volume

created a managed volume in the Cassandra example in section 4.1.2. The container named cass-shared specified a volume at /var/lib/cassandra/data:

```
docker run -d \
    -v /var/lib/cassandra/data \          Specify volume mount
    --name cass-shared \                  point inside container
    alpine echo Data Container
```

When you created this container, the Docker daemon created directories to store the contents of the three volumes somewhere in a part of the host file system that it controls. To find out exactly where this folder is, you can use the docker inspect command filtered for the Volumes key. The important thing to take away from this output is that Docker created each of the volumes in a directory controlled by the Docker daemon on the host:

```
docker inspect -f "{{json .Volumes}}" cass-shared
```

The inspect subcommand will output a list of container mount points and the corresponding path on the host directory tree. The output will look like this:

```
{"/var/lib/cassandra/data":"/mnt/sda1/var/lib/docker/vfs/dir/632fa59c..."}
```

The Volumes key points to a value that is itself a map. In this map each key is a mount point in the container, and the value is the location of the directory on the host file system. Here we've inspected a container with one volume. The map is sorted by the lexicographical ordering of its keys and is independent of the ordering specified when the container is created.

> **TIP** VirtualBox (Docker Machine or Boot2Docker) users should keep in mind that the host path specified in each value is relative to their virtual machine root file system and not the root of their host. Managed volumes are created on the machine that's running the Docker daemon, but VirtualBox will create bind mount volumes that reference directories or files on the host machine.

Docker-managed volumes may seem difficult to work with if you're manually building or linking tools together on your desktop, but in larger systems where specific locality of the data is less important, managed volumes are a much more effective way to organize your data. Using them decouples volumes from other potential concerns of the system. By using Docker-managed volumes, you're simply stating, "I need a place to put some data that I'm working with." This is a requirement that Docker can fill on any machine with Docker installed. Further, when you're finished with a volume and you ask Docker to clean things up for you, Docker can confidently remove any directories or files that are no longer being used by a container. Using volumes in this way helps manage clutter. As Docker middleware or plugins evolve, managed volume users will be able to adopt more advanced features like portable volumes.

Sharing access to data is a key feature of volumes. If you have decoupled volumes from known locations on the file system, you need to know how to share volumes between containers without exposing the exact location of managed containers. The next section describes two ways to share data between containers using volumes.

4.3   Sharing volumes

Suppose you have a web server running inside a container that logs all the requests it receives to /logs/access. If you want to move those logs off your web server into storage that's more permanent, you might do that with a script inside another container. Sharing volumes between containers is where their value becomes more obvious. Just as there are two types of volume, there are two ways to share volumes between containers.

4.3.1   Host-dependent sharing

You've already read about the tools needed to implement host-dependent sharing. Two or more containers are said to use host-dependent sharing when each has a bind mount volume for a single known location on the host file system. This is the most obvious way to share some disk space between containers. You can see it in action in the following example:

```
mkdir ~/web-logs-example                                ◄────┐  Set up a known location

docker run --name plath -d \                            Bind mount the location into
    -v ~/web-logs-example:/data \                       a log-writing container
    dockerinaction/ch4_writer_a

docker run --rm \
    -v ~/web-logs-example:/reader-data \                Bind mount the same location
    alpine:latest \                                     into a container for reading
    head /reader-data/logA

cat ~/web-logs-example/logA                             ◄────┐  View the logs from the host
Stop the
writer ┌──►  docker stop plath
```

In this example you created two containers: one named plath that writes lines to a file and another that views the top part of the file. These containers share a common bind mount volume. Outside any container you can see the changes by listing the contents of the directory you created or viewing the new file.

Explore ways that containers might be linked together in this way. The next example starts four containers—two log writers and two readers:

```
docker run --name woolf -d \
    --volume ~/web-logs-example:/data \
    dockerinaction/ch4_writer_a

docker run --name alcott -d \
    -v ~/web-logs-example:/data \
    dockerinaction/ch4_writer_b

docker run --rm --entrypoint head \
    -v ~/web-logs-example:/towatch:ro \
    alpine:latest \
    /towatch/logA

docker run --rm \
    -v ~/web-logs-example:/toread:ro \
    alpine:latest \
    head /toread/logB
```

In this example, you created four containers, each of which mounted the same directory as a volume. The first two containers are writing to different files in that volume. The third and fourth containers mount the volume at a different location and as read-only. This is a toy example, but it clearly demonstrates a feature that could be useful given the variety of ways that people build images and software.

Host-dependent sharing requires you to use bind mount volumes but—for the reasons mentioned at the end of section 4.2.1—bind mount volumes and therefore host-dependent sharing might cause problems or be too expensive to maintain if you're working with a large number of machines. The next section demonstrates a shortcut to share both managed volumes and bind mount volumes with a set of containers.

4.3.2 *Generalized sharing and the volumes-from flag*

The docker run command provides a flag that will copy the volumes from one or more containers to the new container. The flag --volumes-from can be set multiple times to specify multiple source containers.

You used this flag in section 4.1.2 to copy the managed volume defined by a volume container into each of the containers running Cassandra. The example is realistic but fails to illustrate a few specific behaviors of the --volumes-from flag and managed containers:

```
docker run --name fowler \
    -v ~/example-books:/library/PoEAA \
    -v /library/DSL \
    alpine:latest \
    echo "Fowler collection created."
```

```
docker run --name knuth \
    -v /library/TAoCP.vol1 \
    -v /library/TAoCP.vol2 \
    -v /library/TAoCP.vol3 \
    -v /library/TAoCP.vol4.a \
    alpine:latest \
    echo "Knuth collection created"

docker run --name reader \
    --volumes-from fowler \
    --volumes-from knuth \
    alpine:latest ls -l /library/

docker inspect --format "{{json .Volumes}}" reader
```

List all volumes as they were copied into new container

Checkout volume list for reader

In this example you created two containers that defined Docker-managed volumes as well as a bind mount volume. To share these with a third container without the --volumes-from flag, you'd need to inspect the previously created containers and then craft bind mount volumes to the Docker-managed host directories. Docker does all this on your behalf when you use the --volumes-from flag. It copies any volume present on a referenced source container into the new container. In this case, the container named reader copied all the volumes defined by both fowler and knuth.

You can copy volumes directly or transitively. This means that if you're copying the volumes from another container, you'll also copy the volumes that it copied from some other container. Using the containers created in the last example yields the following:

```
docker run --name aggregator \
    --volumes-from fowler \
    --volumes-from knuth \
    alpine:latest \
    echo "Collection Created."

docker run --rm \
    --volumes-from aggregator \
    alpine:latest \
    ls -l /library/
```

Create an aggregation

Consume volumes from a single source and list them

Copied volumes always have the same mount point. That means that you can't use --volumes-from in three situations.

In the first situation, you can't use --volumes-from if the container you're building needs a shared volume mounted to a different location. It offers no tooling for remapping mount points. It will only copy and union the mount points specified by the specified containers. For example, if the student in the last example wanted to mount the library to a location like /school/library, they wouldn't be able to do so.

The second situation occurs when the volume sources conflict with each other or a new volume specification. If one or more sources create a managed volume with the same mount point, then a consumer of both will receive only one of the volume definitions:

```
docker run --name chomsky --volume /library/ss \
    alpine:latest echo "Chomsky collection created."
```

```
docker run --name lamport --volume /library/ss \
    alpine:latest echo "Lamport collection created."

docker run --name student \
    --volumes-from chomsky --volumes-from lamport \
    alpine:latest ls -l /library/

docker inspect -f "{{json .Volumes}}" student
```

When you run the example, the output of docker inspect will show that the last container has only a single volume listed at /library/ss and its value is the same as one of the other two. Each source container defines the same mount point, and you create a race condition by copying both to the new container. Only one of the two copy operations can succeed.

A real-world example where this would be limiting is if you were copying the volumes of several web servers into a single container for inspection. If those servers are all running the same software or share common configuration (which is more likely than not in a containerized system), then all those servers might use the same mount points. In that case, the mount points would conflict, and you'd be able to access only a subset of the required data.

The third situation where you can't use --volumes-from is if you need to change the write permission of a volume. This is because --volumes-from copies the full volumes definition. For example, if your source has a volume mounted with read/write access, and you want to share that with a container that should have only read access, using --volumes-from won't work.

Sharing volumes with the --volumes-from flag is an important tool for building portable application architectures, but it does introduce some limitations. Using Docker-managed volumes decouples containers from the data and file system structure of the host machine, and that's critical for most production environments. The files and directories that Docker creates for managed volumes still need to be accounted for and maintained. To understand how Docker works with these files and how to keep your Docker environment clean, you need to understand the managed volume life cycle.

4.4   The managed volume life cycle

By this point in the chapter you should have quite a few containers and volumes to clean up. I've omitted cleanup instructions thus far so that you have a wealth of material to use in this section. Managed volumes have life cycles that are independent of any container, but as of this writing you can only reference them by the containers that use them.

4.4.1   Volume ownership

Managed volumes are second-class entities. You have no way to share or delete a specific managed volume because you have no way to identify a managed volume.

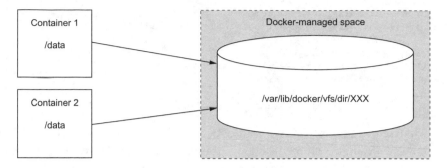

Figure 4.6   These two containers have an ownership relationship with a single managed volume.

Managed volumes are only created when you omit a bind mount source, and they're only identifiable by the containers that use them.

The highest fidelity way to identify volumes is to define a single container for each managed volume. In doing so, you can be very specific about which volumes you consume. More importantly, doing so helps you delete specific volumes. Unless you resort to examining volume mappings on a container and manually cleaning up the Docker-managed space, removing volumes requires a referencing container, and that makes it important to understand which containers own each managed volume. See figure 4.6.

A container owns all managed volumes mounted to its file system, and multiple containers can own a volume like in the fowler, knuth, and reader example. Docker tracks these references on managed volumes to ensure that no currently referenced volume is deleted.

4.4.2   *Cleaning up volumes*

Cleaning up managed volumes is a manual task. This default functionality prevents accidental destruction of potentially valuable data. Docker can't delete bind mount volumes because the source exists outside the Docker scope. Doing so could result in all manner of conflicts, instability, and unintentional data loss.

Docker can delete managed volumes when deleting containers. Running the docker rm command with the -v option will attempt to delete any managed volumes referenced by the target container. Any managed volumes that are referenced by other containers will be skipped, but the internal counters will be decremented. This is a safe default, but it can lead to the problematic scenario shown in figure 4.7.

If you delete every container that references a managed volume but fail to use the -v flag, you'll make that volume an orphan. Removing orphaned volumes requires messy manual steps, but depending on the size of the volumes it may be worth the effort. Alternatively, there are orphan volume cleanup scripts that you might consider using. You should carefully check those before running them. You'll need to run those scripts as a privileged user, and if they contain malware, you could be handing over full control of your system.

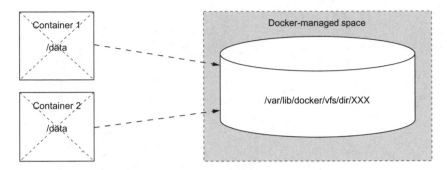

Figure 4.7 **The user created an orphan volume by deleting the two owners of that volume without instructing Docker to remove the volumes attached to those containers.**

It's a better idea to avoid the situation by getting into the habit of using the -v option and using the volume container pattern discussed in section 4.5 for critical data.

Docker creates volumes in another way that we haven't discussed. Image metadata can provide volume specifications. Chapter 7 includes details on this mechanism. In these cases, you may not even be aware of the volumes created for new containers. This is the primary reason to train yourself to use the -v option.

Orphan volumes render disk space unusable until you've cleaned them up. You can minimize this problem by remembering to clean them up and using a volume container pattern.

> **CLEANUP** Before reading further, take a few moments to clean up the containers that you've created. Use docker ps -a to get a list of those containers and remember to use the -v flag on docker rm to prevent orphan volumes.

The following is a concrete example of removing a container from one of the earlier examples:

```
docker rm -v student
```

Alternatively, if you're using a POSIX-compliant shell, you can remove all stopped containers and their volumes with the following command:

```
docker rm -v $(docker ps -aq)
```

However you accomplish the task, cleaning up volumes is an important part of resource management. Now that you have a firm grasp on the volume life cycle, sharing mechanisms, and use cases, you should be ready to learn about advanced volume patterns.

4.5 *Advanced container patterns with volumes*

In the real world, volumes are a used to accomplish a wide range of file system customizations and container interactions. This section focuses on a couple of advanced but common patterns that you may encounter or have a reason to employ in your own systems.

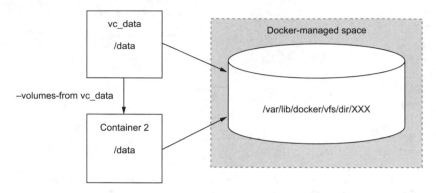

Figure 4.8   Container 2 copied vc_data's volume references.

4.5.1   *Volume container pattern*

Sections 4.1.3 and 4.3.2 use a pattern called a volume container, which is a container that does little more than provide a handle to volumes. This is useful if you come across a case for sharing a set of volumes with many containers, or if you can categorize a set of volumes that fit a common use case; see figure 4.8.

A volume container doesn't need to be running because stopped containers maintain their volume references. Several of the examples you've read so far used the volume container pattern. The example containers cass-shared, fowler, knuth, chomsky, and lamport all ran a simple `echo` command to print something to the terminal and then exited. Then you used the stopped containers as sources for the `--volumes-from` flag when creating consumer containers.

Volume containers are important for keeping a handle on data even in cases where a single container should have exclusive access to some data. These handles make it possible to easily back up, restore, and migrate data.

Suppose you wanted to update your database software (use a new image). If your database container writes its state to a volume and that volume was defined by a volume container, the migration would be as simple as shutting down the original database container and starting the new one with the volume container as a volume source. Backup and restore operations could be handled similarly. This, of course, assumes that the new database software is able to read the storage format of the old software, and it looks for the data at the same location.

> **TIP**   Using a container name prefix such as vc_ would be a great hint for humans or scripts not to use the -v option when deleting a container. The specific prefix is not as important as establishing some convention that people on your team and the tools you build can rely on.

Volume containers are most useful when you control and are able to standardize on mount point naming conventions. This is because every container that copies volumes from a volume container inherits its mount point definitions. For example, a volume container that defines a volume mounted at /logs will only be useful to other containers that expect to be able to access a volume mounted at /logs. In this way, a volume and its mount point become a sort of contract between containers. For this reason, images that have specific volume requirements should clearly communicate those in their documentation or find a way to do so programmatically.

An example where two containers disagree might be where a volume container contributes a volume mounted at /logs, but the container that uses --volumes-from is expecting to find logs at /var/logs. In this case, the consuming container would be unable to access the material it needs, and the system would fail.

Consider another example with a volume container named vc_data that contributes two volumes: /data and /app. A container that has a dependency on the /data volume provided by vc_data but uses /app for something else would break if both volumes were copied in this way. These two containers are incompatible, but Docker has no way of determining intent. The error wouldn't be discovered until after the new container was created and failed in some way.

The volume container pattern is more about simplicity and convention than anything else. It's a fundamental tool for working with data in Docker and can be extended in a few interesting ways.

4.5.2 *Data-packed volume containers*

You can extend the volume container pattern and value added by packing containers with data, as illustrated in figure 4.9. Once you've adapted your containers to use volumes, you'll find all sorts of occasions to share volumes. Volume containers are in a unique position to seed volumes with data. The data-packed volume container extension formalizes that notion. It describes how images can be used to distribute static resources like configuration or code for use in containers created with other images.

A data-packed volume container is built from an image that copies static content from its image to volumes it defines. In doing so, these containers can be used to distribute critical architecture information like configuration, key material, and code.

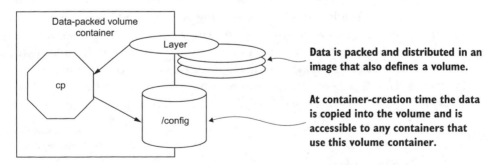

Figure 4.9   A data-packed volume container that contributes and populates a volume mounted at /config

You can build these by hand if you have an image that has the data you'd like to make available by running and defining the volume and running a `cp` command at container-creation time:

Copy image content into a volume

```
docker run --name dpvc \
    -v /config \
    dockerinaction/ch4_packed /bin/sh -c 'cp /packed/* /config/'

docker run --rm --volumes-from dpvc \
    alpine:latest ls /config                         ← List shared material

docker run --rm --volumes-from dpvc \
    alpine:latest cat /config/packedData             ← View shared material

docker rm -v dpvc        ← Remember to use –v when you clean up
```

The commands in this code share files distributed by a single image. You created three containers: one data-packed volume container and two that copied its volume and inspected the contents of the volume. Again, this is a toy example, but it demonstrates the way that you might consider distributing configuration in your own situations. Using data-packed volume containers to inject material into a new container is the basis for the polymorphic container pattern discussed in the next section.

4.5.3   *Polymorphic container pattern*

As I stated earlier in the chapter, a polymorphic tool is one that you interact with in a consistent way but might have several implementations that do different things. Using volumes, you can inject different behavior into containers without modifying an image. A polymorphic container is one that provides some functionality that's easily substituted using volumes. For example, you may have an image that contains the binaries for Node.JS and by default executes a command that runs the Node.JS program located at /app/app.js. The image might contain some default implementation that simply prints "This is a Node.JS application" to the terminal.

You can change the behavior of containers created from this image by injecting your own app.js implementation using a volume mounted at /app/app.js. It might make more sense to layer that new functionality in a new image, but there are some cases when this is the best solution. The first is during development when you might not want to build a new image each time you iterate. The second is during operational events.

Consider a situation where an operational issue has occurred. In order to triage the issue, you might need tools available in an image that you had not anticipated when the image was built. But if you mount a volume where you make additional tools available, you can use the `docker exec` command to run additional processes in a container:

```
docker run --name tools dockerinaction/ch4_tools      ← Create data-packed volume
                                                          container with tools
docker run --rm \
    --volumes-from tools \
    alpine:latest \
    ls /operations/*          ← List shared tools
```

```
docker run -d --name important_application \
    --volumes-from tools \
    dockerinaction/ch4_ia
```

Start another container with shared tools

Use shared tool in running container

```
docker exec important_application /operations/tools/someTool
```

Shut down the application

```
docker rm -vf important_application
```

```
docker rm -v tools
```

Clean up the tools

You can inject files into otherwise static containers to change all types of behavior. Most commonly, you'll use polymorphic containers to inject application configuration. Consider a multi-state deployment pipeline where an application's configuration would change depending on where you deploy it. You might use data-packed volume containers to contribute environment-specific configuration at each stage, and then your application would look for its configuration at some known location:

```
docker run --name devConfig \
    -v /config \
    dockerinaction/ch4_packed_config:latest \
    /bin/sh -c 'cp /development/* /config/'

docker run --name prodConfig \
    -v /config \
    dockerinaction/ch4_packed_config:latest \
    /bin/sh -c 'cp /production/* /config/'

docker run --name devApp \
    --volumes-from devConfig \
    dockerinaction/ch4_polyapp

docker run --name prodApp \
    --volumes-from prodConfig \
    dockerinaction/ch4_polyapp
```

In this example, you start the same application twice but with a different configuration file injected. Using this pattern you can build a simple version-controlled configuration distribution system.

4.6 Summary

One of the first major hurdles in learning how to use Docker is understanding volumes and the file system. This chapter covers volumes in depth, including the following:

- Volumes allow containers to share files with the host or other containers.
- Volumes are parts of the host file system that Docker mounts into containers at specified locations.
- There are two types of volumes: Docker-managed volumes that are located in the Docker part of the host file system and bind mount volumes that are located anywhere on the host file system.
- Volumes have life cycles that are independent of any specific container, but a user can only reference Docker-managed volumes with a container handle.

- The orphan volume problem can make disk space difficult to recover. Use the -v option on `docker rm` to avoid the problem.
- The volume container pattern is useful for keeping your volumes organized and avoiding the orphan volume problem.
- The data-packed volume container pattern is useful for distributing static content for other containers.
- The polymorphic container pattern is a way to compose minimal functional components and maximize reuse.

Network exposure

In the previous chapter you read about how to use volumes and work with files in a container. This chapter deals with another common form of input and output: network access.

If you want to run a website, database, email server, or any software that depends on networking, like a web browser inside a Docker container, then you need to understand how to connect that container to the network. After reading this chapter you'll be able to create containers with network exposure appropriate for the application you're running, use network software in one container from another, and understand how containers interact with the host and the host's network.

This chapter is focused on single-host Docker networking. Multi-host Docker is the subject of chapter 12. That chapter describes strategies for service discovery and the role container linking plays in that situation. You'll need the information in this chapter before any of that will make sense.

5.1   *Networking background*

A quick overview of relevant networking concepts will be helpful for understanding the topics in this chapter. This section includes only high-level detail; so if you're an expert, feel free to skip ahead.

Networking is all about communicating between processes that may or may not share the same local resources. To understand the material in this chapter you only need to consider a few basic network abstractions that are commonly used by processes. The better understanding you have of networking, the more you'll learn about the mechanics at work. But a deep understanding isn't required to use the tools provided by Docker. If anything, the material contained herein should prompt you to independently research selected topics as they come up. Those basic abstractions used by processes include protocols, network interfaces, and ports.

5.1.1   *Basics: protocols, interfaces, and ports*

A *protocol* with respect to communication and networking is a sort of language. Two parties that agree on a protocol can understand what each other is communicating. This is key to effective communication. Hypertext Transfer Protocol (HTTP) is one popular network protocol that many people have heard of. It's the protocol that provides the World Wide Web. A huge number of network protocols and several layers of communication are created by those protocols. For now, it's only important that you know what a protocol is so that you can understand network interfaces and ports.

A network *interface* has an address and represents a location. You can think of interfaces as analogous to real-world locations with addresses. A network interface is like a mailbox. Messages are delivered to a mailbox for recipients at that address, and messages are taken from a mailbox to be delivered elsewhere.

Whereas a mailbox has a postal address, a network interface has an *IP address*, which is defined by the Internet Protocol. The details of IP are interesting but outside of the scope of this book. The important thing to know about IP addresses is that they are unique in their network and contain information about their location on their network.

It's common for computers to have two kinds of *interfaces*: an Ethernet interface and a loopback interface. An Ethernet interface is what you're likely most familiar with. It's used to connect to other interfaces and processes. A loopback interface isn't connected to any other interface. At first this might seem useless, but it's often useful to be able to use network protocols to communicate with other programs on the same computer. In those cases a loopback is a great solution.

In keeping with the mailbox metaphor, a *port* is like a recipient or a sender. There might be several people who receive messages at a single address. For example, a single address might receive messages for Wendy Webserver, Deborah Database, and

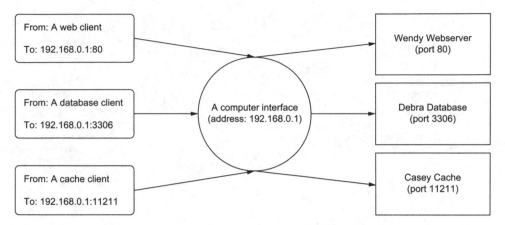

Figure 5.1   Processes use the same interface and are uniquely identified in the same way multiple people might use the same mailbox.

Casey Cache, as illustrated in figure 5.1. Each recipient should only open his or her own messages.

In reality, ports are just numbers and defined as part of the Transmission Control Protocol (TCP). Again the details of the protocol are beyond the scope of this book, but I encourage you to read about it some time. People who created standards for protocols, or companies that own a particular product, decide what port number should be used for specific purposes. For example, web servers provide HTTP on port 80 by default. MySQL, a database product, serves its protocol on port 3306 by default. Memcached, a fast cache technology, provides its protocol on port 11211. Ports are written on TCP messages just like names are written on envelopes.

Interfaces, protocols, and ports are all immediate concerns for software and users. By learning about these things, you develop a better appreciation for the way programs communicate and how your computer fits into the bigger picture.

5.1.2   *Bigger picture: networks, NAT, and port forwarding*

Interfaces are single points in larger networks. Networks are defined in the way that interfaces are linked together, and that linkage determines an interface's IP address.

Sometimes a message has a recipient that an interface is not directly linked to, so instead it's delivered to an intermediary that knows how to route the message for delivery. Coming back to the mail metaphor, this is similar to how real-world mail carriers operate.

When you place a message in your outbox, a mail carrier picks it up and delivers it to a local routing facility. That facility is itself an interface. It will take the message and send it along to the next stop on the route to a destination. A local routing facility for a mail carrier might forward a message to a regional facility, and then to a local facility for the destination, and finally to the recipient. It's common for network routes to

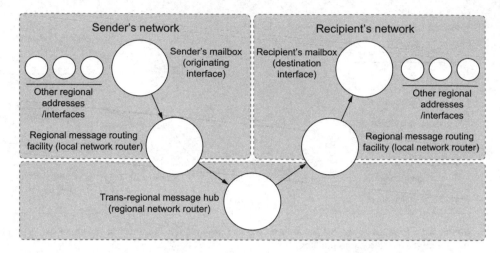

Figure 5.2   The path of a message in a postal system and a computer network

follow a similar pattern. Figure 5.2 illustrates the described route and draws the relationships between physical message routing and network routing.

This chapter is concerned with interfaces that exist on a single computer, so the networks and routes we consider won't be anywhere near that complicated. In fact, this chapter is about two specific networks and the way containers are attached to them. The first network is the one that your computer is connected to. The second is a virtual network that Docker creates to connect all of the running containers to the network that the computer is connected to. That second network is called a *bridge*.

Just as the name implies, a bridge is an interface that connects multiple networks so that they can function as a single network, as shown in figure 5.3. Bridges work by selectively forwarding traffic between the connected networks based on another type of network address. To understand the material in this chapter, you only need to be comfortable with this abstract idea.

This has been a very rough introduction to some nuanced topics. I've really only scratched the surface in order to help you understand how to use Docker and the networking facilities that it simplifies.

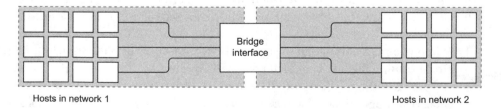

Figure 5.3   A bridge interface connecting two distinct networks

5.2 *Docker container networking*

Docker is concerned with two types of networking: single-host virtual networks and multi-host networks. Local virtual networks are used to provide container isolation. Multi-host virtual networks provide an overlay where any container on a participating host can have its own routable IP address from any other container in the network.

This chapter covers single-host virtual networks in depth. Understanding how Docker isolates containers on the network is critical for the security-minded. People building networked applications need to know how containerization will impact their deployment requirements.

Multi-host networking is still in beta at the time of this writing. Implementing it requires a broader understanding of other ecosystem tools in addition to understanding the material covering single-host networking. Until multi-host networking settles, it's best to get started by understanding how Docker builds local virtual networks.

5.2.1 *The local Docker network topology*

Docker uses features of the underlying operating system to build a specific and customizable virtual network topology. The virtual network is local to the machine where Docker is installed and is made up of routes between participating containers and the wider network where the host is attached. You can change the behavior of that network structure and in some cases change the structure itself by using command-line options for starting the Docker daemon and each container. Figure 5.4 illustrates two containers attached to the virtual network and its components.

Containers have their own private loopback interface and a separate Ethernet interface linked to another virtual interface in the host's namespace. These two linked interfaces form a link between the host's network stack and the stack created for each container. Just like typical home networks, each container is assigned a unique private IP address that's not directly reachable from the external network. Connections are routed through the Docker bridge interface called docker0. You can think of the

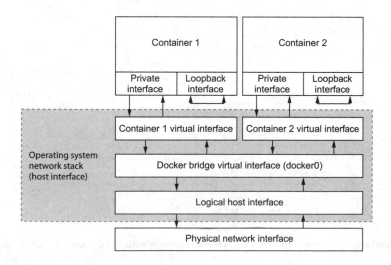

Figure 5.4 The default local Docker network topology and two attached containers

docker0 interface like your home router. Each of the virtual interfaces created for containers is linked to docker0, and together they form a network. This bridge interface is attached to the network where the host is attached.

Using the docker command-line tool, you can customize the IP addresses used, the host interface that docker0 is connected to, and the way containers communicate with each other. The connections between interfaces describe how exposed or isolated any specific network container is from the rest of the network. Docker uses kernel namespaces to create those private virtual interfaces, but the namespace itself doesn't provide the network isolation. Network exposure or isolation is provided by the host's firewall rules (every modern Linux distribution runs a firewall). With the options provided, there are four archetypes for network containers.

5.2.2   *Four network container archetypes*

All Docker containers follow one of four archetypes. These archetypes define how a container interacts with other local containers and the host's network. Each serves a different purpose, and you can think of each as having a different level of isolation. When you use Docker to create a container, it's important to carefully consider what you want to accomplish and use the strongest possible container without compromising that goal. Figure 5.5 illustrates each archetype, where the strongest containers (most isolated) are on the left and the weakest are on the right.

The four are archetypes are these:

- Closed containers
- Bridged containers
- Joined containers
- Open containers

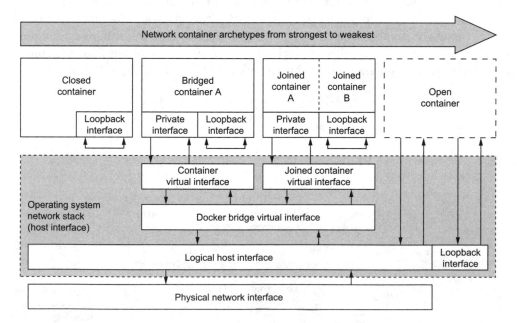

Figure 5.5   Four container network archetypes and their interaction with the Docker network topology

Over the next four subsections I introduce each archetype. Few readers will have an occasion to use all four. In reading about how to build them and when to use them, you'll be able to make that distinction yourself.

5.3 *Closed containers*

The strongest type of network container is one that doesn't allow any network traffic. These are called closed containers. Processes running in such a container will have access only to a loopback interface. If they need to communicate only with themselves or each other, this will be suitable. But any program that requires access to the network or the internet won't operate correctly in such a container. For example, if the software needs to download updates, it won't be able to because it can't use the network.

Most readers will be coming from a server software or web application background, and in that context it can be difficult to imagine a practical use for a container that has no network access. There are so many ways to use Docker that it's easy to forget about volume containers, backup jobs, offline batch processing, or diagnostic tools. The challenge you face is not justifying Docker for each feature but knowing which features best fit the use cases that you might be taking for granted.

Docker builds this type of container by simply skipping the step where an externally accessible network interface is created. As you can see in figure 5.6, the closed archetype has no connection to the Docker bridge interface. Programs in these containers can talk only to themselves.

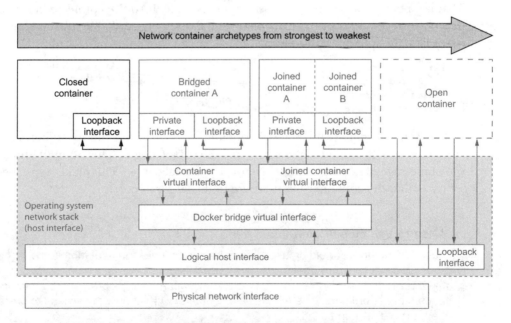

Figure 5.6   The closed container archetype and relevant components

All Docker containers, including closed containers, have access to a private loopback interface. You may have experience working with loopback interfaces already. It's common for people with moderate experience to have used localhost or 127.0.0.1 as an address in a URL. In these cases you were telling a program to bind to or contact a service bound to your computer's loopback network interface.

By creating private loopback interfaces for each container, Docker enables programs run inside a container to communicate through the network but without that communication leaving the container.

You can tell Docker to create a closed container by specifying none with the --net flag as an argument to the docker run command:

```
docker run --rm \                                    Create a closed
    --net none \                                     container
    alpine:latest \
    ip addr                    List the interfaces
```

Running this example, you can see that the only network interface available is the loopback interface, bound to the address 127.0.0.1. This configuration means three things:

- Any program running in the container can connect to or wait for connections on that interface.
- Nothing outside the container can connect to that interface.
- No program running inside that container can reach anything outside the container.

That last point is important and easily demonstrable. If you're connected to the internet, try to reach a popular service that should always be available. In this case, try to reach Google's public DNS service:

```
docker run --rm \                                    Create a closed
    --net none \                                     container
    alpine:latest \
    ping -w 2 8.8.8.8          Ping Google
```

In this example you create a closed container and try to test the speed between your container and the public DNS server provided by Google. This attempt should fail with a message like "ping: send-to: Network is unreachable." This makes sense because we know that the container has no route to the larger network.

> ## When to use closed containers
>
> Closed containers should be used when the need for network isolation is the highest or whenever a program doesn't require network access. For example, running a terminal text editor shouldn't require network access. Running a program to generate a random password should be run inside a container without network access to prevent the theft of that number.

There aren't many ways to customize the network configuration for a closed container. Although this type may seem overly limiting, it's the safest of the four options and can be extended to be more accommodating. These are not the default for Docker containers, but as a best practice you should try to justify using anything weaker before doing so. Docker creates bridged containers by default.

5.4 Bridged containers

Bridged containers relax network isolation and in doing so make it simpler to get started. This archetype is the most customizable and should be hardened as a best practice. Bridged containers have a private loopback interface and another private interface that's connected to the rest of the host through a network bridge.

This section is the longest of the chapter. Bridged containers are the most common network container archetype (see figure 5.7), and this section introduces several new options that you can use with other archetypes. Everything covered before section 5.6 is in the context of bridged containers.

All interfaces connected to docker0 are part of the same virtual subnet. This means they can talk to each other and communicate with the larger network through the docker0 interface.

5.4.1 Reaching out

The most common reason to choose a bridged container is that the process needs access to the network. To create a bridged container you can either omit the `--net`

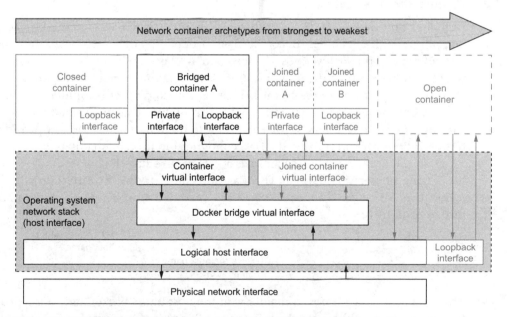

Figure 5.7   The bridged container archetype and relevant components

option to the docker run command or you can set its value to bridge. I use each form in the following examples:

```
docker run --rm \
    --net bridge \                          Join the bridge
    alpine:latest \                         network
    ip addr          List the container interfaces
```

Just like the first example for closed containers, this command will create a new container from the latest alpine image and list the available network interfaces. This time it will list two interfaces: an Ethernet interface and a local loopback. The output will include details like the IP address and subnet mask of each interface, the maximum packet size (MTU), and various interface metrics.

Now that you've verified that your container has another interface with an IP address, try to access the network again. This time omit the --net flag to see that bridge is the default Docker network container type:

```
docker run --rm \                             Note omission of
    alpine:latest \          Run ping command  the --net option
    ping -w 2 8.8.8.8        against Google
```

Pinging Google's public DNS server from this bridged container works, and no additional options are required. After running this command you'll see your container run a ping test for two seconds and report on the network statistics gathered.

Now you know that if you have some software that needs to access the internet, or some other computer on a private network, you can use a bridged container.

5.4.2   Custom name resolution

Domain Name System (DNS) is a protocol for mapping host names to IP addresses. This mapping enables clients to decouple from a dependency on a specific host IP and instead depend on whatever host is referred to by a known name. One of the most basic ways to change outbound communications is by creating names for IP addresses.

It is typical for containers on the bridge network and other computers on your network to have IP addresses that aren't publicly routable. This means that unless you're running your own DNS server, you can't refer to them by a name. Docker provides different options for customizing the DNS configuration for a new container.

First, the docker run command has a --hostname flag that you can use to set the host name of a new container. This flag adds an entry to the DNS override system inside the container. The entry maps the provided host name to the container's bridge IP address:

```
docker run --rm \
    --hostname barker \                       Set the container
    alpine:latest \                           host name
    nslookup barker        Resolve the host name
                           to an IP address
```

This example creates a new container with the host name barker and runs a program to look up the IP address for the same name. Running this example will generate output that looks something like the following:

```
Server:    10.0.2.3
Address 1: 10.0.2.3

Name:      barker
Address 1: 172.17.0.22 barker
```

The IP address on the last line is the bridge IP address for the new container. The IP address provided on the line labeled Server is the address of the server that provided the mapping.

Setting the host name of a container is useful when programs running inside a container need to look up their own IP address or must self-identify. Because other containers don't know this hostname, its uses are limited. But if you use an external DNS server, you can share those hostnames.

The second option for customizing the DNS configuration of a container is the ability to specify one or more DNS servers to use. To demonstrate, the following example creates a new container and sets the DNS server for that container to Google's public DNS service:

```
docker run --rm \                ┌─  Set primary
    --dns 8.8.8.8 \         ◄───┘   DNS server
    alpine:latest \                       ┌─  Resolve IP address
    nslookup docker.com              ◄───┘   of docker.com
```

Using a specific DNS server can provide consistency if you're running Docker on a laptop and often move between internet service providers. It's a critical tool for people building services and networks. There are a few important notes on setting your own DNS server:

- *The value must be an IP address.* If you think about it, the reason is obvious; the container needs a DNS server to perform the lookup on a name.
- *The* --dns=[] *flag can be set multiple times to set multiple DNS servers (in case one or more are unreachable).*
- *The* --dns=[] *flag can be set when you start up the Docker daemon that runs in the background.* When you do so, those DNS servers will be set on every container by default. But if you stop the daemon with containers running and change the default when you restart the daemon, the running containers will still have the old DNS settings. You'll need to restart those containers for the change to take effect.

The third DNS-related option, --dns-search=[], allows you to specify a DNS search domain, which is like a default host name suffix. With one set, any host names that don't have a known top-level domain (like .com or .net) will be searched for with the specified suffix appended.

```
docker run --rm \                       ┌─  Set search
    --dns-search docker.com \     ◄───┘   domain
    busybox:latest \                        ┌─  Look up shortcut for
    nslookup registry.hub              ◄───┘   registry.hub.docker.com
```

This command will resolve to the IP address of registry.hub.docker.com because the DNS search domain provided will complete the host name.

This feature is most often used for trivialities like shortcut names for internal corporate networks. For example, your company might maintain an internal documentation wiki that you can simply reference at http://wiki/. But this can be much more powerful.

Suppose you maintain a single DNS server for your development and test environments. Rather than building environment-aware software (with hard-coded environment-specific names like myservice.dev.mycompany.com), you might consider using DNS search domains and using environment-unaware names (like myservice):

```
docker run --rm \
    --dns-search dev.mycompany \          ◀—| Note dev prefix
    busybox:latest \                               Resolves to
    nslookup myservice                      ◀—| myservice.dev.mycompany

docker run --rm \
    --dns-search test.mycompany \         ◀—| Note test prefix
    busybox:latest \                               Resolves to
    nslookup myservice                      ◀—| myservice.test.mycompany
```

Using this pattern, the only change is the context in which the program is running. Like providing custom DNS servers, you can provide several custom search domains for the same container. Simply set the flag as many times as you have search domains. For example:

```
docker run --rm \
    --dns-search mycompany \
    --dns-search myothercompany ...
```

This flag can also be set when you start up the Docker daemon to provide defaults for every container created. Again, remember that these options are only set for a container when it is created. If you change the defaults when a container is running, that container will maintain the old values.

The last DNS feature to consider provides the ability to override the DNS system. This uses the same system that the --hostname flag uses. The --add-host=[] flag on the docker run command lets you provide a custom mapping for an IP address and host name pair:

```
docker run --rm \
    --add-host test:10.10.10.255 \        ◀—| Add host entry
    alpine:latest \                                Resolves to
    nslookup test                           ◀—| 10.10.10.255
```

Like --dns and --dns-search, this option can be specified multiple times. But unlike those other options, this flag can't be set as a default at daemon startup.

This feature is a sort of name resolution scalpel. Providing specific name mappings for individual containers is the most fine-grained customization possible. You can use this to effectively block targeted host names by mapping them to a known IP address like 127.0.0.1. You could use it to route traffic for a particular destination through a proxy. This is often used to route unsecure traffic through secure channels like an SSH tunnel. Adding these overrides is a trick that has been used for years by web developers who run their own local copies of a web application. If you spend some time thinking about the interface that name-to-IP address mappings provide, I'm sure you can come up with all sorts of uses.

All the custom mappings live in a file at /etc/hosts inside your container. If you want to see what overrides are in place, all you have to do is inspect that file. Rules for editing and parsing this file can be found online and are a bit beyond the scope of this book:

```
docker run --rm \
    --hostname mycontainer \          Set host name
    --add-host docker.com:127.0.0.1 \
    --add-host test:10.10.10.2 \       Create another
    alpine:latest \                    host entry
    cat /etc/hosts                     View all entries
```
Create host entry

This should produce output that looks something like the following:

```
172.17.0.45    mycontainer
127.0.0.1      localhost
::1            localhost ip6-localhost ip6-loopback
fe00::0        ip6-localnet
ff00::0        ip6-mcastprefix
ff02::1        ip6-allnodes
ff02::2        ip6-allrouters
10.10.10.2     test
127.0.0.1      docker.com
```

DNS is a powerful system for changing behavior. The name-to-IP address map provides a simple interface that people and programs can use to decouple themselves from specific network addresses. If DNS is your best tool for changing outbound traffic behavior, then the firewall and network topology is your best tool for controlling inbound traffic.

5.4.3 Opening inbound communication

Bridged containers aren't accessible from the host network by default. Containers are protected by your host's firewall system. The default network topology provides no route from the host's external interface to a container interface. That means there's just no way to get to a container from outside the host. The flow of inbound network traffic is shown in figure 5.8.

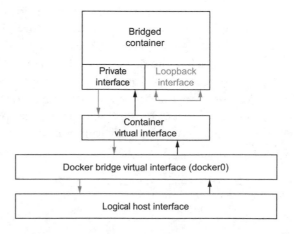

Figure 5.8 An inbound traffic route to a bridged container

Containers wouldn't be very useful if there were no way to get to them through the network. Luckily, that's not the case. The `docker run` command provides a flag, `-p=[]` or `--publish=[]`, that you can use to create a mapping between a port on the host's network stack and the new container's interface. You've used this a few times earlier in this book, but it's worth mentioning again. The format of the mapping can have four forms:

- `<containerPort>`

  This form binds the container port to a dynamic port on all of the host's interfaces:

  ```
  docker run -p 3333 ...
  ```

- `<hostPort>:<containerPort>`

  This form binds the specified container port to the specified port on each of the host's interfaces:

  ```
  docker run -p 3333:3333 ...
  ```

- `<ip>::<containerPort>`

  This form binds the container port to a dynamic port on the interface with the specified IP address:

  ```
  docker run -p 192.168.0.32::2222 ...
  ```

- `<ip>:<hostPort>:<containerPort>`

  This form binds the container port to the specified port on the interface with the specified IP address:

  ```
  docker run -p 192.168.0.32:1111:1111 ...
  ```

These examples assume that your host's IP address is 192.168.0.32. This is arbitrary but useful to demonstrate the feature. Each of the command fragments will create a route from a port on a host interface to a specific port on the container's interface. The different forms offer a range of granularity and control. This flag is another that can be repeated as many times as you need to provide the desired set of mappings.

The `docker run` command provides an alternate way to accomplish opening channels. If you can accept a dynamic or ephemeral port assignment on the host, you can use the `-P`, or `--publish-all`, flag. This flag tells the Docker daemon to create mappings, like the first form of the `-p` option for all ports that an image reports, to expose. Images carry a list of ports that are exposed for simplicity and as a hint to users where contained services are listening. For example, if you know that an image like dockerinaction/ch5_expose exposes ports 5000, 6000, and 7000, each of the following commands do the same thing:

```
docker run -d --name dawson \
    -p 5000 \
    -p 6000 \                          Expose all ports
    -p 7000 \
    dockerinaction/ch5_expose
```

```
docker run -d --name woolery \
    -P \                              ◀──┐  Expose relevant ports
    dockerinaction/ch5_expose
```

It's easy to see how this can save a user some typing, but it begs two questions. First, how is this used if the image doesn't expose the port you want to use? Second, how do you discover which dynamic ports were assigned?

The docker run command provides another flag, --expose, that takes a port number that the container should expose. This flag can be set multiple times, once for each port:

```
docker run -d --name philbin \
    --expose 8000 \                   ◀──┐  Expose another port
    -P \                              ◀──┐  Publish all ports
    dockerinaction/ch5_expose
```

Using --expose in this way will add port 8000 to the list of ports that should be bound to dynamic ports using the -P flag. After running the example, you can see what these ports were mapped to by using docker ps, docker inspect, or a new command, docker port. The port subcommand takes either the container name or ID as an argument and produces a simple list with one port map entry per line:

```
docker port philbin
```

Running this command should produce a list like the following:

```
5000/tcp -> 0.0.0.0:49164
6000/tcp -> 0.0.0.0:49165
7000/tcp -> 0.0.0.0:49166
8000/tcp -> 0.0.0.0:49163
```

With the tools covered in this section, you should be able to manage routing any inbound traffic to the correct bridged container running on your host. There's one other subtle type of communication: inter-container communication.

5.4.4   Inter-container communication

As a reminder, all the containers covered so far use the Docker bridge network to communicate with each other and the network that the host is on. All local bridged containers are on the same bridge network and can communicate with each other by default. Figure 5.9 illustrates the network relationship between five containers on the same host.

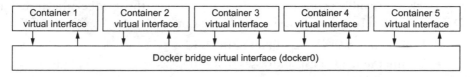

Figure 5.9   Five containers connected to the same Docker bridge (docker0)

In order to make sure that you have a full appreciation for this openness, the following command demonstrates how containers can communicate over this network:

```
docker run -it --rm dockerinaction/ch5_nmap -sS -p 3333 172.17.0.0/24
```

This command will run a program called nmap to scan all the interfaces attached to the bridge network. In this case it's looking for any interface that's accepting connections on port 3333. If you had such a service running in another container, this command would have discovered it, and you could use another program to connect to it.

Allowing communication in this way makes it simple to build cooperating containers. No additional work needs to be done to build pipes between containers. It's as free as an open network. This may be tolerable but can be risky for users who are unaware. It's common for software to ship with low-security features like default passwords or disabled encryption. Naïve users may expect that the network topology or some local firewall will protect containers from open access. This is true to some extent, but by default any container is fully accessible from any other local container.

When you start the Docker daemon, you can configure it to disallow network connections between containers. Doing so is a best practice in multi-tenant environments. It minimizes the points (called an attack surface) where an attacker might compromise other containers. You can achieve this by setting --icc=false when you start the Docker daemon:

```
docker -d --icc=false ...
```

When inter-container communication is disabled, any traffic from one container to another will be blocked by the host's firewall except where explicitly allowed. These exceptions are covered in section 5.4.

Disabling inter-container communication is an important step in any Docker-enabled environment. In doing so, you create an environment where explicit dependencies must be declared in order to work properly. At best, a more promiscuous configuration allows containers to be started when their dependencies aren't ready. At worst, leaving inter-container communication enabled allows compromised programs within containers to attack other local containers.

5.4.5   *Modifying the bridge interface*

Before moving on to the next archetype, this seems like an appropriate time to demonstrate the configuration options that modify the bridge interface. Outside this section, examples will always assume that you're working with the default bridge configuration.

Docker provides three options for customizing the bridge interface that the Docker daemon builds on first startup. These options let the user do the following:

- Define the address and subnet of the bridge
- Define the range of IP addresses that can be assigned to containers
- Define the maximum transmission unit (MTU)

To define the IP address of the bridge and the subnet range, use the --bip flag when you start the Docker daemon. There are all sorts of reasons why you might want to use a different IP range for your bridge network. When you encounter one of those situations, making the change is as simple as using one flag.

Using the --bip flag (which stands for *bridge IP*), you can set the IP address of the bridge interface that Docker will create and the size of the subnet using a classless inter-domain routing (CIDR) formatted address. CIDR notation provides a way to specify an IP address and its routing prefix. See appendix B for a brief primer on CIDR notation. There are several guides online detailing how to build CIDR formatted addresses, but if you're familiar with bit masking, the following example will be sufficient to get you started.

Suppose you want to set your bridge IP address to 192.168.0.128 and allocate the last 128 addresses in that subnet prefix to the bridge network. In that case, you'd set the value of --bip to 192.168.0.128/25. To be explicit, using this value will create the docker0 interface, set its IP address to 192.168.0.128, and allow IP addresses that range from 192.168.0.128 to 192.168.0.255. The command would be similar to this:

```
docker -d --bip "192.168.0.128" ...
```

With a network defined for the bridge, you can go on to customize which IP addresses in that network can be assigned to new containers. To do so, provide a similar CIDR notation description to the --fixed-cidr flag.

Working from the previous situation, if you wanted to reserve only the last 64 addresses of the network assigned to the bridge interface, you would use 192.168.0.192/26. When the Docker daemon is started with this set, new containers will receive an IP address between 192.168.0.192 and 192.168.0.255. The only caveat with this option is that the range specified must be a subnet of the network assigned to the bridge (if you're confused, there's lots of great documentation and tooling on the internet to help):

```
docker -d --fixed-cidr "192.168.0.192/26"
```

I'm not going to spend too much effort on the last setting. Network interfaces have a limit to the maximum size of a packet (a packet is an atomic unit of communication). By protocol, Ethernet interfaces have a maximum packet size of 1500 bytes. This is the configured default. In some specific instances you'll need to change the MTU on the Docker bridge. When you encounter such a scenario, you can use the --mtu flag to set the size in bytes:

```
docker -d –mtu 1200
```

Users who are more comfortable with Linux networking primitives may like to know that they can provide their own custom bridge interface instead of using the default bridge. To do so, configure your bridge interface and then tell the Docker daemon to use it instead of docker0 when you start the daemon. The flag to use is -b or --bridge.

If you've configured a bridge named `mybridge`, you'd start Docker with a command like the following:

```
docker -d -b mybridge ...
```

```
docker -d --bridge mybridge ...
```

Building custom bridges requires a deeper understanding of Linux kernel tools than is necessary for this book. But you should know that this ability is available if you do the research required.

5.5   *Joined containers*

The next less isolated network container archetype is called a joined container. These containers share a common network stack. In this way there's no isolation between joined containers. This means reduced control and security. Although this isn't the least secure archetype, it's the first one where the walls of a jail have been torn down.

Docker builds this type of container by providing access to the interfaces created for a specific container to another new container. Interfaces are in this way shared like managed volumes. Figure 5.10 shows the network architecture of two joined containers.

The easiest way to see joined containers in action is to use a special case and join it with a new container. The first command starts a server that listens on the loopback interface. The second command lists all the open ports. The second command lists

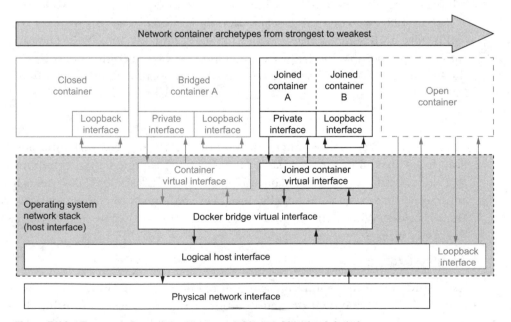

Figure 5.10   Two containers share the same bridge and loopback interface.

the open port created by the first command because both containers share the same network interface:

```
docker run -d --name brady \
    --net none alpine:latest \
    nc -l 127.0.0.1:3333

docker run -it \
    --net container:brady \
    alpine:latest netstat -al
```

By running these two commands you create two containers that share the same network interface. Because the first container is created as a closed container, the two will only share that single loopback interface. The container value of the --net flag lets you specify the container that the new container should be joined with. Either the container name or its raw ID identifies the container that the new container should reuse.

Containers joined in this way will maintain other forms of isolation. They will maintain different file systems, different memory, and so on. But they will have the exact same network components. That may sound concerning, but this type of container can be useful.

In the last example you joined two containers on a network interface that has no access to the larger network. In doing so, you expanded the usefulness of a closed container. You might use this pattern when two different programs with access to two different pieces of data need to communicate but shouldn't share direct access to the other's data. Alternatively, you might use this pattern when you have network services that need to communicate but network access or service discovery mechanisms like DNS are unavailable.

Setting aside security concerns, using joined containers reintroduces port conflict issues. A user should be aware of this whenever they're joining two containers. It's likely if they're joining containers that run similar services that they will create conflicts. Under those circumstances, the conflicts will need to be resolved using more traditional methods like changing application configuration. These conflicts can occur on any shared interfaces. When programs are run outside a container, they share access to the host's interfaces with every other program running on the computer, so this specific scope increase is still an improvement on today's status quo.

When two containers are joined, all interfaces are shared, and conflicts might happen on any of them. At first it might seem silly to join two containers that need bridge access. After all, they can already communicate over the Docker bridge subnet. But consider situations where one process needs to monitor the other through otherwise protected channels. Communication between containers is subject to firewall rules. If one process needs to communicate with another on an unexposed port, the best thing to do may be to join the containers.

> ### The best reasons to use joined containers
>
> Use joined containers when you want to use a single loopback interface for communication between programs in different containers.
>
> Use joined containers if a program in one container is going to change the joined network stack and another program is going to use that modified network.
>
> Use joined containers when you need to monitor the network traffic for a program in another container.

Before you start talking about how insecure Docker is because it allows any new container to join a running one, keep in mind that issuing any commands to Docker requires privileged access. Attackers with privileged access can do whatever they want, including attacking the code or data running in any container directly. In that context, this kind of network stack manipulation is no big deal.

In contexts where people build multi-tenant systems, it's a huge deal. If you're building or considering using such a service, the first thing you should do is set up multiple accounts and try do gain access to one from the other. If you can, think twice about using the service for anything important. Joining another user's network stack or mounting their volumes is a magnificent problem.

Joined containers are a bit weaker but are not the weakest type of network container. That title belongs to open containers.

5.6 *Open containers*

Open containers are dangerous. They have no network container and have full access to the host's network. This includes access to critical host services. Open containers provide absolutely no isolation and should be considered only in cases when you have no other option. The only redeeming quality is that unprivileged containers are still unable to actually reconfigure the network stack. Figure 5.11 shows the network architecture of an open container.

This type of container is created when you specify `host` as the value of the `--net` option on the `docker run` command:

```
docker run --rm \                    Create an open
   --net host \               ◀──    container
   alpine:latest ip addr
```

Running this command will create a container from the latest alpine image and without any network jail. When you execute `ip addr` inside that container, you can inspect all the host machine's network interfaces. You should see several interfaces listed, including one named docker0. As you may have noticed, this example creates a container that executes a discrete task and then immediately removes the container.

Using this configuration, processes can bind to protected network ports numbered lower than 1024.

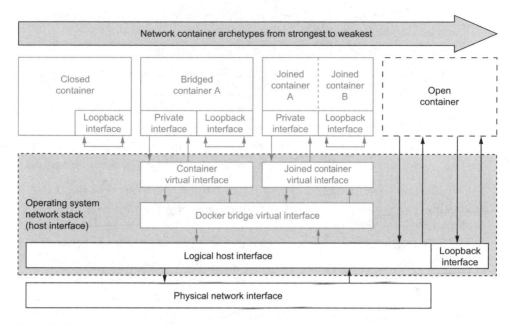

Figure 5.11   An open container is a container with full access to the host networking resources.

5.7   *Inter-container dependencies*

Now that you've learned what kind of network containers you can build with Docker and how those containers interact with the network, you need to learn how to use network software in one container from another. You've seen how containers use the bridge network to communicate and may have started thinking about how to piece together a small system. When you consider that the bridge network assigns IP addresses to containers dynamically at creation time, local service discovery can seem complicated.

One way to solve the problem would be to use a local DNS server and a registration hook when containers start. Another would be to write your programs to scan the local network for IP addresses listening on known ports. Both approaches handle dynamic environments but require a non-trivial workload and additional tooling. Each of these approaches will fail if arbitrary inter-container communication has been disabled. You could force all traffic out and back through the host's interface to known published ports. But there are several occasions when you'll need privileged access to a network port. Docker provides another tool that you've already seen to handle this use case.

5.7.1   *Introducing links for local service discovery*

When you create a new container, you can tell Docker to link it to any other container. That target container must be running when the new container is created. The reason is simple. Containers hold their IP address only when they're running. If they're stopped, they lose that lease.

Adding a link on a new container does three things:

- Environment variables describing the target container's end point will be created.
- The link alias will be added to the DNS override list of the new container with the IP address of the target container.
- Most interestingly, if inter-container communication is disabled, Docker will add specific firewall rules to allow communication between linked containers.

The first two features of links are great for basic service discovery, but the third feature enables users to harden their local container networks without sacrificing container-to-container communication.

The ports that are opened for communication are those that have been exposed by the target container. So the --expose flag provides a shortcut for only one particular type of container to host port mapping when ICC is enabled. When ICC is disabled, --expose becomes a tool for defining firewall rules and explicit declaration of a container's interface on the network. In the same context, links become a more static declaration of local runtime service dependencies. Here's a simple example; these images don't actually exist:

```
docker run -d --name importantData \            Named target
    --expose 3306 \                             of a link
    dockerinaction/mysql_noauth \
    service mysql_noauth start

docker run -d --name importantWebapp \          Create link and set
    --link imporantData:db \                    alias to db
    dockerinaction/ch5_web startapp.sh -db tcp://db:3306

docker run -d --name buggyProgram \             This container has no
    dockerinaction/ch5_buggy                    route to importantData.
```

Reading through this example, you can see that I've started some foolishly configured MySQL server (a popular database server). The name implies that the server has disabled any authentication requirements and anyone who can connect to the server can access the data. I then started an important web application that needs access to the data in the importantData container. I added a link from the importantWebapp container to the importantData container. Docker will add information to that new container that will describe how to connect to importantData. This way, when the web application opens a database connection to tcp://db:3306, it will connect to the database. Lastly, I started another container that's known to contain buggy code. It's running as a nonprivileged user, but it may be possible for an attacker to inspect the bridge network if the program is compromised.

If I'm running with inter-container communication enabled, attackers could easily steal the data from the database in the importantData container. They would be able to do a simple network scan to identify the open port and then gain access by simply opening a connection. Even a casual traffic observer might think this connection appropriate because no container dependencies have been strongly modeled.

If I were running this example with inter-container communication disabled, an attacker would be unable to reach any other containers from the container running the compromised software.

This is a fairly silly example. Please don't think that simply disabling inter-container communication will protect resources if those resources don't protect themselves. With appropriately configured software, strong network rules, and declared service dependencies, you can build systems that achieve good defense in depth.

5.7.2 *Link aliases*

Links are one-way network dependencies created when one container is created and specifies a link to another. As mentioned previously, the `--link` flag used for this purpose takes a single argument. That argument is a map from a container name or ID to an alias. The alias can be anything as long as it's unique in the scope of the container being created. So, if three containers named a, b, and c already exist and are running, then I could run the following:

```
docker run --link a:alias-a --link b:alias-b --link c:alias-c ...
```

But if I made a mistake and assigned some or all containers to the same alias, then that alias would only contain connection information for one of the other containers. In this case, the firewall rules would still be created but would be nearly useless without that connection information.

Link aliases create a higher-level issue. Software running inside a container needs to know the alias of the container or host it's connecting to so it can perform the lookup. Similar to host names, link aliases become a symbol that multiple parties must agree on for a system to operate correctly. Link aliases function as a contract.

A developer may build their application to assume that a database will be have an alias of "database" and always look for a it at tcp://database:3306 because a DNS override with that host name would exist. This expected host name approach would work as long as the person or process building the container either creates a link aliased to a database or uses `--add-host` to create the host name. Alternatively, the application could always look for connection information from an environment variable named `DATABASE_PORT`. The environment variable approach will work only when a link is created with that alias.

The trouble is that there are no dependency declarations or runtime dependency checks. It's easy for the person building the container to do so without providing the required linkage. Docker users must either rely on documentation to communicate these dependencies or include custom dependency checking and fail-fast behavior on container startup. I recommend building the dependency-checking code first. For example, the following script is included in dockerinaction/ch5_ff to validate that a link named "database" has been set at startup:

```
#!/bin/sh

if [ -z ${DATABASE_PORT+x} ]
then
    echo "Link alias 'database' was not set!"
    exit
else
    exec "$@"
fi
```

You can see this script at work by running the following:

```
docker run -d --name mydb --expose 3306 \          ◀── Create valid
    alpine:latest nc -l 0.0.0.0:3306                    link target

docker run -it --rm \                              Test
    dockerinaction/ch5_ff echo This "shouldn't" work.  without
                                                   link

docker run -it --rm \                              Test with incorrect
    --link mydb:wrongalias \               ◀──     link alias
    dockerinaction/ch5_ff echo Wrong.

docker run -it --rm \
    --link mydb:database \                 ◀── Test correct alias
    dockerinaction/ch5_ff echo It worked.

                                           Shut down link
docker stop mydb && docker rm mydb         ◀── target container
```

This example script relies on the environment modifications made by Docker when links are created. You'll find these very useful when you start building your own images in chapter 7.

5.7.3 *Environment modifications*

I've mentioned that creating a link will add connection information to a new container. This connection information is injected in the new container by adding environment variables and a host name mapping in the DNS override system. Let's start with an example to inspect the link modifications:

```
docker run -d --name mydb \                        ◀── Create valid
    --expose 2222 --expose 3333 --expose 4444/udp \    link target
    alpine:latest nc -l 0.0.0.0:2222

docker run -it --rm \
    --link mydb:database \                 ◀── Create link and list
    dockerinaction/ch5_ff env                   environment variables

docker stop mydb && docker rm mydb
```

This should output a block of lines that include the following:

```
DATABASE_PORT=tcp://172.17.0.23:3333
DATABASE_PORT_3333_TCP=tcp://172.17.0.23:3333
DATABASE_PORT_2222_TCP=tcp://172.17.0.23:2222
DATABASE_PORT_4444_UDP=udp://172.17.0.23:4444
DATABASE_PORT_2222_TCP_PORT=2222
DATABASE_PORT_3333_TCP_PORT=3333
DATABASE_PORT_4444_UDP_PORT=4444
DATABASE_PORT_3333_TCP_ADDR=172.17.0.23
DATABASE_PORT_2222_TCP_ADDR=172.17.0.23
DATABASE_PORT_4444_UDP_ADDR=172.17.0.23
DATABASE_PORT_2222_TCP_PROTO=tcp
DATABASE_PORT_3333_TCP_PROTO=tcp
DATABASE_PORT_4444_UDP_PROTO=udp
DATABASE_NAME=/furious_lalande/database
```

These are a sample of environment variables created for a link. All the variables relating to a specific link will use the link alias as a prefix. There will always be a single variable with the _NAME suffix that includes the name of the current container, a slash, and the link alias. For each port exposed by the linked container, there will be four individual environment variables with the exposed port in the variable name. The patterns are as follows:

- `<ALIAS>_PORT_<PORT NUMBER>_<PROTOCOL TCP or UDP>_PORT`
  This variable will simply contain the port number. That is curious because the value will be contained in the variable name. This could be useful if you're filtering the list of environment variables for those containing the string `TCP_PORT`. Doing so would render the list of ports.

- `<ALIAS>_PORT_<PORT NUMBER>_<PROTOCOL TCP or UDP>_ADDR`
  The values of variables with this pattern will be the IP address of the container serving the connection. If the alias is the same, these should all have the same value.

- `<ALIAS>_PORT_<PORT NUMBER>_<PROTOCOL TCP or UDP>_PROTO`
  Like variables with the _PORT suffix, the values of these variables are actually contained within the variable name. It's important not to assume that the protocol will always be TCP. UDP is also supported.

- `<ALIAS>_PORT_<PORT NUMBER>_<PROTOCOL TCP or UDP>`
  Variables of this form contain all the previous information encoded in URL form.

One additional environment variable of the form `<ALIAS>_<PORT>` will be created and will contain connection information for one of the exposed ports in URL form.

These environment variables are available for any need application developers might have in connecting to linked containers. But if developers have the port and protocol predetermined, then all they really need is host name resolution and they can rely on DNS for that purpose.

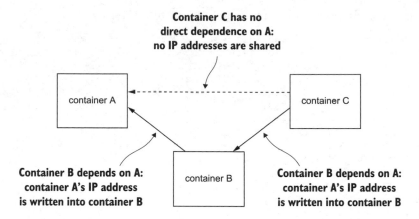

Figure 5.12   Links are not transitive. There's no link from container C to container A.

5.7.4   *Link nature and shortcomings*

The nature of links is such that dependencies are directional, static, and nontransitive. Nontransitive means that linked containers won't inherit links. More explicitly, if I link container B to container A, and then link container C to container B, there will be no link from container C to container A. Consider the container relationship in figure 5.12.

Links work by determining the network information of a container (IP address and exposed ports) and then injecting that into a new container. Because this is done at container creation time, and Docker can't know what a container's IP address will be before that container is running, links can only be built from new containers to existing containers. This is not to say that communication is one way but rather that discovery is one way. This also means that if a dependency stops for some reason, the link will be broken. Remember that containers maintain IP address leases only when they're running. So if a container is stopped or restarted, it will lose its IP lease and any linked containers will have stale data.

This property has caused some to criticize the value of links. The issue is that the deeper a dependency fails, the greater the domino effect of required container restarts. This might be an issue for some, but you must consider the specific impact.

If a critical service like a database fails, an availability event has already occurred. The chosen service discovery method impacts the recovery routine. An unavailable service might recover on the same or different IP address. Links will break only if the IP address changes and will require restarts. This leads some to jump to more dynamic lookup systems like DNS.

But even DNS systems have time-to-live (TTL) values that might slow the propagation of IP address changes. If an IP address changes during recovery, it might feel easier to use DNS, but recovery would only happen more quickly if connections to the database can fail, reconnect attempts can time out, and the DNS TTL expires in less time than it takes to restart a container. In abandoning container linking, you'll be forced to enable inter-container communication.

If your applications are slow to start and you need to handle IP address changes on service recovery, you may want to consider DNS. Otherwise, consider the static dependency chain that has been modeled using container links. Building a system that restarts appropriate containers on a dependency failure would be an achievable exercise.

This chapter focused on single-host Docker networking, and in that scope links are incredibly useful tools. Most environments span more than one computer. Service portability is the idea that a service could be running on any machine, in any container in a larger environment. It's the idea that a system where any process might run anywhere is more robust than systems with strict locality constraints. I think this is true, but it's important to show how Docker can be used in either situation.

5.8 *Summary*

Networking is a broad subject that would take several books to properly cover. This chapter should help readers with a basic understanding of network fundamentals adopt the single-host networking facilities provided by Docker. In reading this material, you learned the following:

- Docker provides four network container archetypes: closed containers, bridged containers, joined containers, and open containers.
- Docker creates a bridge network that binds participating containers to each other and to the network that the host is attached to.
- The bridge interface created by Docker can be replaced or customized using `docker` command-line options when the Docker daemon is started.
- Options on the `docker run` command can be used to expose ports on a container's interface, bind ports exposed by a container to the host's network interface, and link containers to each other.
- Disabling arbitrary inter-container communication is simple and builds a system with defense in depth.
- Using links provides a low-overhead local service discovery mechanism and maps specific container dependencies.

6
Limiting risk with isolation

This chapter covers

- Setting resource limits
- Sharing container memory
- Users, permissions, and administrative privileges
- Granting access to specific Linux features
- Working with enhanced Linux isolation and security tools: SELinux and AppArmor

Containers provide isolated process contexts, not whole system virtualization. The semantic difference may seem subtle, but the impact is drastic. Chapter 1 touches on the differences a bit. Chapters 2 through 5 each cover a different isolation feature set of Docker containers. This chapter covers the remaining four and also includes information about enhancing security on your system.

The features covered in this chapter focus on managing or limiting the risks of running software. You will learn how to give containers resource allowances, open access to shared memory, run programs as specific users, control the type of changes that a container can make to your computer, and integrate with other

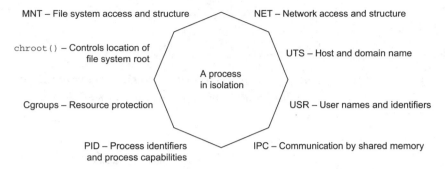

MNT – File system access and structure

NET – Network access and structure

chroot() – Controls location of
file system root

UTS – Host and domain name

A process
in isolation

Cgroups – Resource protection

USR – User names and identifiers

PID – Process identifiers
and process capabilities

IPC – Communication by shared memory

Figure 6.1   Eight-sided containers

Linux isolation tools. Some of these topics involve Linux features that are beyond the scope of this book. In those cases I try to give you an idea about their purpose and some basic usage examples, and you can integrate them with Docker. Figure 6.1 shows the eight namespaces and features that are used to build Docker containers.

One last reminder, Docker and the technology it uses are evolving projects. Once you get the learning tools presented in this chapter, remember to check for developments, enhancements, and new best practices when you go to build something valuable.

6.1   Resource allowances

Physical system resources like memory and time on the CPU are scarce. If the resource consumption of processes on a computer exceeds the available physical resources, the processes will experience performance issues and may stop running. Part of building a system that creates strong isolation includes providing resource allowances on individual containers.

If you want to make sure that a program won't overwhelm others on your computer, the easiest thing to do is set a limit on the resources that it can use. Docker provides three flags on the docker run and docker create commands for managing three different types of resource allowances that you can set on a container. Those three are memory, CPU, and devices.

6.1.1   Memory limits

Memory limits are the most basic restriction you can place on a container. They restrict the amount of memory that processes inside a container can use. Memory limits are useful for making sure that one container can't overwhelm the others running on a single system. You can put a limit in place by using the -m or --memory flag on the docker run or docker create commands. The flag takes a value and a unit. The format is as follows:

```
<number><optional unit>where unit = b, k, m or g
```

In the context of these commands, b refers to bytes, k to kilobytes, m to megabytes, and g to gigabytes. Put this new knowledge to use and start up a database application that you'll use in other examples:

```
docker run -d --name ch6_mariadb \
    --memory 256m \                    ◀─┐ Set a memory constraint
    --cpu-shares 1024 \
    --user nobody \
    --cap-drop all \
    dockerfile/mariadb
```

With this command you install database software called MariaDB and start a container with a memory limit of 256 megabytes. You might have noticed a few extra flags on this command. This chapter covers each of those, but you may already be able to guess what they do. Something else to note is that you don't expose any ports or bind any ports to the host's interfaces. It will be easiest to connect to this database by linking to it from another container. Before we get to that, I want to make sure you have a full understanding of what happens here and how to use memory limits.

The most important thing to understand about memory limits is that they're not reservations. They don't guarantee that the specified amount of memory will be available. They're only a protection from overconsumption.

Before you put a memory allowance in place, you should consider two things. First, can the software you're running operate under the proposed memory allowance? Second, can the system you're running on support the allowance?

The first question is often difficult to answer. It's not common to see minimum requirements published with open source software these days. Even if it were, though, you'd have to understand how the memory requirements of the software scale based on the size of the data you're asking it to handle. For better or worse, people tend to overestimate and adjust based on trial and error. In the case of memory-sensitive tools like databases, skilled professionals such as database administrators can make better-educated estimates and recommendations. Even then, the question is often answered by another: how much memory do you have? And that leads to the second question.

Can the system you're running on support the allowance? It's possible to set a memory allowance that's bigger than the amount of available memory on the system. On hosts that have swap space (virtual memory that extends onto disk), a container may realize the allowance. It's always possible to impose an allowance that's greater than any physical memory resource. In those cases the limitations of the system will always cap the container.

Finally, understand that there are several ways that software can fail if it exhausts the available memory. Some programs may fail with a memory access fault, whereas others may start writing out-of-memory errors to their logging. Docker neither detects this problem nor attempts to mitigate the issue. The best it can do is apply the restart logic you may have specified using the `--restart` flag described in chapter 2.

6.1.2 CPU

Processing time is just as scarce as memory, but the effect of starvation is performance degradation instead of failure. A paused process that is waiting for time on the CPU is still working correctly. But a slow process may be worse than a failing one if it's running some important data-processing program, a revenue-generating web application, or a back-end service for your app. Docker lets you limit a container's CPU resources in two ways.

First, you can specify the relative weight of a container. Linux uses this to determine the percentage of CPU time the container should use relative to other running containers. That percentage is for the sum of the computing cycles of all processors available to the container.

To set the CPU shares of a container and establish its relative weight, both `docker run` and `docker create` offer a `--cpu-shares` flag. The value provided should be an integer (which means you shouldn't quote it). Start another container to see how CPU shares work:

```
docker run -d -P --name ch6_wordpress \
--memory 512m \
--cpu-shares 512 \          ◀─┐ Set a relative process weight
--user nobody \
--cap-drop net_raw \
--link ch6_mariadb \
wordpress:4.1
```

This command will download and start WordPress version 4.1. It's written in PHP and is a great example of software that has been challenged by adapting to security risks. Here we've started it with a few extra precautions. If you'd like to see it running on your computer, use `docker port ch6_wordpress` to get the port number (I'll call it <port>) that the service is running on and open http://localhost:<port> in your web browser. Remember, if you're using Boot2Docker, you'll need to use `boot2docker ip` to determine the IP address of the virtual machine where Docker is running. When you have that, substitute that value for localhost in the preceding URL.

When you started the MariaDB container, you set its relative weight (cpu-shares) to 1024, and you set the relative weight of WordPress to 512. These settings create a system where the MariaDB container gets two CPU cycles for every one WordPress cycle. If you started a third container and set its `--cpu-shares` value to 2048, it would get half of the CPU cycles, and MariaDB and WordPress would split the other half at

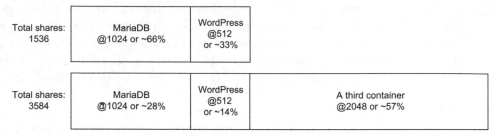

Figure 6.2 Relative weight and CPU shares

the same proportions as they were before. Figure 6.2 shows how portions change based on the total weight of the system.

CPU shares differ from memory limits in that they're enforced only when there is contention for time on the CPU. If other processes and containers are idle, then the container may burst well beyond its limits. This is preferable because it makes sure that CPU time is not wasted and that limited processes will yield if another process needs the CPU. The intent of this tool is to prevent one or a set of processes from overwhelming a computer, not to hinder performance of those processes. The defaults won't limit the container, and it will be able to use 100% of the CPU.

The second feature Docker exposes is the ability to assign a container to a specific CPU set. Most modern hardware uses multi-core CPUs. Roughly speaking, a CPU can process as many instructions in parallel as it has cores. This is especially useful when you're running many processes on the same computer.

A context switch is the task of changing from executing one process to executing another. Context switching is expensive and may cause a noticeable impact on the performance of your system. In some cases it may make sense to try to minimize context switching by making sure that some critical processes are never executed on the same set of CPU cores. You can use the --cpuset-cpus flag on docker run or docker create to limit a container to execute only on a specific set of CPU cores.

You can see the CPU set restrictions in action by stressing one of your machine cores and examining your CPU workload:

```
# Start a container limited to a single CPU and run a load generator
docker run -d \
    --cpuset-cpus 0 \                          ◄─┐ Restrict to CPU number 0
    --name ch6_stresser dockerinaction/ch6_stresser

# Start a container to watch the load on the CPU under load
docker run -it --rm dockerinaction/ch6_htop
```

Once you run the second command, you'll see htop display the running processes and the workload of the available CPUs. The ch6_stresser container will stop running after 30 seconds, so it's important not to delay when you run this experiment.

When you finish with htop, press Q to quit. Before moving on, remember to shut down and remove the container named ch6_stresser:

```
docker rm -vf ch6_stresser
```

I thought this was exciting when I first used it. To get the best appreciation, repeat this experiment a few different times using different values for the --cpuset-cpus flag. If you do, you'll see the process assigned to different cores or different sets of cores. The value can be either list or range forms:

- 0,1,2—A list including the first three cores of the CPU
- 0-2—A range including the first three cores of the CPU

6.1.3 *Access to devices*

Devices are the last resource type. This control differs from memory and CPU limits in that access to devices is not a limit. This is more like resource authorization control.

Linux systems have all sorts of devices, including hard drives, optical drives, USB drives, mouse, keyboard, sound devices, and webcams. Containers have access to some of these devices by default, and Docker creates others for each container (like virtual terminals).

On occasion it may be important to share other devices between a host and a specific container. Consider a situation where you're running some computer vision software that requires access to a webcam. In that case you'll need to grant access to the container running your software to the webcam device attached to the system; you can use the --device flag to specify a set of devices to mount into the new container. The following example would map your webcam at /dev/video0 to the same location within a new container. Running this example will work only if you have a webcam at /dev/video0:

```
docker -it --rm \
    --device /dev/video0:/dev/video0 \            ◄──┐ Mount video0
    ubuntu:latest ls -al /dev
```

The value provided must be a map between the device file on the host operating system and the location inside the new container. The device flag can be set many times to grant access to different devices.

People in situations with custom hardware or proprietary drivers will find this kind of access to devices useful. It's preferable to resorting to modifying their host operating system.

6.2 *Shared memory*

Linux provides a few tools for sharing memory between processes running on the same computer. This form of inter-process communication (IPC) performs at memory speeds. It's often used when the latency associated with network or pipe-based IPC drags software performance down below requirements. The best examples of shared memory-based IPC use are in scientific computing and some popular database technologies like PostgreSQL.

Docker creates a unique IPC namespace for each container by default. The Linux IPC namespace partitions share memory primitives such as named shared memory blocks and semaphores, as well as message queues. It's okay if you're not sure what these are. Just know that they're tools used by Linux programs to coordinate processing. The IPC namespace prevents processes in one container from accessing the memory on the host or in other containers.

6.2.1 *Sharing IPC primitives between containers*

I've created an image named `dockerinactionch6_ipc` that contains both a producer and consumer. They communicate using shared memory. The following will help you understand the problem with running these in separate containers:

```
docker -d -u nobody --name ch6_ipc_producer \        ◀── Start producer
    dockerinaction/ch6_ipc -producer
docker -d -u nobody --name ch6_ipc_consumer \        ◀── Start consumer
    dockerinaction/ch6_ipc -consumer
```

These commands start two containers. The first creates a message queue and begins broadcasting messages on it. The second should pull from the message queue and write the messages to the logs. You can see what each is doing by using the following commands to inspect the logs of each:

```
docker logs ch6_ipc_producer

docker logs ch6_ipc_consumer
```

Notice that something is wrong with the containers you started. The consumer never sees any messages on the queue. Each process used the same key to identify the shared memory resource, but they referred to different memory. The reason is that each container has its own shared memory namespace.

If you need to run programs that communicate with shared memory in different containers, then you'll need to join their IPC namespaces with the `--ipc` flag. The `--ipc` flag has a container mode that will create a new container in the same IPC namespace as another target container. This is just like the `--net` flag covered in chapter 5. Figure 6.3 illustrates the relationship between containers and their namespaced shared memory pools.

Use the following commands to test joined IPC namespaces for yourself:

```
docker rm -v ch6_ipc_consumer            ◀── Remove original consumer
```
Start new consumer ──▶
```
docker -d --name ch6_ipc_consumer \
    --ipc container:ch6_ipc_producer \       ◀── Join IPC namespace
    dockerinaction/ch6_ipc -consumer
```

These commands rebuild the consumer container and reuse the IPC namespace of the `ch6_ipc_producer` container. This time the consumer should be able to access the

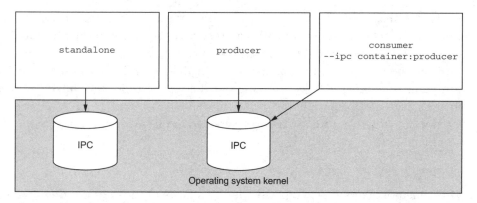

Figure 6.3   Three containers and their shared memory pools. Producer and consumer share a single pool.

same memory location where the server is writing. You can see this working by using the following commands to inspect the logs of each:

```
docker logs ch6_ipc_producer
```

```
docker logs ch6_ipc_consumer
```

Remember to clean up your running containers before moving on:

- The v option will clean up volumes.
- The f option will kill the container if it is running.
- The rm command takes a list of containers.

```
docker rm -vf ch6_ipc_producer ch6_ipc_consumer
```

There are obvious security implications to reusing the shared memory namespaces of containers. But this option is available if you need it. Sharing memory between containers is a safer alternative than sharing memory with the host.

6.2.2   *Using an open memory container*

Memory isolation is a desirable trait. If you encounter a situation where you need to operate in the same namespace as the rest of the host, you can do so using an open memory container:

```
docker -d --name ch6_ipc_producer \                    ◀─┤ Start a producer
    --ipc host \                          ◀──  Use open memory container
    dockerinaction/ch6_ipc –producer
```

```
docker -d --name ch6_ipc_consumer \                    ◀─┤ Start a consumer
    --ipc host \                          ◀──  Use open memory container
    dockerinaction/ch6_ipc -consumer
```

These containers will be able to communicate with each other and any other processes running on the host computer immediately. As you can see in this example, you enable this feature by specifying host on the --ipc flag. You might use this in cases when you need to communicate with a process that must run on the host, but in general you should try to avoid this if possible.

Feel free to check out the source code for this example. It's an ugly but simple C program. You can find it by checking out the source repository linked to from the image's page on Docker Hub.

You can clean up the containers you created in this section using the same cleanup command as in section 6.2.1:

```
docker rm -vf ch6_ipc_producer ch6_ipc_consumer
```

Open memory containers are a risk, but it's a far better idea to use them than to run those processes outside a container.

6.3 *Understanding users*

Docker starts containers as the root user inside that container by default. The root user has almost full privileged access to the state of the container. Any processes running as that user inherit those permissions. It follows that if there's a bug in one of those processes, they might damage the container. There are ways to limit the damage, but the most effective way to prevent these types of issues is not to use the root user.

There are reasonable exceptions when using the root user is the best if not only available option. You use the root user for building images and at runtime when there's no other option. There are other similar situations when you want to run system administration software inside a container. In those cases the process needs privileged access not only to the container but also to the host operating system. This section covers the range of solutions to these problems.

6.3.1 *Introduction to the Linux user namespace*

Linux recently released a new user (USR) namespace that allows users in one namespace to be mapped to users in another. The new namespace operates like the process identifier (PID) namespace.

Docker hasn't yet been integrated with the USR namespace. This means that a container running with a user ID (number, not name) that's the same as a user on the host machine has the same host file permissions as that user. This isn't a problem. The file system available inside a container has been mounted in such a way that changes that are made inside that container will stay inside that container's file system. But this does impact volumes.

When Docker adopts the USR namespace, you'll be able to map user IDs on the host to user IDs in a container namespace. So, I could map user 1000 on my host to user 2 in the container. This is particularly useful for resolving file permissions issues in cases like reading and writing to volumes.

6.3.2 *Working with the run-as user*

Before you create a container, it would be nice to be able to tell what username (and user ID) is going to be used by default. The default is specified by the image. There's currently no way to examine an image to discover attributes like the default user. This information is not included on Docker Hub. And there's no command to examine image metadata.

The closest feature available is the docker inspect command. If you missed it in chapter 2, the inspect subcommand displays the metadata of a specific container. Container metadata includes the metadata of the image it was created from. Once you've created a container—let's call it bob—you can get the username that the container is using with the following commands:

```
docker create --name bob busybox:latest ping localhost
```

Display all of bob's metadata →
```
docker inspect bob

docker inspect --format "{{.Config.User}}" bob
```
← **Show only run-as user defined by bob's image**

If the result is blank, the container will default to running as the root user. If it isn't blank, either the image author specifically named a default run-as user or you set a specific run-as user when you created the container. The --format or -f option used in the second command allows you to specify a template to render the output. In this case you've selected the User field of the Config property of the document. The value can be any valid GoLang template, so if you're feeling up to it, you can get creative with the results.

There are problems with this approach. First, the run-as user might be changed by whatever script the image uses to start up. These are sometimes referred to as boot, or init, scripts. The metadata returned by docker inspect includes only the configuration that the container was started with. So if the user changes, it won't be reflected there. Second, you have to create a container from an image in order to get the information. That can be dangerous.

Currently, the only way to fix both problems would be to look inside the image. You could expand the image files after you download them and examine the metadata and init scripts by hand, but doing so is time-consuming and easy to get wrong. For the time being, it may be better to run a simple experiment to determine the default user. This will solve the first problem but not the second:

Outputs: root →
```
docker run --rm --entrypoint "" busybox:latest whoami

docker run --rm --entrypoint "" busybox:latest id
```
← **Outputs: uid=0(root) gid=0(root) groups=10(wheel)**

This demonstrates two commands that you might use to determine the default user of an image (in this case, busybox:latest). Both the whoami and id commands are common among Linux distributions, and so they're likely to be available in any given

Figure 6.4   Root vs. root—a security drama

image. The second command is superior because it shows both the name and ID details for the run-as user. Both these commands are careful to unset the entrypoint of the container. This will make sure that the command specified after the image name is the command that is executed by the container. These are poor substitutes for a first-class image metadata tool, but they get the job done. Consider the brief exchange between two root users in figure 6.4.

You can entirely avoid the default user problem if you change the run-as user when you create the container. The quirk with using this is that the username must exist on the image you're using. Different Linux distributions ship with different users predefined, and some image authors reduce or augment that set. You can get a list of available users in an image with the following command:

```
docker run --rm busybox:latest awk -F: '$0=$1' /etc/passwd
```

I won't go into much detail here, but the Linux user database is stored in a file located at /etc/passwd. This command will read that file and pull a list of the usernames. Once you've identified the user you want to use, you can create a new container with a specific run-as user. Docker provides the --user or -u flag on docker run and docker create for setting the user. This will set the user to "nobody":

```
docker run --rm \
    --user nobody \          ← Set run-as user to nobody          ← Outputs: uid=99(nobody)
    busybox:latest id                                                gid=99(nobody)
```

This command used the "nobody" user. That user is very common and intended for use in restricted-privileges scenarios like running applications. That was just one example. You can use any username defined by the image here, including root. This only scratches the surface of what you can do with the -u or --user flag. The value can accept any user or group pair. It can also accept user and group names or IDs. When you use IDs instead of names, the options start to open up:

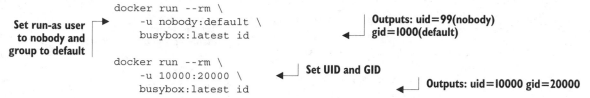

Set run-as user to nobody and group to default

```
docker run --rm \
    -u nobody:default \
    busybox:latest id
```

Outputs: uid=99(nobody) gid=1000(default)

```
docker run --rm \
    -u 10000:20000 \
    busybox:latest id
```

Set UID and GID

Outputs: uid=10000 gid=20000

The second command starts a new container that sets the run-as user and group to a user and group that do not exist in the container. When that happens, the IDs won't resolve to a user or group name, but all file permissions will work as if the user and group did exist. Depending on how the software packaged in the container is configured, changing the run-as user may cause problems. Otherwise, this is a powerful feature that can make file-permission issues simple to resolve.

You should be very careful about which users on your systems are able to control your Docker daemon. If a user can control your Docker daemon, that person can effectively control the root account on your host.

The best way to be confident in your runtime configuration is to pull images from trusted sources or build your own. It's entirely possible to do malicious things like turning a default non-root user into the root user (making your attempt at safety a trap) or opening up access to the root account without authentication. Chapter 7 covers this topic briefly. For now, I'll wrap up with another interesting example:

```
docker run -it --name escalation -u nobody busybox:latest \
    /bin/sh -c "whoami; su -c whoami"
```

Outputs: "nobody" and then "root"

That was too easy. The official BusyBox image has no password set for root (or many other accounts). The official Ubuntu image ships with the account locked; you'd have to start the container with root or promote via an SUID binary (more on these in chapter 7). The impact of such weak authentication is that a process running as any user could self-promote to root in the container. The lesson here is that you might consider learning to start setting passwords or disabling the root account like Ubuntu and others. This means modifying images, so even if you're not a software author, you'll benefit from reading part 2 of this book.

6.3.3 Users and volumes

Now that you've learned how users inside containers share the same user ID space as the users on your host system, you need to learn how those two might interact. The main reason for that interaction is the file permissions on files in volumes. For example, if you're running a Linux terminal, you should be able to use these commands directly; otherwise, you'll need to use the `boot2docker ssh` command to get a shell in your Boot2Docker virtual machine:

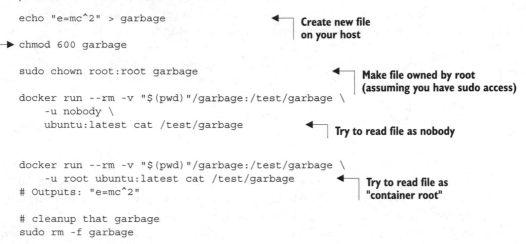

```
echo "e=mc^2" > garbage

chmod 600 garbage

sudo chown root:root garbage

docker run --rm -v "$(pwd)"/garbage:/test/garbage \
    -u nobody \
    ubuntu:latest cat /test/garbage


docker run --rm -v "$(pwd)"/garbage:/test/garbage \
    -u root ubuntu:latest cat /test/garbage
# Outputs: "e=mc^2"

# cleanup that garbage
sudo rm -f garbage
```

Make file readable only by its owner

Create new file on your host

Make file owned by root (assuming you have sudo access)

Try to read file as nobody

Try to read file as "container root"

The second-to-last `docker` command should fail with an error message like "Permission denied." But the last `docker` command should succeed and show you the contents of the file you created in the first command. This means that file permissions on files in volumes are respected inside the container. But this also reflects that the user ID space is shared. Both root on the host and root in the container have user ID 0. So, although the container's nobody user with ID 65534 can't access a file owned by root on the host, the container's root user can.

Unless you want a file to be accessible to a container, don't mount it into that container with a volume.

The good news about this example is that you've seen how file permissions are respected and can solve some more mundane—but practical—operational issues. For example, how do you handle a log file written to a volume?

The preferred way is with volume containers, as described in chapter 4. But even then you need to consider file ownership and permission issues. If logs are written to a volume by a process running as user 1001 and another container tries to access that file as user 1002, then file permissions might prevent the operation.

One way to overcome this obstacle would be to specifically manage the user ID of the running user. You can either edit the image ahead of time by setting the user ID of the user you're going to run the container with, or you can use the desired user and group ID:

```
mkdir logFiles

sudo chown 2000:2000 logFiles

docker run --rm -v "$(pwd)"/logFiles:/logFiles \
    -u 2000:2000 ubuntu:latest \
    /bin/bash -c "echo This is important info > /logFiles/important.log"
```

Set ownership of directory to desired user and group

Write important log file

Set UID:GID to 2000:2000

Append to log from another container ▸
```
docker run --rm -v "$(pwd)"/logFiles:/logFiles \
    -u 2000:2000 ubuntu:latest \
    /bin/bash -c "echo More info >> /logFiles/important.log"
```
◂ ⎤ **Also set UID:GID to 2000:2000**

```
sudo rm -r logFiles
```

After running this example, you'll see that the file could be written to the directory that's owned by user 2000. Not only that, but any container that uses a user or group with write access to the directory could write a file in that directory or to the same file if the permissions allow. This trick works for reading, writing, and executing files.

6.4 Adjusting OS feature access with capabilities

Docker can adjust the feature authorization of processes within containers. In Linux these feature authorizations are called capabilities, but as native support expands to other operating systems, other back-end implementations would need to be provided. Whenever a process attempts to make a gated system call, the capabilities of that process are checked for the required capability. The call will succeed if the process has the required capability and fail otherwise.

When you create a new container, Docker drops a specific set of capabilities by default. This is done to further isolate the running process from the administrative functions of the operating system. In reading this list of dropped capabilities, you might be able to guess at the reason for their removal. At the time of this writing, this set includes the following:

- *SETPCAP*—Modify process capabilities
- *SYS_MODULE*—Insert/remove kernel modules
- *SYS_RAWIO*—Modify kernel memory
- *SYS_PACCT*—Configure process accounting
- *SYS_NICE*—Modify priority of processes
- *SYS_RESOURCE*—Override resource limits
- *SYS_TIME*—Modify the system clock
- *SYS_TTY_CONFIG*—Configure TTY devices
- *AUDIT_WRITE*—Write the audit log
- *AUDIT_CONTROL*—Configure audit subsystem
- *MAC_OVERRIDE*—Ignore kernel MAC policy
- *MAC_ADMIN*—Configure MAC configuration
- *SYSLOG*—Modify kernel print behavior
- *NET_ADMIN*—Configure the network
- *SYS_ADMIN*—Catchall for administrative functions

The default set of capabilities provided to Docker containers provides a reasonable feature reduction, but there will be times when you need to add or reduce this set further. For example, the capability NET_RAW can be dangerous. If you wanted to be a bit more careful than the default configuration, you could drop NET_RAW from the list of capabilities. You can drop capabilities from a container using the `--cap-drop` flag on `docker create` or `docker run`.

```
docker run --rm -u nobody \
    ubuntu:latest \
    /bin/bash -c "capsh --print | grep net_raw"

docker run --rm -u nobody \                    ◄─── Drop NET_RAW
    --cap-drop net_raw \                             capability
    ubuntu:latest \
    /bin/bash -c "capsh --print | grep net_raw"
```

In Linux documentation you'll often see capabilities named in all uppercase and prefixed with CAP_, but that prefix won't work if provided to the capability-management options. Use unprefixed and lowercase names for the best results.

Similar to the `--cap-drop` flag, the `--cap-add` flag will add capabilities. If you needed to add the SYS_ADMIN capability for some reason, you'd use a command like the following:

```
docker run --rm -u nobody \
    ubuntu:latest \
    /bin/bash –c "capsh --print | grep sys_admin"   ◄─── SYS_ADMIN is
                                                          not included
docker run --rm -u nobody \
    --cap-add sys_admin \          ◄─── Add SYS_ADMIN
    ubuntu:latest \
    /bin/bash –c "capsh --print | grep sys_admin"
```

Like other container-creation options, both `--cap-add` and `--cap-drop` can be specified multiple times to add or drop multiple capabilities. These flags can be used to build containers that will let a process perform exactly and only what is required for proper operation.

6.5   *Running a container with full privileges*

In those cases when you need to run a system administration task inside a container, you can grant that container privileged access to your computer. Privileged containers maintain their file system and network isolation but have full access to shared memory and devices and possess full system capabilities. You can perform several interesting tasks, like running Docker inside a container, with privileged containers.

The bulk of the uses for privileged containers is administrative. Take, for example, an environment where the root file system is read-only, or installing software outside a container has been disallowed, or you have no direct access to a shell on the host. If you wanted to run a program to tune the operating system (for something like load balancing) and you had access to run a container on that host, then you could simply run that program in a privileged container.

If you find a situation that can be solved only with the reduced isolation of a privileged container, use the `--privileged` flag on `docker create` or `docker run` to enable this mode:

```
docker run --rm \
    --privileged \
    ubuntu:latest id
```
◀── **Check out our IDs**

```
docker run --rm \
    --privileged \
    ubuntu:latest capsh -print
```
◀── **Check out our Linux capabilities**

```
docker run --rm \
    --privileged \
    ubuntu:latest ls /dev
```
◀── **Check out list of mounted devices**

```
docker run --rm \
    --privileged \
    ubuntu:latest ifconfig
```
◀── **Examine network configuration**

Privileged containers are still partially isolated. For example, the network namespace will still be in effect. If you need to tear down that namespace, you'll need to combine this with `--net host` as well.

6.6 *Stronger containers with enhanced tools*

Docker uses reasonable defaults and a "batteries included" toolset to ease adoption and promote best practices. But you can enhance the containers it builds if you bring additional tools. Tools you can use to harden your containers include AppArmor and SELinux. If you use the LXC container provider, you can also provide custom LXC configuration and get into fine-tuning containers. If you're using LXC, you can even use a Linux feature called seccomp-bpf (secure computing with system call filtering).

Whole books have been written about each of these tools. They bring their own nuances, benefits, and required skillsets. Their use is—without question—worth the effort. Support for each varies by Linux distribution, so you may be in for a bit of work. But once you've adjusted your host configuration, the Docker integration is simpler.

Security research

The information security space is very complicated and constantly evolving. It's easy to feel overwhelmed when reading through open conversations between InfoSec professionals. These are often highly skilled people with long memories and very different contexts from developers or general users. If you can take any one thing away from open InfoSec conversations, it is that balancing system security with user needs is complex.

One of the best things you can do if you're new to this space is start with articles, papers, blogs, and books before you jump into conversations. This will give you an opportunity to digest one perspective and gain some deeper insight before switching to thought from a different perspective. When you've had an opportunity to form your own insight and opinions, these conversations become much more valuable.

(continued)

It's very difficult to read one paper or learn one thing and know the best possible way to build a hardened solution. Whatever your situation, the system will evolve to include improvements from several sources. So the best thing you can do is take each tool and learn it by itself. Don't be intimidated by the depth some tools require for a strong understanding. The effort will be worth the result, and you'll understand the systems you use much better for it.

Docker isn't a perfect solution. Some would argue that it's not even a security tool. But what improvements it provides are far better than the alternative where people forego any isolation due to perceived cost. If you've read this far, maybe you'd be willing to go further with these auxiliary topics.

6.6.1 *Specifying additional security options*

Docker provides a single flag for specifying options for Linux Security Modules (LSM) at container creation or runtime. LSM is a framework that Linux adopted to act as an interface layer between the operating system and security providers.

AppArmor and SELinux are both LSM providers. They both provide mandatory access control (MAC—the system defines access rules) and replace the standard Linux discretionary access control (file owners define access rules).

The flag available on `docker run` and `docker create` is `--security-opt`. This flag can be set multiple times to pass multiple values. The values can currently be one of six formats:

- To set a SELinux user label, use the form `label:user:<USERNAME>` where `<USERNAME>` is the name of the user you want to use for the label.
- To set a SELinux role label, use the form `label:role:<ROLE>` where `<ROLE>` is the name of the role you want to apply to processes in the container.
- To set a SELinux type label, use the form `label:type:<TYPE>` where `<TYPE>` is the type name of the processes in the container.
- To set a SELinux level label, use the form `label:level:<LEVEL>` where `<LEVEL>` is the level where processes in the container should run. Levels are specified as low-high pairs. Where abbreviated to the low level only, SELinux will interpret the range as single level.
- To disable SELinux label confinement for a container, use the form `label:disable`.
- To apply an AppArmor profile on the container, use the form `label:apparmor:<PROFILE>` where `<PROFILE>` is the name of the AppArmor profile to use.

As you can guess from these options, SELinux is a labeling system. A set of labels, called a *context*, is applied to every file and system object. A similar set of labels is applied to every user and process. At runtime when a process attempts to interact with a file or system resource, the sets of labels are evaluated against a set of allowed rules. The result of that evaluation determines whether the interaction is allowed or blocked.

The last option will set an AppArmor profile. AppArmor is frequently substituted for SELinux because it works with file paths instead of labels and has a training mode that you can use to passively build profiles based on observed application behavior. These differences are often cited as reasons why AppArmor is easier to adopt and maintain.

6.6.2 *Fine-tuning with LXC*

Docker was originally built to use software called Linux Containers (LXC). LXC is a container runtime provider—a tool that actually works with Linux to create namespaces and all the components that go into building a container.

As Docker matured and portability became a concern, a new container runtime called libcontainer was built, replacing LXC. Docker ships with libcontainer by default, but Docker uses an interface layer so that users can change the container execution provider. LXC is a more mature library than libcontainer and provides many additional features that diverge from the goals of Docker. If you're running a system where you can and want to use LXC, you can change the container provider and take advantage of those additional features. Before investing too heavily, know that some of those additional features will greatly reduce the portability of your containers.

To use LXC, you need to install it and make sure the Docker daemon was started with the LXC driver enabled. Use the `--exec-driver=lxc` option when you start the Docker daemon. The daemon is usually configured to start as one of your system's services. Check the installation instructions on www.docker.com to find details for your distribution.

Once Docker is configured for LXC, you can use the `--lxc-conf` flag on `docker run` or `docker create` to set the LXC configuration for a container:

```
docker run -d \
    --lxc-conf="lxc.cgroup.cpuset.cpus=0,1" \     ◄─── Limited to two
    --name ch6_stresser dockerinaction/ch6_stresser      CPU cores by LXC

docker run -it --rm dockerinaction/ch6_htop

docker rm -vf ch6_stresser
```

As when you ran a similar example earlier in this chapter, when you've finished with htop, press Q to quit.

If you decide to use the LXC provider and specify LXC-specific options for your containers, Docker won't be aware of that configuration. Certain configurations can be provided that conflict with the standard container changes made for every Docker container. For this reason, you should always carefully validate the configuration against the actual impact to a container.

6.7   *Build use-case-appropriate containers*

Containers are a cross-cutting concern. There are more reasons and ways that people could use them than I could ever enumerate. So it's important, when you use Docker to build containers to serve your own purposes, that you take the time to do so in a way that's appropriate for the software you're running.

The most secure tactic for doing so would be to start with the most isolated container you can build and justify reasons for weakening those restrictions. In reality, people tend to be a bit more reactive than proactive. For that reason I think Docker hits a sweet spot with the default container construction. It provides reasonable defaults without hindering the productivity of users.

Docker containers are not the most isolated by default. Docker does not require that you enhance those defaults. It will let you do silly things in production if you want to. This makes Docker seem much more like a tool than a burden and something people generally want to use rather than feel like they have to use. For those who would rather not do silly things in production, Docker provides a simple interface to enhance container isolation.

6.7.1   *Applications*

Applications are the whole reason we use computers. Most applications are programs that other people wrote and work with potentially malicious data. Consider your web browser.

A web browser is a type of application that's installed on almost every computer. It interacts with web pages, images, scripts, embedded video, Flash documents, Java applications, and anything else out there. You certainly didn't create all that content, and most people were not contributors on web browser projects. How can you trust your web browser to handle all that content correctly?

Some more cavalier readers might just ignore the problem. After all, what's the worst thing that could happen? Well, if an attacker gains control of your web browser (or other application), they will gain all the capabilities of that application and the permissions of the user it's running as. They could trash your computer, delete your files, install other malware, or even launch attacks against other computers from yours. So, this isn't a good thing to ignore. The question remains: how do you protect yourself when this is a risk you need to take?

The best approach is to isolate the risk. First, make sure the application is running as a user with limited permissions. That way, if there's a problem, it won't be able to change the files on your computer. Second, limit the system capabilities of the browser. In doing so, you make sure your system configuration is safer. Third, set limits on how much of the CPU and memory the application can use. Limits help reserve resources to keep the system responsive. Finally, it's a good idea to specifically whitelist devices that it can access. That will keep snoops off your webcam, USB, and the like.

6.7.2 *High-level system services*

High-level system services are a bit different from applications. They're not part of the operating system, but your computer makes sure they're started and kept running. These tools typically sit alongside applications outside the operating system, but they often require privileged access to the operating system to operate correctly. They provide important functionality to users and other software on a system. Examples include cron, syslogd, dbus, sshd, and docker.

If you're unfamiliar with these tools (hopefully not all of them), it's all right. They do things like keep system logs, run scheduled commands, and provide a way to get a secure shell on the system from the network, and docker manages containers.

Although running services as root is common, few of them actually need full privileged access. Use capabilities to tune their access for the specific features they need.

6.7.3 *Low-level system services*

Low-level services control things like devices or the system's network stack. They require privileged access to the components of the system they provide (for example, firewall software needs administrative access to the network stack).

It's rare to see these run inside containers. Tasks such as file-system management, device management, and network management are core host concerns. Most software run in containers is expected to be portable. So machine-specific tasks like these are a poor fit for general container use cases.

The best exceptions are short-running configuration containers. For example, in an environment where all deployments happen with Docker images and containers, you'd want to push network stack changes in the same way you push software. In this case, you might push an image with the configuration to the host and make the changes with a privileged container. The risk in this case is reduced because you authored the configuration to be pushed, the container is not long running, and changes like these are simple to audit.

6.8 *Summary*

This chapter introduced the isolation features provided by Linux and talked about how Docker uses those to build configurable containers. With this knowledge, you will be able to customize that container isolation and use Docker for any use case. The following points were covered in this chapter:

- Docker uses cgroups, which let a user set memory limits, CPU weight, and CPU core restrictions and restrict access to specific devices.
- Docker containers each have their own IPC namespace that can be shared with other containers or the host in order to facilitate communication over shared memory.

- Docker does not yet support the USR namespace, so user and group IDs inside a container are equivalent to the same IDs on the host machine.
- You can and should use the `-u` option on `docker run` and `docker create` to run containers as non-root users.
- Avoid running containers in privileged mode whenever possible.
- Linux capabilities provide operating system feature authorization. Docker drops certain capabilities in order to provide reasonably isolating defaults.
- The capabilities granted to any container can be set with the `--cap-add` and `--cap-drop` flags.
- Docker provides tooling for integrating with enhanced isolation technologies like SELinux and AppArmor. These are powerful tools that any serious Docker adopter should investigate.

Part 2

Packaging Software
for Distribution

It may not be a frequent occasion, but inevitably a Docker user will need to create an image. There are times when the software you need is not packaged in an image. Other times you will need a feature that has not been enabled in an available image. The four chapters in this part will help you understand how to originate, customize, and specialize the images you intend to deploy or share using Docker.

Packaging software in images 7

This chapter covers

- Manual image construction and practices
- Images from a packaging perspective
- Working with flat images
- Image versioning best practices

The goal of this chapter is to help you understand the concerns of image design, learn the tools for building images, and discover advanced image patterns. You will accomplish these things by working through a thorough real-world example. Before getting started, you should have a firm grasp on the concepts in part 1 of this book.

You can create a Docker image by either modifying an existing image inside a container or defining and executing a build script called a Dockerfile. This chapter focuses on the process of manually changing an image, the fundamental mechanics of image manipulation, and the artifacts that are produced. Dockerfiles and build automation are covered in chapter 8.

7.1 Building Docker images from a container

It's easy to get started building images if you're already familiar with using containers. Remember, a union file system (UFS) mount provides a container's file system.

127

Any changes that you make to the file system inside a container will be written as new layers that are owned by the container that created them.

Before you work with real software, the next section details the typical workflow with a Hello World example.

7.1.1   *Packaging Hello World*

The basic workflow for building an image from a container includes three steps. First, you need to create a container from an existing image. You will choose the image based on what you want to be included with the new finished image and the tools you will need to make the changes.

The second step is to modify the file system of the container. These changes will be written to a new layer on the union file system for the container. We'll revisit the relationship between images, layers, and repositories later in this chapter.

Once the changes have been made, the last step is to commit those changes. Once the changes are committed, you'll be able to create new containers from the resulting image. Figure 7.1 illustrates this workflow.

With these steps in mind, work through the following commands to create a new image named hw_image.

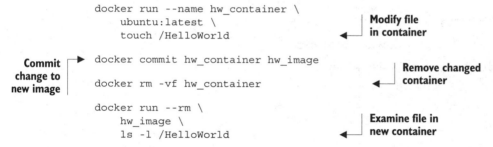

If that seems stunningly simple, you should know that it does become a bit more nuanced as the images you produce become more sophisticated, but the basic steps will always be the same.

Now that you have an idea of the workflow, you should try to build a new image with real software. In this case, you'll be packaging a program called Git.

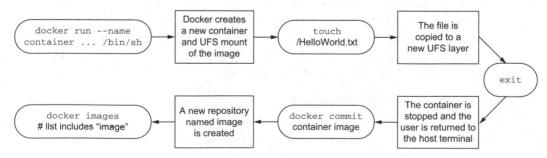

Figure 7.1   Building an image from a container

7.1.2 *Preparing packaging for Git*

Git is a popular, distributed version-control tool. Whole books have been written about the topic. If you're unfamiliar with it, I recommend that you spend some time learning how to use Git. At the moment, though, you only need to know that it's a program you're going to install onto an Ubuntu image.

To get started building your own image, the first thing you'll need is a container created from an appropriate base image:

```
docker run -it --name image-dev ubuntu:latest /bin/bash
```

This will start a new container running the bash shell. From this prompt, you can issue commands to customize your container. Ubuntu ships with a Linux tool for software installation called `apt-get`. This will come in handy for acquiring the software that you want to package in a Docker image. You should now have an interactive shell running with your container. Next, you need to install Git in the container. Do that by running the following command:

```
apt-get -y install git
```

This will tell APT to download and install Git and all its dependencies on the container's file system. When it's finished, you can test the installation by running the `git` program:

```
git version
# Output something like:
# git version 1.9.1
```

Package tools like `apt-get` make installing and uninstalling software easier than if you had to do everything by hand. But they provide no isolation to that software and dependency conflicts often occur. You can be sure that other software you install outside this container won't impact the version of Git you have installed.

Now that Git has been installed on your Ubuntu container, you can simply exit the container:

```
exit
```

The container should be stopped but still present on your computer. Git has been installed in a new layer on top of the ubuntu:latest image. If you were to walk away from this example right now and return a few days later, how would you know exactly what changes were made? When you're packaging software, it's often useful to review the list of files that have been modified in a container, and Docker has a command for that.

7.1.3 *Reviewing file system changes*

Docker has a command that shows you all the file-system changes that have been made inside a container. These changes include added, changed, or deleted files and directories. To review the changes that you made when you used APT to install Git, run the `diff` subcommand:

```
docker diff image-dev
```
◄──┐ **# Outputs a LONG list of file changes...**

Lines that start with an A are files that were added. Those starting with a C were changed. Finally those with a D were deleted. Installing Git with APT in this way made several changes. For that reason, it might be better to see this at work with a few specific examples:

```
docker run --name tweak-a busybox:latest touch /HelloWorld        ◄──┐ Add new file
docker diff tweak-a                                                   │ to busybox
# Output:
#   A /HelloWorld

docker run --name tweak-d busybox:latest rm /bin/vi               ◄──┐ Remove existing
docker diff tweak-d                                                   │ file from busybox
# Output:
#   C /bin
#   D /bin/vi

docker run --name tweak-c busybox:latest touch /bin/vi            ◄──┐ Change existing
docker diff tweak-c                                                   │ file in busybox
# Output:
#   C /bin
#   C /bin/busybox
```

Always remember to clean up your workspace, like this:

```
docker rm -vf tweak-a
docker rm -vf tweak-d
docker rm -vf tweak-c
```

Now that you've seen the changes you've made to the file system, you're ready to commit the changes to a new image. As with most other things, this involves a single command that does several things.

7.1.4 *Committing a new image*

You use the docker commit command to create an image from a modified container. It's a best practice to use the -a flag that signs the image with an author string. You should also always use the -m flag, which sets a commit message. Create and sign a new image that you'll name ubuntu-git from the image-dev container where you installed Git:

```
docker commit -a "@dockerinaction" -m "Added git" image-dev ubuntu-git
# Outputs a new unique image identifier like:
# bbf1d5d430cdf541a72ad74dfa54f6faec41d2c1e4200778e9d4302035e5d143
```

Once you've committed the image, it should show up in the list of images installed on your computer. Running docker images should include a line like this:

```
REPOSITORY     TAG      IMAGE ID      CREATED        VIRTUAL SIZE
ubuntu-git     latest   bbf1d5d430cd  5 seconds ago  226 MB
```

Make sure it works by testing Git in a container created from that image:

```
docker run --rm ubuntu-git git version
```

Now you've created a new image based on an Ubuntu image and installed Git. That's a great start, but what do you think will happen if you omit the command override? Try it to find out:

```
docker run --rm ubuntu-git
```

Nothing appears to happen when you run that command. That's because the command you started the original container with was committed with the new image. The command you used to start the container that the image was created by was /bin/bash. When you create a container from this image using the default command, it will start a shell and immediately exit. That's not a terribly useful default command.

I doubt that any users of an image named ubuntu-git would expect that they'd need to manually invoke Git each time. It would be better to set an entrypoint on the image to git. An entrypoint is the program that will be executed when the container starts. If the entrypoint isn't set, the default command will be executed directly. If the entrypoint is set, the default command and its arguments will be passed to the entrypoint as arguments.

To set the entrypoint, you'll need to create a new container with the --entrypoint flag set and create a new image from that container:

```
docker run --name cmd-git --entrypoint git ubuntu-git          ◄──── Show standard
                                                                     git help and exit
docker commit -m "Set CMD git" \
    -a "@dockerinaction" cmd-git ubuntu-git          ◄──── Commit new image
                                                           to same name
Cleanup └──► docker rm -vf cmd-git

docker run --name cmd-git ubuntu-git version          ◄──┘ Test
```

Now that the entrypoint has been set to git, users no longer need to type the command at the end. This might seem like a marginal savings with this example, but many tools that people use are not as succinct. Setting the entrypoint is just one thing you can do to make images easier for people to use and integrate into their projects.

7.1.5 Configurable image attributes

When you use docker commit, you commit a new layer to an image. The file-system snapshot isn't the only thing included with this commit. Each layer also includes metadata describing the execution context. Of the parameters that can be set when a container is created, all the following will carry forward with an image created from the container:

- All environment variables
- The working directory
- The set of exposed ports
- All volume definitions
- The container entrypoint
- Command and arguments

If these values weren't specifically set for the container, the values will be inherited from the original image. Part 1 of this book covers each of these, so I won't reintroduce them here. But it may be valuable to examine two detailed examples. First, consider a container that introduces two environment variable specializations:

```
docker run --name rich-image-example \
    -e ENV_EXAMPLE1=Rich -e ENV_EXAMPLE2=Example \
    busybox:latest
docker commit rich-image-example rie

docker run --rm rie \
    /bin/sh -c "echo \$ENV_EXAMPLE1 \$ENV_EXAMPLE2"
```

Create environment variable specialization

Commit image

Outputs: Rich Example

Next, consider a container that introduces an entrypoint and command specialization as a new layer on top of the previous example:

```
docker run --name rich-image-example-2 \
    --entrypoint "/bin/sh" \
    rie \
    -c "echo \$ENV_EXAMPLE1 \$ENV_EXAMPLE2"
docker commit rich-image-example-2 rie

docker run --rm rie
```

Set default entrypoint

Set default command

Commit image

Different command with same output

This example builds two additional layers on top of BusyBox. In neither case are files changed, but the behavior changes because the context metadata has been altered. These changes include two new environment variables in the first new layer. Those environment variables are clearly inherited by the second new layer, which sets the entrypoint and default command to display their values. The last command uses the final image without specifying any alternative behavior, but it's clear that the previous defined behavior has been inherited.

Now that you understand how to modify an image, take the time to dive deeper into the mechanics of images and layers. Doing so will help you produce high-quality images in real-world situations.

7.2   *Going deep on Docker images and layers*

By this point in the chapter, you've built a few images. In those examples you started by creating a container from an image like ubuntu:latest or busybox:latest. Then you made changes to the file system or context within that container. Finally, everything seemed to just work when you used the `docker commit` command to create a new image. Understanding how the container's file system works and what the `docker commit` command actually does will help you become a better image author. This section dives into that subject and demonstrates the impact to authors.

7.2.1   *An exploration of union file systems*

Understanding the details of union file systems (UFS) is important for image authors for two reasons:

- Authors need to know the impact that adding, changing, and deleting files have on resulting images.
- Authors need have a solid understanding of the relationship between layers and how layers relate to images, repositories, and tags.

Start by considering a simple example. Suppose you want to make a single change to an existing image. In this case the image is ubuntu:latest, and you want to add a file named mychange to the root directory. You should use the following command to do this:

```
docker run --name mod_ubuntu ubuntu:latest touch /mychange
```

The resulting container (named `mod_ubuntu`) will be stopped but will have written that single change to its file system. As discussed in chapters 3 and 4, the root file system is provided by the image that the container was started from. That file system is implemented with something called a union file system.

A union file system is made up of layers. Each time a change is made to a union file system, that change is recorded on a new layer on top of all of the others. The "union" of all of those layers, or top-down view, is what the container (and user) sees when accessing the file system. Figure 7.2 illustrates the two perspectives for this example.

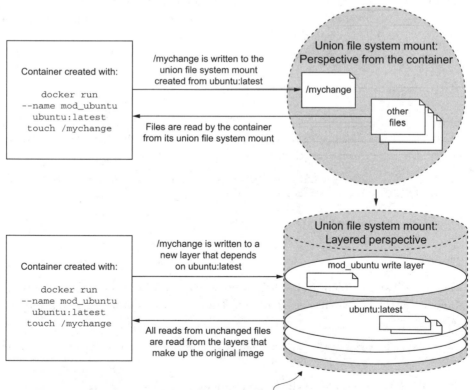

By looking at the union file system from the side—the perspective of its layers—you can begin to understand the relationship between different images and how file changes impact image size.

Figure 7.2   A simple file write example on a union file system from two perspectives

When you read a file from a union file system, that file will be read from the top-most layer where it exists. If a file was not created or changed on the top layer, the read will fall through the layers until it reaches a layer where that file does exist. This is illustrated in figure 7.3.

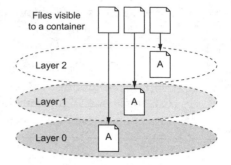

Figure 7.3 Reading files that are located on different layers

All this layer functionality is hidden by the union file system. No special actions need to be taken by the software running in a container to take advantage of these features. Understanding layers where files were added covers one of three types of file system writes. The other two are deletions and file changes.

Like additions, both file changes and deletions work by modifying the top layer. When a file is deleted, a delete record is written to the top layer, which overshadows any versions of that file on lower layers. When a file is changed, that change is written to the top layer, which again shadows any versions of that file on lower layers. The changes made to the file system of a container are listed with the docker diff command you used earlier in the chapter:

```
docker diff mod_ubuntu
```

This command will produce the output:

```
A /mychange
```

The A in this case indicates that the file was added. Run the next two commands to see how a file deletion is recorded:

```
docker run --name mod_busybox_delete busybox:latest rm /etc/profile
docker diff mod_busybox_delete
```

This time the output will have two rows:

```
C /etc
D /etc/profile
```

The D indicates a deletion, but this time the parent folder of the file was also included. The C indicates that it was changed. The next two commands demonstrate a file change:

```
docker run --name mod_busybox_change busybox:latest touch /etc/profile
docker diff mod_busybox_change
```

The diff subcommand will show two changes:

```
C /etc
C /etc/profile
```

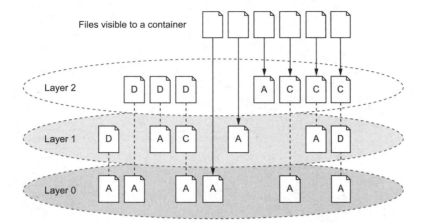

Figure 7.4   Various file addition, change, and deletion combinations over a three-layered image

Again, the C indicates a change, and the two items are the file and the folder where it's located. If a file nested five levels deep were changed, there would be a line for each level of the tree. File-change mechanics are the most important thing to understand about union file systems.

Most union file systems use something called copy-on-write, which is easier to understand if you think of it as copy-on-change. When a file in a read-only layer (not the top layer) is modified, the whole file is first copied from the read-only layer into the writable layer before the change is made. This has a negative impact on runtime performance and image size. Section 7.2.3 covers the way this should influence your image design.

Take a moment to solidify your understanding of the system by examining how the more comprehensive set of scenarios is illustrated in figure 7.4. In this illustration files are added, changed, deleted, and added again over a range of three layers.

Knowing how file system changes are recorded, you can begin to understand what happens when you use the docker commit command to create a new image.

7.2.2   *Reintroducing images, layers, repositories, and tags*

You've created an image using the docker commit command, and you understand that it commits the top-layer changes to an image. But we've yet to define *commit*.

Remember, a union file system is made up of a stack of layers where new layers are added to the top of the stack. Those layers are stored separately as collections of the changes made in that layer and metadata for that layer. When you commit a container's changes to its file system, you're saving a copy of that top layer in an identifiable way.

When you commit the layer, a new ID is generated for it, and copies of all the file changes are saved. Exactly how this happens depends on the storage engine that's

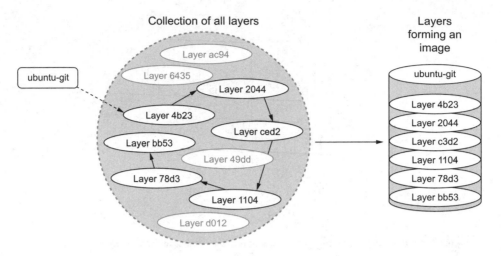

Figure 7.5   An image is the collection of layers produced by traversing the parent graph from a top layer.

being used on your system. It's less important for you to understand the details than it is for you to understand the general approach. The metadata for a layer includes that generated identifier, the identifier of the layer below it (parent), and the execution context of the container that the layer was created from. Layer identities and metadata form the graph that Docker and the UFS use to construct images.

An image is the stack of layers that you get by starting with a given top layer and then following all the links defined by the parent ID in each layer's metadata, as shown in figure 7.5.

Images are stacks of layers constructed by traversing the layer dependency graph from some starting layer. The layer that the traversal starts from is the top of the stack. This means that a layer's ID is also the ID of the image that it and its dependencies form. Take a moment to see this in action by committing the mod_ubuntu container you created earlier:

```
docker commit mod_ubuntu
```

That commit subcommand will generate output that includes a new image ID like this:

```
6528255cda2f9774a11a6b82be46c86a66b5feff913f5bb3e09536a54b08234d
```

You can create a new container from this image using the image ID as it's presented to you. Like containers, layer IDs are large hexadecimal numbers that can be difficult for a person to work with directly. For that reason, Docker provides repositories.

In chapter 3, a *repository* is roughly defined as a named bucket of images. More specifically, repositories are location/name pairs that point to a set of specific layer identifiers. Each repository contains at least one tag that points to a specific layer identifier and thus the image definition. Let's revisit the example used in chapter 3:

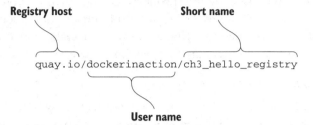

This repository is located in the registry hosted at quay.io. It's named for the user (dockerinaction) and a unique short name (ch3_hello_registry). Pulling this repository would pull all the images defined for each tag in the repository. In this example, there's only one tag, latest. That tag points to a layer with the short form ID 07c0f84777ef, as illustrated in figure 7.6.

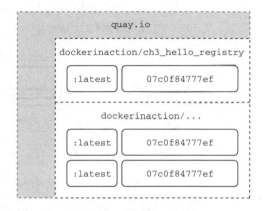

Figure 7.6   A visual representation of repositories

Repositories and tags are created with the docker tag, docker commit, or docker build commands. Revisit the mod_ubuntu container again and put it into a repository with a tag:

```
docker commit mod_ubuntu myuser/myfirstrepo:mytag
# Outputs:
# 82ec7d2c57952bf57ab1ffdf40d5374c4c68228e3e923633734e68a11f9a2b59
```

The generated ID that's displayed will be different because another copy of the layer was created. With this new friendly name, creating containers from your images requires little effort. If you want to copy an image, you only need to create a new tag or repository from the existing one. You can do that with the docker tag command. Every repository contains a "latest" tag by default. That will be used if the tag is omitted like in the previous command:

```
docker tag myuser/myfirstrepo:mytag myuser/mod_ubuntu
```

By this point you should have a strong understanding of basic UFS fundamentals as well as how Docker creates and manages layers, images, and repositories. With these in mind, let's consider how they might impact image design.

All layers below the writable layer created for a container are immutable, meaning they can never be modified. This property makes it possible to share access to images instead of creating independent copies for every container. It also makes individual layers highly reusable. The other side of this property is that anytime you make changes to an image, you need to add a new layer, and old layers are never removed. Knowing that images will inevitably need to change, you need to be aware of any image limitations and keep in mind how changes impact image size.

7.2.3   *Managing image size and layer limits*

If images evolved in the same way that most people manage their file systems, Docker images would quickly become unusable. For example, suppose you wanted to make a different version of the ubuntu-git image you created earlier in this chapter. It may seem natural to modify that ubuntu-git image. Before you do, create a new tag for your ubuntu-git image. You'll be reassigning the latest tag:

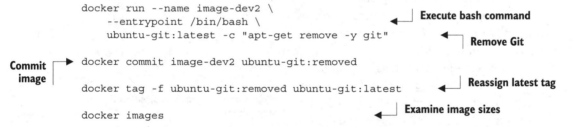

```
docker tag ubuntu-git:latest ubuntu-git:1.9          ◄──┐  Create new tag: 1.9
```

The first thing you'll do in building your new image is remove the version of Git you installed:

```
docker run --name image-dev2 \
    --entrypoint /bin/bash \          ◄──┐  Execute bash command
    ubuntu-git:latest -c "apt-get remove -y git"   ◄──┐  Remove Git
```

Commit ──►
image
```
docker commit image-dev2 ubuntu-git:removed

docker tag -f ubuntu-git:removed ubuntu-git:latest   ◄──┐  Reassign latest tag

docker images          ◄──┐  Examine image sizes
```

The image list and sizes reported will look something like the following:

```
REPOSITORY     TAG        IMAGE ID        CREATED          VIRTUAL SIZE
ubuntu-git     latest     826c66145a59    10 seconds ago   226.6 MB
ubuntu-git     removed    826c66145a59    10 seconds ago   226.6 MB
ubuntu-git     1.9        3e356394c14e    41 hours ago     226 MB
...
```

Notice that even though you removed Git, the image actually increased in size. Although you could examine the specific changes with docker diff, you should be quick to realize that the reason for the increase has to do with the union file system.

Remember, UFS will mark a file as deleted by actually adding a file to the top layer. The original file and any copies that existed in other layers will still be present in the image. It's important to minimize image size for the sake of the people and systems that will be consuming your images. If you can avoid causing long download times and significant disk usage with smart image creation, then your consumers will benefit. There's also another risk with this approach that you should be aware of.

The union file system on your computer may have a layer count limit. These limits vary, but a limit of 42 layers is common on computers that use the AUFS system. This number may seem high, but it's not unreachable. You can examine all the layers in an image using the `docker history` command. It will display the following:

- Abbreviated layer ID
- Age of the layer
- Initial command of the creating container
- Total file size of that layer

By examining the history of the ubuntu-git:removed image, you can see that three layers have already been added on the top of the original ubuntu:latest image:

```
docker history ubuntu-git:removed
```

Outputs are something like:

```
IMAGE         CREATED          CREATED BY                     SIZE
826c66145a59  24 minutes ago   /bin/bash -c apt-get remove    662 kB
3e356394c14e  42 hours ago     git                            0 B
bbf1d5d430cd  42 hours ago     /bin/bash                      37.68 MB
b39b81afc8ca  3 months ago     /bin/sh -c #(nop) CMD [/bin    0 B
615c102e2290  3 months ago     /bin/sh -c sed -i 's/^#\s*\    1.895 kB
837339b91538  3 months ago     /bin/sh -c echo '#!/bin/sh'    194.5 kB
53f858aaaf03  3 months ago     /bin/sh -c #(nop) ADD file:    188.1 MB
511136ea3c5a  22 months ago                                   0 B
```

You can flatten images if you export them and then reimport them with Docker. But that's a bad idea because you lose the change history as well as any savings customers might get when they download images with the same lower levels. Flattening images defeats the purpose. The smarter thing to do in this case is to create a branch.

Instead of fighting the layer system, you can solve both the size and layer growth problems by using the layer system to create branches. The layer system makes it trivial to go back in the history of an image and make a new branch. You are potentially creating a new branch every time you create a container from the same image.

In reconsidering your strategy for your new ubuntu-git image, you should simply start from ubuntu:latest again. With a fresh container from ubuntu:latest, you could install whatever version of Git you want. The result would be that both the original ubuntu-git image you created and the new one would share the same parent, and the new image wouldn't have any of the baggage of unrelated changes.

Branching increases the likelihood that you'll need to repeat steps that were accomplished in peer branches. Doing that work by hand is prone to error. Automating image builds with Dockerfiles is a better idea.

Occasionally the need arises to build a full image from scratch. This practice can be beneficial if your goal is to keep images small and if you're working with technologies that have few dependencies. Other times you may want to flatten an image to trim an image's history. In either case, you need a way to import and export full file systems.

7.3   *Exporting and importing flat file systems*

On some occasions it's advantageous to build images by working with the files destined for an image outside the context of the union file system or a container. To fill this need, Docker provides two commands for exporting and importing archives of files.

The `docker export` command will stream the full contents of the flattened union file system to stdout or an output file as a tarball. The result is a tarball that contains all the files from the container perspective. This can be useful if you need to use the file system that was shipped with an image outside the context of a container. You can use the `docker cp` command for this purpose, but if you need several files, exporting the full file system may be more direct.

Create a new container and use the export subcommand to get a flattened copy of its filesystem:

```
docker run --name export-test \
    dockerinaction/ch7_packed:latest ./echo For Export          Export file
                                                                 system contents
docker export --output contents.tar export-test

docker rm export-test

tar -tf contents.tar                Show archive contents
```

This will produce a file in the current directory named contents.tar. That file should contain two files. At this point you could extract, examine, or change those files to whatever end. If you had omitted the `--output` (or `-o` for short), then the contents of the file system would be streamed in tarball format to stdout. Streaming the contents to stdout makes the `export` command useful for chaining with other shell programs that work with tarballs.

The `docker import` command will stream the content of a tarball into a new image. The `import` command recognizes several compressed and uncompressed forms of tarballs. An optional Dockerfile instruction can also be applied during file-system import. Importing file systems is a simple way to get a complete minimum set of files into an image.

To see how useful this is, consider a statically linked Go version of Hello World. Create an empty folder and copy the following code into a new file named hello-world.go:

```
package main
import "fmt"
func main() {
        fmt.Println("hello, world!")
}
```

You may not have Go installed on your computer, but that's no problem for a Docker user. By running the next command, Docker will pull an image containing the Go compiler, compile and statically link the code (which means it can run all by itself), and place that program back into your folder:

```
docker run --rm -v "$(pwd)":/usr/src/hello \
    -w /usr/src/hello golang:1.3 go build -v
```

If everything works correctly, you should have an executable program (binary file) in the same folder, named hello. Statically linked programs have no external file dependencies at runtime. That means this statically linked version of Hello World can run in a container with no other files. The next step is to put that program in a tarball:

```
tar -cf static_hello.tar hello
```

Now that the program has been packaged in a tarball, you can import it using the docker import command:

```
docker import -c "ENTRYPOINT [\"/hello\"]" - \
    dockerinaction/ch7_static < static_hello.tar
```
Tar file streamed via UNIX pipe

In this command you use the -c flag to specify a Dockerfile command. The command you use sets the entrypoint for the new image. The exact syntax of the Dockerfile command is covered in chapter 8. The more interesting argument on this command is the hyphen (-) at the end of the first line. This hyphen indicates that the contents of the tarball will be streamed through stdin. You can specify a URL at this position if you're fetching the file from a remote web server instead of from your local file system.

You tagged the resulting image as the dockerinaction/ch7_static repository. Take a moment to explore the results:

```
docker run dockerinaction/ch7_static
docker history dockerinaction/ch7_static
```
Outputs: hello, world!

You'll notice that the history for this image has only a single entry (and layer):

```
IMAGE           CREATED          CREATED BY       SIZE
edafbd4a0ac5    11 minutes ago                    1.824 MB
```

In this case, the image we produced was small for two reasons. First, the program we produced was only just over 1.8 MB, and we included no operating system files or support programs. This is a minimalistic image. Second, there's only one layer. There are no deleted or unused files carried with the image in lower layers. The downside to using single-layer (or flat) images is that your system won't benefit from layer reuse. That might not be a problem if all your images are small enough. But the overhead may be significant if you use larger stacks or languages that don't offer static linking.

There are trade-offs to every image design decision, including whether or not to use flat images. Regardless of the mechanism you use to build images, your users need a consistent and predictable way to identify different versions.

7.4 *Versioning best practices*

Pragmatic versioning practices help users make the best use of images. The goal of an effective versioning scheme is to communicate clearly and provide adoption flexibility.

It's generally insufficient to build or maintain only a single version of your software unless it's your first. If you're releasing the first version of your software, you should be mindful of your users' adoption experience immediately. The reason why versions are

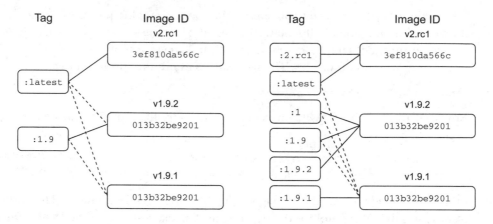

Figure 7.7   Two different tagging schemes (left and right) for the same repository with three images. Dotted lines represent old relationships between a tag and an image.

important is that they identify contracts that your adopters depend on. Unexpected software changes cause problems.

With Docker, the key to maintaining multiple versions of the same software is proper repository tagging. The understanding that every repository contains multiple tags and that multiple tags can reference the same image is at the core of a pragmatic tagging scheme.

The docker tag command is unlike the other two commands that can be used to create tags. It's the only one that's applied to existing images. To understand how to use tags and how they impact the user adoption experience, consider the two tagging schemes for a repository shown in figure 7.7.

There are two problems with the tagging scheme on the left side of figure 7.7. First, it provides poor adoption flexibility. A user can choose to declare a dependency on 1.9 or latest. When a user adopts version 1.9 and that implementation is actually 1.9.1, they may develop dependencies on behavior defined by that build version. Without a way to explicitly depend on that build version, they will experience pain when 1.9 is updated to point to 1.9.2.

The best way to eliminate this problem is to define and tag versions at a level where users can depend on consistent contracts. This is not advocating a three-tiered versioning system. It means only that the smallest unit of the versioning system you use captures the smallest unit of contract iteration. By providing multiple tags at this level, you can let users decide how much version drift they want to accept.

Consider the right side of figure 7.7. A user who adopts version 1 will always use the highest minor and build version under that major version. Adopting 1.9 will always use the highest build version for that minor version. Adopters who need to carefully migrate between versions of their dependencies can do so with control and at times of their choosing.

The second problem is related to the latest tag. On the left, latest currently points to an image that's not otherwise tagged, and so an adopter has no way of knowing what version of the software that is. In this case, it's referring to a release candidate for the next major version of the software. An unsuspecting user may adopt the latest tag with the impression that it's referring to the latest build of an otherwise tagged version.

There are other problems with the latest tag. It's adopted more frequently than it should be. This happens because it's the default tag, and Docker has a young community. The impact is that a responsible repository maintainer should always make sure that its repository's latest refers to the latest stable build of its software instead of the true latest.

The last thing to keep in mind is that in the context of containers, you're versioning not only your software but also a snapshot of all of your software's packaged dependencies. For example, if you package software with a particular distribution of Linux, like Debian, then those additional packages become part of your image's interface contract. Your users will build tooling around your images and in some cases may come to depend on the presence of a particular shell or script in your image. If you suddenly rebase your software on something like CentOS but leave your software otherwise unchanged, your users will experience pain.

In situations where the software dependencies change, or the software needs to be distributed on top of multiple bases, then those dependencies should be included with your tagging scheme.

The Docker official repositories are ideal examples to follow. Consider this tag list for the official golang repository, where each row represents a distinct image:

```
1.3.3,             1.3
1.3.3-onbuild,     1.3-onbuild
1.3.3-cross,       1.3-cross
1.3.3-wheezy,      1.3-wheezy
1.4.2,             1.4,          1,            latest
1.4.2-onbuild,     1.4-onbuild,  1-onbuild,    onbuild
1.4.2-cross,       1.4-cross,    1-cross,      cross
1.4.2-wheezy,      1.4-wheezy,   1-wheezy,     wheezy
```

The columns are neatly organized by their scope of version creep with build-level tags on the left and major versions to the right. Each build in this case has an additional base image component, which is annotated in the tag.

Users know that the latest version is actually version 1.4.2. If an adopter needs the latest image built on the debian:wheezy platform, they can use the wheezy tag. Those who need a 1.4 image with ONBUILD triggers can adopt 1.4-onbuild. This scheme puts the control and responsibility for upgrades in the hands of your adopters.

7.5   *Summary*

This is the first chapter to cover the creation of Docker images, tag management, and other distribution concerns such as image size. Learning this material will help you build images and become a better consumer of images. The following are the key points in the chapter:

- New images are created when changes to a container are committed using the `docker commit` command.
- When a container is committed, the configuration it was started with will be encoded into the configuration for the resulting image.
- An image is a stack of layers that's identified by its top layer.
- An image's size on disk is the sum of the sizes of its component layers.
- Images can be exported to and imported from a flat tarball representation using the `docker export` and `docker import` commands.
- The `docker tag` command can be used to assign several tags to a single repository.
- Repository maintainers should keep pragmatic tags to ease user adoption and migration control.
- Tag your latest stable build with the `latest` tag.
- Provide fine-grained and overlapping tags so that adopters have control of the scope of their dependency version creep.

Build automation and advanced image considerations

A Dockerfile is a file that contains instructions for building an image. The instructions are followed by the Docker image builder from top to bottom and can be used to change anything about an image. Building images from Dockerfiles makes tasks like adding files to a container from your computer simple one-line instructions. This section covers the basics of working with Dockerfile builds and the best reasons to use them, a lean overview of the instructions, and how to add future build behavior. We'll get started with a familiar example.

8.1   *Packaging Git with a Dockerfile*

Let's start by revisiting the Git on Ubuntu example. Having previously built a similar image by hand, you should recognize many of the details and advantages of working with a Dockerfile.

First, create a new directory and from that directory create a new file with your favorite text editor. Name the new file Dockerfile. Write the following five lines and then save the file:

```
# An example Dockerfile for installing Git on Ubuntu
FROM ubuntu:latest
MAINTAINER "dockerinaction@allingeek.com"
RUN apt-get install -y git
ENTRYPOINT ["git"]
```

Before dissecting this example, build a new image from it with the docker build command from the same directory containing the Dockerfile. Tag the new image with auto:

```
docker build --tag ubuntu-git:auto .
```

Outputs several lines about steps and output from apt-get and will finally display a message like this:

```
Successfully built 0bca8436849b
```

Running this command starts the build process. When it's completed, you should have a brand-new image that you can test. View the list of all your ubuntu-git images and test the newest one with this command:

```
docker images
```

The new build tagged "auto" should now appear in the list:

```
REPOSITORY    TAG       IMAGE ID       CREATED          VIRTUAL SIZE
ubuntu-git    auto      0bca8436849b   10 seconds ago   225.9 MB
ubuntu-git    latest    826c66145a59   10 minutes ago   226.6 MB
ubuntu-git    removed   826c66145a59   10 minutes ago   226.6 MB
ubuntu-git    1.9       3e356394c14e   41 hours ago     226 MB
...
```

Now you can run a Git command using the new image:

```
docker run --rm ubuntu-git:auto
```

These commands demonstrate that the image you built with the Dockerfile works and is functionally equivalent to the one you built by hand. Examine what you did to accomplish this.

First, you created a Dockerfile with four instructions:

- FROM ubuntu:latest—Tells Docker to start from the latest Ubuntu image just as you did when creating the image manually.

- `MAINTAINER`—Sets the maintainer name and email for the image. Providing this information helps people know whom to contact if there's a problem with the image. This was accomplished earlier when you invoked `commit`.
- `RUN apt-get install -y git`—Tells the builder to run the provided command to install Git.
- `ENTRYPOINT ["git"]`—Sets the entrypoint for the image to `git`.

Dockerfiles, like most scripts, can include comments. Any line beginning with a # will be ignored by the builder. It's important for Dockerfiles of any complexity to be well documented. In addition to improving Dockerfile maintainability, comments help people audit images that they're considering for adoption and spread best practices.

The only special rule about Dockerfiles is that the first instruction must be `FROM`. If you're starting from an empty image and your software has no dependencies, or you'll provide all the dependencies, then you can start from a special empty repository named `scratch`.

After you saved the Dockerfile, you started the build process by invoking the `docker build` command. The command had one flag set and one argument. The `--tag` flag (or `-t` for short) specifies the full repository designation that you want to use for the resulting image. In this case you used `ubuntu-git:auto`. The argument that you included at the end was a single period. That argument told the builder the location of the Dockerfile. The period told it to look for the file in the current directory.

The `docker build` command has another flag, `--file` (or `-f` for short), that lets you set the name of the Dockerfile. Dockerfile is the default, but with this flag you could tell the builder to look for a file named BuildScript. This flag sets only the name of the file, not the location of the file. That must always be specified in the location argument.

The builder works by automating the same tasks that you'd use to create images by hand. Each instruction triggers the creation of a new container with the specified modification. After the modification has been made, the builder commits the layer and moves on to the next instruction and container created from the fresh layer.

The builder validated that the image specified by the `FROM` instruction was installed as the first step of the build. If it were not, Docker would have automatically tried to pull the image. Take a look at the output from the `build` command that you ran:

```
Sending build context to Docker daemon 2.048 kB
Sending build context to Docker daemon
Step 0 : FROM ubuntu:latest
 ---> b39b81afc8ca
```

You can see that in this case the base image specified by the `FROM` instruction is `ubuntu:latest`, which should have already been installed on your machine. The abbreviated image ID of the base image is included in the output.

The next instruction sets the maintainer information on the image. This creates a new container and then commits the resulting layer. You can see the result of this operation in the output for step 1:

```
Step 1 : MAINTAINER "dockerinaction@allingeek.com"
 ---> Running in 938ff06bf8f4
 ---> 80a695671201
Removing intermediate container 938ff06bf8f4
```

The output includes the ID of the container that was created and the ID of the committed layer. That layer will be used as the top of the image for the next instruction, RUN. The output for the RUN instruction was clouded with all the output for the command apt-get install -y git. If you're not interested in this output, you can invoke the docker build command with the --quiet or -q flag. Running in quiet mode will suppress output from the intermediate containers. Without the container output, the RUN step produces output that looks like this:

```
Step 2 : RUN apt-get install -y git
 ---> Running in 4438c3b2c049
 ---> 1c20f8970532
Removing intermediate container 4438c3b2c049
```

Although this step usually takes much longer to complete, you can see the instruction and input as well as the ID of the container where the command was run and the ID of the resulting layer. Finally, the ENTRYPOINT instruction performs all the same steps, and the output is similarly unsurprising:

```
Step 3 : ENTRYPOINT git
 ---> Running in c9b24b0f035c
 ---> 89d726cf3514
Removing intermediate container c9b24b0f035c
```

A new layer is being added to the resulting image after each step in the build. Although this means you could potentially branch on any of these steps, the more important implication is that the builder can aggressively cache the results of each step. If a problem with the build script occurs after several other steps, the builder can restart from the same position after the problem has been fixed. You can see this in action by breaking your Dockerfile.

Add this line to the end of your Dockerfile:

```
RUN This will not work
```

Then run the build again:

```
docker build --tag ubuntu-git:auto .
```

The output will show which steps the builder was able to skip in favor of cached results:

```
Sending build context to Docker daemon 2.048 kB
Sending build context to Docker daemon
```

```
Step 0 : FROM ubuntu:latest
 ---> b39b81afc8ca
Step 1 : MAINTAINER "dockerinaction@allingeek.com"
 ---> Using cache
 ---> 80a695671201
Step 2 : RUN apt-get install -y git
 ---> Using cache
 ---> 1c20f8970532
Step 3 : ENTRYPOINT git
 ---> Using cache
 ---> 89d726cf3514
Step 4 : RUN This will not work
 ---> Running in f68f0e0418b5
/bin/sh: 1: This: not found
INFO[0001] The command [/bin/sh -c This will not work] returned a non-zero
  code: 127
```

Note use of cache

Steps 1 through 3 were skipped because they were already built during your last build. Step 4 failed because there's no program with the name `This` in the container. The container output was valuable in this case because the error message informs you about the specific problem with the Dockerfile. If you fix the problem, the same steps will be skipped again, and the build will succeed, resulting in output like `Successfully built d7a8ee0cebd4`.

The use of caching during the build can save time if the build includes downloading material, compiling programs, or anything else that is time-intense. If you need a full rebuild, you can use the `--no-cache` flag on `docker build` to disable the use of the cache. But make sure you're disabling the cache only when absolutely required.

This short example uses 4 of the 14 Dockerfile instructions. The example was limited in that all the files that were added to the image were downloaded from the network; it modified the environment in a very limited way and provided a very general tool. The next example with a more specific purpose and local code will provide a more complete Dockerfile primer.

8.2 *A Dockerfile primer*

Dockerfiles are expressive and easy to understand due to their terse syntax that allows for comments. You can keep track of changes to Dockerfiles with any version-control system. Maintaining multiple versions of an image is as simple as maintaining multiple Dockerfiles. The Dockerfile build process itself uses extensive caching to aid rapid development and iteration. The builds are traceable and reproducible. They integrate easily with existing build systems and many continuous build and integration tools. With all these reasons to prefer Dockerfile builds to hand-made images, it's important to learn how to write them.

The examples in this section cover each of the Dockerfile instructions except for one. The ONBUILD instruction has a specific use case and is covered in the next section. Every instruction is covered here at an introductory level. For deep coverage of each instruction, the best reference will always be the Docker documentation online at https://docs.docker.com/reference/builder/. Docker also provides a best practices section in its documentation: http://docs.docker.com/reference/builder.

8.2.1   *Metadata instructions*

The first example builds a base image and two other images with distinct versions of the mailer program you used in chapter 2. The purpose of the program is to listen for messages on a TCP port and then send those messages to their intended recipients. The first version of the mailer will listen for messages but only log those messages. The second will send the message as an HTTP POST to the defined URL.

One of the best reasons to use Dockerfile builds is that they simplify copying files from your computer into an image. But it's not always appropriate for certain files to be copied to images. The first thing to do when starting a new project is to define which files should never be copied into any images. You can do this in a file called .dockerignore. In this example you'll be creating three Dockerfiles, and none needs to be copied into the resulting images.

Use your favorite text editor to create a new file named .dockerignore and copy in the following lines:

```
.dockerignore
mailer-base.df
mailer-logging.df
mailer-live.df
```

Save and close the file when you've finished. This will prevent the .dockerignore file, or files named mailer-base.df, mailer-log.df, or mailer-live.df, from ever being copied into an image during a build. With that bit of accounting finished, you can begin working on the base image.

Building a base image helps create common layers. Each of the different versions of the mailer will be built on top of an image called mailer-base. When you create a Dockerfile, you need to keep in mind that each Dockerfile instruction will result in a new layer being created. Instructions should be combined whenever possible because the builder won't perform any optimization. Putting this in practice, create a new file named mailer-base.df and add the following lines:

```
FROM debian:wheezy
MAINTAINER Jeff Nickoloff "dia@allingeek.com"
RUN groupadd -r -g 2200 example && \
    useradd -rM -g example -u 2200 example
ENV APPROOT="/app" \
    APP="mailer.sh" \
    VERSION="0.6"
LABEL base.name="Mailer Archetype" \
      base.version="${VERSION}"
WORKDIR $APPROOT
ADD . $APPROOT                        This file does
ENTRYPOINT ["/app/mailer.sh"]    ◄─┘ not exist yet
EXPOSE 33333
# Do not set the default user in the base otherwise
```

```
# implementations will not be able to update the image
# USER example:example
```

Put it all together by running the `docker build` command from the directory where the mailer-base file is located. The `-f` flag tells the builder which filename to use as input:

```
docker build -t dockerinaction/mailer-base:0.6 -f mailer-base.df .
```

Five new instructions are introduced in this Dockerfile. The first new instruction is `ENV`. `ENV` sets environment variables for an image similar to the `--env` flag on `docker run` or `docker create`. In this case, a single `ENV` instruction is used to set three distinct environment variables. That could have been accomplished with three subsequent `ENV` instructions, but doing so would result in the creation of three layers. You can keep things looking well structured by using a backslash to escape the newline character (just like shell scripting):

```
Step 3 : ENV APPROOT "/app" APP "mailer.sh" VERSION "0.6"
 ---> Running in 05cb87a03b1b
 ---> 054f1747aa8d
Removing intermediate container 05cb87a03b1b
```

Environment variables declared in the Dockerfile are made available to the resulting image but can be used in other Dockerfile instructions as substitutions. In this Dockerfile the environment variable `VERSION` was used as a substitution in the next new instruction, `LABEL`:

```
Step 4 : LABEL base.name "Mailer Archetype" base.version "${VERSION}"
 ---> Running in 0473087065c4
 ---> ab76b163e1d7
Removing intermediate container 0473087065c4
```

The `LABEL` instruction is used to define key/value pairs that are recorded as additional metadata for an image or container. This mirrors the `--label` flag on `docker run` and `docker create`. Like the `ENV` instruction before it, multiple labels can and should be set with a single instruction. In this case, the value of the `VERSION` environment variable was substituted for the value of the `base.version` label. By using an environment variable in this way, the value of `VERSION` will be available to processes running inside a container as well as recorded to an appropriate label. This increases maintainability of the Dockerfile because it's more difficult to make inconsistent changes when the value is set in a single location.

The next two instructions are `WORKDIR` and `EXPOSE`. These are similar in operation to their corresponding flags on the `docker run` and `docker create` commands. An environment variable was substituted for the argument to the `WORKDIR` command:

```
Step 5 : WORKDIR $APPROOT
 ---> Running in 073583e0d554
 ---> 363129ccda97
Removing intermediate container 073583e0d554
```

The result of the WORKDIR instruction will be an image with the default working directory set to /app. Setting WORKDIR to a location that doesn't exist will create that location just like the command-line option. Last, the EXPOSE command creates a layer that opens TCP port 33333:

```
Step 7 : EXPOSE 33333
 ---> Running in a6c4f54b2907
 ---> 86e0b43f234a
Removing intermediate container a6c4f54b2907
```

The parts of this Dockerfile that you should recognize are the FROM, MAINTAINER, and ENTRYPOINT instructions. In brief, the FROM instruction sets the layer stack to start from the debian:wheezy image. Any new layers built will be placed on top of that image. The MAINTAINER instruction sets the Author value in the image metadata. The ENTRYPOINT instruction sets the executable to be run at container startup. Here, it's setting the instruction to exec ./mailer.sh and using the shell form of the instruction.

The ENTRYPOINT instruction has two forms: the shell form and an exec form. The shell form looks like a shell command with whitespace-delimited arguments. The exec form is a string array where the first value is the command to execute and the remaining values are arguments. A command specified using the shell form would be executed as an argument to the default shell. Specifically, the command used in this Dockerfile will be executed as /bin/sh -c 'exec ./mailer.sh' at runtime. Most importantly, if the shell form is used for ENTRYPOINT, then all other arguments provided by the CMD instruction or at runtime as extra arguments to docker run will be ignored. This makes the shell form of ENTRYPOINT less flexible.

You can see from the build output that the ENV and LABEL instructions each resulted in a single step and layer. But the output doesn't show that the environment variable values were substituted correctly. To verify that, you'll need to inspect the image:

```
docker inspect dockerinaction/mailer-base:0.6
```

> **TIP** Remember, the docker inspect command can be used to view the metadata of either a container or an image. In this case, you used it to inspect an image.

The relevant lines are these:

```
"Env": [
    "PATH=/usr/local/sbin:/usr/local/bin:/usr/sbin:/usr/bin:/sbin:/bin",
    "APPROOT=/app",
    "APP=mailer.sh",
    "VERSION=0.6"
],
...
"Labels": {
    "base.name": "Mailer Archetype",
    "base.version": "0.6"
},
...
"WorkingDir": "/app"
```

The metadata makes it clear that the environment variable substitution works. You can use this form of substitution in the ENV, ADD, COPY, WORKDIR, VOLUME, EXPOSE, and USER instructions.

The last commented line is a metadata instruction USER. It sets the user and group for all further build steps and containers created from the image. In this case, setting it in a base image would prevent any downstream Dockerfiles from installing software. That would mean that those Dockerfiles would need to flip the default back and forth for permission. Doing so would create at least two additional layers. The better approach would be to set up the user and group accounts in the base image and let the implementations set the default user when they've finished building.

The most curious thing about this Dockerfile is that the ENTRYPOINT is set to a file that doesn't exist. The entrypoint will fail when you try to run a container from this base image. But now that the entrypoint is set in the base image, that's one less layer that will need to be duplicated for specific implementations of the mailer. The next two Dockerfiles build mailer.sh different implementations.

8.2.2 *File system instructions*

Images that include custom functionality will need to modify the file system. A Dockerfile defines three instructions that modify the file system: COPY, VOLUME, and ADD. The Dockerfile for the first implementation should be placed in a file named mailer-logging.df:

```
FROM dockerinaction/mailer-base:0.6
COPY ["./log-impl", "${APPROOT}"]
RUN chmod a+x ${APPROOT}/${APP} && \
    chown example:example /var/log
USER example:example
VOLUME ["/var/log"]
CMD ["/var/log/mailer.log"]
```

In this Dockerfile you used the image generated from mailer-base as the starting point. The three new instructions are COPY, VOLUME, and CMD. The COPY instruction will copy files from the file system where the image is being built into the build container. The COPY instruction takes at least two arguments. The last argument is the destination, and all other arguments are source files. This instruction has only one unexpected feature: any files copied will be copied with file ownership set to root. This is the case regardless of how the default user is set before the COPY instruction. It's better to delay any RUN instructions to change file ownership until all the files that you need to update have been copied into the image.

The COPY instruction will honor both shell style and exec style arguments, just like ENTRYPOINT and other instructions. But if any of the arguments contains whitespace, then you'll need to use the exec form.

> **TIP** Using the exec (or string array) form wherever possible is the best practice. At a minimum, a Dockerfile should be consistent and avoid mixing styles.

This will make your Dockerfiles more readable and ensure that instructions behave as you'd expect without detailed understanding of their nuances.

The second new instruction is VOLUME. This behaves exactly as you'd expect if you understand what the `--volume` flag does on a call to `docker run` or `docker create`. Each value in the string array argument will be created as a new volume definition in the resulting layer. Defining volumes at image build time is more limiting than at run-time. You have no way to specify a bind-mount volume or read-only volume at image build time. This instruction will only create the defined location in the file system and then add a volume definition to the image metadata.

The last instruction in this Dockerfile is CMD. CMD is closely related to the ENTRYPOINT instruction. They both take either shell or exec forms and are both used to start a process within a container. But there are a few important differences.

The CMD command represents an argument list for the entrypoint. The default entrypoint for a container is /bin/sh. If no entrypoint is set for a container, then the values are passed, because the command will be wrapped by the default entrypoint. But if the entrypoint is set and is declared using the exec form, then you use CMD to set default arguments. This base for this Dockerfile defines the ENTRYPOINT as the mailer command. This Dockerfile injects an implementation of mailer.sh and defines a default argument. The argument used is the location that should be used for the log file.

Before building the image, you'll need to create the logging version of the mailer program. Create a directory at ./log-impl. Inside that directory create a file named mailer.sh and copy the following script into the file:

```
#!/bin/sh
printf "Logging Mailer has started.\n"
while true
do
    MESSAGE=$(nc -l -p 33333)
    printf "[Message]: %s\n" "$MESSAGE" > $1
    sleep 1
done
```

The structural specifics of this script are unimportant. All you need to know is that this script will start a mailer daemon on port 33333 and write each message that it receives to the file specified in the first argument to the program. Use the following command to build the `mailer-logging` image from the directory containing mailer-logging.df:

```
docker build -t dockerinaction/mailer-logging -f mailer-logging.df .
```

The results of this image build should be anti-climactic. Go ahead and start up a named container from this new image:

```
docker run -d --name logging-mailer dockerinaction/mailer-logging
```

The logging mailer should now be built and running. Containers that link to this implementation will have their messages logged to /var/log/mailer.log. That's not very interesting or useful in a real-world situation, but it might be handy for testing. An implementation that sends email would be better for operational monitoring.

The next implementation example uses the Simple Email Service provided by Amazon Web Services to send email. Get started with another Dockerfile. Name this file mailer-live.df:

```
FROM dockerinaction/mailer-base:0.6
ADD ["./live-impl", "${APPROOT}"]
RUN apt-get update && \
    apt-get install -y curl python && \
    curl "https://bootstrap.pypa.io/get-pip.py" -o "get-pip.py" && \
    python get-pip.py && \
    pip install awscli && \
    rm get-pip.py && \
    chmod a+x "${APPROOT}/${APP}"
RUN apt-get install -y netcat
USER example:example
CMD ["mailer@dockerinaction.com", "pager@dockerinaction.com"]
```

This Dockerfile includes one new instruction, ADD. The ADD instruction operates similarly to the COPY instruction with two important differences. The ADD instruction will

- Fetch remote source files if a URL is specified
- Extract the files of any source determined to be an archive file

The auto-extraction of archive files is the more useful of the two. Using the remote fetch feature of the ADD instruction isn't good practice. The reason is that although the feature is convenient, it provides no mechanism for cleaning up unused files and results in additional layers. Instead, you should use a chained RUN instruction like the third instruction of mailer-live.df.

The other instruction to note in this Dockerfile is the CMD instruction, where two arguments are passed. Here you're specifying the From and To fields on any emails that are sent. This differs from mailer-logging.df, which specifies only one argument.

Next, create a new subdirectory named live-impl under the location containing mailer-live.df. Add the following script to a file in that directory named mailer.sh:

```
#!/bin/sh
printf "Live Mailer has started.\n"
while true
do
  MESSAGE=$(nc -l -p 33333)
  aws ses send-email --from $1 \
    --destination {\"ToAddresses\":[\"$2\"]} \
    --message "{\"Subject\":{\"Data\":\"Mailer Alert\"},\
                \"Body\":{\"Text\":{\"Data\":\"$MESSAGE}\"}}}"
  sleep 1
done
```

The key takeaway from this script is that, like the other mailer implementation, it will wait for connections on port 33333, take action on any received messages, and then sleep for a moment before waiting for another message. This time, though, the script will send an email using the Simple Email Service command-line tool. Build and start a container with these two commands:

```
docker build -t dockerinaction/mailer-live -f mailer-live.df .
docker run -d --name live-mailer dockerinaction/mailer-live
```

If you link a watcher to these, you'll find that the logging mailer works as advertised. But the live mailer seems to be having difficulty connecting to the Simple Email Service to send the message. With a bit of investigation, you'll eventually realize that the container is misconfigured. The aws program requires certain environment variables to be set.

You'll need to set AWS_ACCESS_KEY_ID, AWS_SECRET_ACCESS_KEY, and AWS_DEFAULT_REGION in order to get this example working. Discovering execution preconditions this way can be frustrating for users. Section 8.4.1 details an image design pattern that reduces this friction and helps adopters.

Before you get to design patterns, you need to learn about the final Dockerfile instruction. Remember, not all images contain applications. Some are built as platforms for downstream images. Those cases specifically benefit from the ability to inject downstream build-time behavior.

8.3   *Injecting downstream build-time behavior*

Only one Dockerfile instruction isn't covered in the primer. That instruction is ONBUILD. The ONBUILD instruction defines instructions to execute if the resulting image is used as a base for another build. For example, you could use ONBUILD instructions to compile a program that's provided by a downstream layer. The upstream Dockerfile copies the contents of the build directory into a known location and then compiles the code at that location. The upstream Dockerfile would use a set of instructions like this:

```
ONBUILD COPY [".", "/var/myapp"]
ONBUILD RUN go build /var/myapp
```

The instructions following ONBUILD instructions aren't executed when their containing Dockerfile is built. Instead, those instructions are recorded in the resulting image's metadata under ContainerConfig.OnBuild. The previous instructions would result in the following metadata inclusions:

```
...
"ContainerConfig": {
...
    "OnBuild": [
        "COPY [\".\", \"/var/myapp\"]",
        "RUN go build /var/myapp"
    ],
    ...
```

This metadata is carried forward until the resulting image is used as the base for another Dockerfile build. When a downstream Dockerfile uses the upstream image (the one with the ONBUILD instructions) in a FROM instruction, those ONBUILD instructions are executed after the FROM instruction and before the next instruction in a Dockerfile.

Consider the following example to see exactly when ONBUILD steps are injected into a build. You need to create two Dockerfiles and execute two build commands to get the full experience. First, create an upstream Dockerfile that defines the ONBUILD instructions. Name the file base.df and add the following instructions:

```
FROM busybox:latest
WORKDIR /app
RUN touch /app/base-evidence
ONBUILD RUN ls -al /app
```

You can see that the image resulting from building base.df will add an empty file named base-evidence to the /app directory. The ONBUILD instruction will list the contents of the /app directory at build time, so it's important that you not run the build in quiet mode if you want to see exactly when changes are made to the file system.

The next file to create is the downstream Dockerfile. When this is built, you will be able to see exactly when the changes are made to the resulting image. Name the file downstream.df and include the following contents:

```
FROM dockerinaction/ch8_onbuild
RUN touch downstream-evidence
RUN ls -al .
```

This Dockerfile will use an image named dockerinaction/ch8_onbuild as a base, so that's the repository name you'll want to use when you build the base. Then you can see that the downstream build will create a second file and then list the contents of /app again.

With these two files in place, you're ready to start building. Run the following to create the upstream image:

```
docker build -t dockerinaction/ch8_onbuild -f base.df .
```

The output of the build should look like this:

```
Sending build context to Docker daemon 3.072 kB
Sending build context to Docker daemon
Step 0 : FROM busybox:latest
---> e72ac664f4f0
Step 1 : WORKDIR /app
---> Running in 4e9a3df4cf17
---> a552ff53eedc
Removing intermediate container 4e9a3df4cf17
Step 2 : RUN touch /app/base-evidence
---> Running in 352819bec296
---> bf38c3e396b2
Removing intermediate container 352819bec296
Step 3 : ONBUILD run ls -al /app
---> Running in fd70cef7e6ca
---> 6a53dbe28364
```

```
Removing intermediate container fd70cef7e6ca
Successfully built 6a53dbe28364
```

Then build the downstream image with this command:

```
docker build -t dockerinaction/ch8_onbuild_down -f downstream.df .
```

The results clearly show when the ONBUILD instruction (from the base image) is executed:

```
Sending build context to Docker daemon 3.072 kB
Sending build context to Docker daemon
Step 0 : FROM dockerinaction/ch8_onbuild
# Executing 1 build triggers
Trigger 0, RUN ls -al /app
Step 0 : RUN ls -al /app
---> Running in dd33ddea1fd4
    total 8
    drwxr-xr-x    2 root      root    4096 Apr 20 23:08 .
    drwxr-xr-x   30 root      root    4096 Apr 20 23:08 ..
    -rw-r--r--    1 root      root       0 Apr 20 23:08 base-evidence
---> 92782cc4e1f6
Removing intermediate container dd33ddea1fd4
Step 1 : RUN touch downstream-evidence
---> Running in 076b7e110b6a
---> 92cc1250b23c
Removing intermediate container 076b7e110b6a
Step 2 : RUN ls -al .
---> Running in b3fe2daac529
    total 8
    drwxr-xr-x    2 root      root    4096 Apr 20 23:08 .
    drwxr-xr-x   31 root      root    4096 Apr 20 23:08 ..
    -rw-r--r--    1 root      root       0 Apr 20 23:08 base-evidence
    -rw-r--r--    1 root      root       0 Apr 20 23:08 downstream-evidence
---> 55202310df7b
Removing intermediate container b3fe2daac529
Successfully built 55202310df7b
```

You can see the builder registering the ONBUILD instruction with the container meta-data in step 3 of the base build. Later, the output of the downstream image build shows which triggers (ONBUILD instructions) it has inherited from the base image. The builder discovers and processes the trigger immediately after step 0, the FROM instruction. The output then includes the result of the RUN instruction specified by the trigger. The output shows that only evidence of the base build is present. Later, when the builder moves on to instructions from the downstream Dockerfile, it lists the contents of the /app directory again. The evidence of both changes is listed.

That example is more illustrative than it is useful. You should consider browsing Docker Hub and looking for images tagged with onbuild suffixes to get an idea about how this is used in the wild. Here are a few of my favorites:

- https://registry.hub.docker.com/_/python/
- https://registry.hub.docker.com/_/golang/
- https://registry.hub.docker.com/_/node/

8.4 *Using startup scripts and multiprocess containers*

Whatever tooling you choose to use, you'll always need to consider a few image design aspects. You'll need to ask yourself whether the software running in your container requires any startup assistance, supervision, monitoring, or coordination with other in-container processes. If so, then you'll need to include a startup script or initialization program with the image and install it as the entrypoint.

8.4.1 *Environmental preconditions validation*

Failure modes are difficult to communicate and can catch someone off guard if they occur at arbitrary times. If container configuration problems always cause failures at startup time for an image, users can be confident that a started container will keep running.

In software design, failing fast and precondition validation are best practices. It makes sense that the same should hold true for image design. The preconditions that should be evaluated are assumptions about the context.

Docker containers have no control over the environment where they're created. They do, however, have control of their own execution. An image author can solidify the user experience of their image by introducing environment and dependency validation prior to execution of the main task. A container user will be better informed about the requirements of an image if containers built from that image fail fast and display descriptive error messages.

For example, WordPress requires certain environment variables to be set or container links to be defined. Without that context, WordPress would be unable to connect to the database where the blog data is stored. It would make no sense to start WordPress in a container without access to the data it's supposed to serve. WordPress images use a script as the container entrypoint. That script validates that the container context is set in a way that's compatible with the contained version of WordPress. If any required condition is unmet (a link is undefined or a variable is unset), then the script will exit before starting WordPress, and the container will stop unexpectedly.

This type of startup script is generally use-case specific. If you're packaging a specific piece of software in an image, you'll need to write the script yourself. Your script should validate as much of the assumed context as possible. This should include the following:

- Presumed links (and aliases)
- Environment variables
- Network access
- Network port availability
- Root file system mount parameters (read-write or read-only)
- Volumes
- Current user

You can use whatever scripting or programming language you want to accomplish the task. In the spirit of building minimal images, it's a good idea to use a language or scripting tool that's already included with the image. Most base images ship with a shell like /bin/sh or /bin/bash. Shell scripts are the most common for that reason.

Consider the following shell script that might accompany a program that depends on a web server. At container startup, this script enforces that either another container has been linked to the web alias and has exposed port 80 or the WEB_HOST environment variable has been defined:

```
#!/bin/bash
set -e

if [ -n "$WEB_PORT_80_TCP" ]; then
  if [ -z "$WEB_HOST" ]; then
    WEB_HOST='web'
  else
    echo >&2 '[WARN]: Linked container, "web" overridden by $WEB_HOST.'
    echo >&2 "===> Connecting to WEB_HOST ($WEB_HOST)"
  fi
fi

if [ -z "$WEB_HOST" ]; then
  echo >&2 '[ERROR]: specify a linked container, "web" or WEB_HOST environ-
  ment variable'
  exit 1
fi
exec "$@" # run the default command
```

If you're unfamiliar with shell scripting, this is an appropriate time to learn it. The topic is approachable, and there are several excellent resources for self-directed learning. This specific script uses a pattern where both an environment variable and a container link are tested. If the environment variable is set, the container link will be ignored. Finally, the default command is executed.

Images that use a startup script to validate configuration should fail fast if someone uses them incorrectly, but those same containers may fail later for other reasons. You can combine startup scripts with container restart policies to make reliable containers. But container restart policies are not perfect solutions. Containers that have failed and are waiting to be restarted aren't running. This means that an operator won't be able to execute another process within a container that's in the middle of a backoff window. The solution to this problem involves making sure the container never stops.

8.4.2 *Initialization processes*

UNIX-based computers usually start an initialization (init) process first. That init process is responsible for starting all the other system services, keeping them running, and shutting them down. It's often appropriate to use an init-style system to launch, manage, restart, and shut down container processes with a similar tool.

Init processes typically use a file or set of files to describe the ideal state of the initialized system. These files describe what programs to start, when to start them, and what actions to take when they stop. Using an init process is the best way to launch multiple programs, clean up orphaned processes, monitor processes, and automatically restart any failed processes.

If you decide to adopt this pattern, you should use the init process as the entry-point of your application-oriented Docker container. Depending on the init program you use, you may need to prepare the environment beforehand with a startup script.

For example, the runit program doesn't pass environment variables to the programs it launches. If your service uses a startup script to validate the environment, it won't have access to the environment variables it needs. The best way to fix that problem might be to use a startup script for the runit program. That script might write the environment variables to some file so the startup script for your application can access them.

There are several open source init programs. Full-featured Linux distributions ship with heavyweight and full-featured init systems like SysV, Upstart, and systemd. Linux Docker images like Ubuntu, Debian, and CentOS typically have their init programs installed but nonfunctioning out of the box. These can be complex to configure and typically have hard dependencies on resources that require root access. For that reason, the community has tended toward the use of lighter-weight init programs.

Popular options include runit, BusyBox init, Supervisord, and DAEMON Tools. These all attempt to solve similar problems, but each has its benefits and costs. Using an init process is a best practice for application containers, but there's no perfect init program for every use case. When evaluating any init program for use in a container, consider these factors:

- Additional dependencies the program will bring into the image
- File sizes
- How the program passes signals to its child processes (or if it does)
- Required user access
- Monitoring and restart functionality (backoff-on-restart features are a bonus)
- Zombie process cleanup features

Whichever init program you decide on, make sure your image uses it to boost adopter confidence in containers created from your image. If the container needs to fail fast to communicate a configuration problem, make sure the init program won't hide that failure.

These are the tools at your disposal to build images that result in durable containers. Durability is not security, and although adopters of your durable images might trust that they will keep running as long as they can, they shouldn't trust your images until they've been hardened.

8.5 *Building hardened application images*

As an image author, it's difficult to anticipate all the scenarios where your work will be used. For that reason, harden the images you produce whenever possible. *Hardening an image* is the process of shaping it in a way that will reduce the attack surface inside any Docker containers based on it.

A general strategy for hardening an application image is to minimize the software included with it. Naturally, including fewer components reduces the number of potential vulnerabilities. Further, building minimal images keeps image download times short and helps adopters deploy and build containers more rapidly.

There are three things that you can do to harden an image beyond that general strategy. First, you can enforce that your images are built from a specific image. Second, you can make sure that regardless of how containers are built from your image, they will have a sensible default user. Last, you should eliminate a common path for root user escalation.

8.5.1   *Content addressable image identifiers*

The image identifiers discussed so far in this book are all designed to allow an author to update images in a transparent way to adopters. An image author chooses what image their work will be built on top of, but that layer of transparency makes it difficult to trust that the base hasn't changed since it was vetted for security problems. Since Docker 1.6, the image identifier has included an optional digest component.

An image ID that includes the digest component is called a content addressable image identifier (CAIID). This refers to a specific layer containing specific content, instead of simply referring to a particular and potentially changing layer.

Now image authors can enforce a build from a specific and unchanging starting point as long as that image is in a version 2 repository. Append an @ symbol followed by the digest in place of the standard tag position.

Use docker pull and observe the line labeled digest in the output to discover the digest of an image from a remote repository. Once you have the digest, you can use it as the identifier to FROM instructions in a Dockerfile. For example, consider the following, which uses a specific snapshot of debian:jessie as a base:

```
docker pull debian:jessie
# Output:
# ...
# Digest: sha256:d5e87cfcb730...

# Dockerfile:
FROM debian@sha256:d5e87cfcb730...
...
```

Regardless of when or how many times the Dockerfile is used to build an image, they will all use the content identified with that CAIID as their base. This is particularly useful for incorporating known updates to a base into your images and identifying the exact build of the software running on your computer.

Although this doesn't directly limit the attack surface of your images, using CAIIDs will prevent it from changing without your knowledge. The next two practices do address the attack surface of an image.

8.5.2 *User permissions*

The known container breakout tactics all rely on having system administrator privileges inside the container. Chapter 6 covers the tools used to harden containers. That chapter includes a deep dive into user management and a brief discussion of the USR Linux namespace. This section covers standard practices for establishing reasonable user defaults for images.

First, please understand that a Docker user can always override image defaults when they create a container. For that reason, there's no way for an image to prevent containers from running as the root user. The best things an image author can do are create other non-root users and establish a non-root default user and group.

Dockerfile includes a USER instruction that sets the user and group in the same way you would with the docker run or docker create command. The instruction itself was covered in the Dockerfile primer. This section is about considerations and best practices.

The best practice and general guidance is to drop privileges as soon as possible. You can do this with the USER instruction before any containers are ever created or with a startup script that's run at container boot time. The challenge for an image author is to determine the earliest appropriate time.

If you drop privileges too early, the active user may not have permission to complete the instructions in a Dockerfile. For example, this Dockerfile won't build correctly:

```
FROM busybox:latest
USER 1000:1000
RUN touch /bin/busybox
```

Building that Dockerfile would result in step 2 failing with a message like touch: /bin/busybox: Permission denied. File access is obviously impacted by user changes. In this case UID 1000 doesn't have permission to change the ownership of the file /bin/busybox. That file is currently owned by root. Reversing the second and third lines would fix the build.

The second timing consideration is the permissions and capabilities needed at runtime. If the image starts a process that requires administrative access at runtime, then it would make no sense to drop user access to a non-root user before that point. For example, any process that needs access to the system port range (1–1024) will need to be started by a user with administrative (at the very least CAP_NET_ADMIN) privileges. Consider what happens when you try to bind to port 80 as a non-root user with Netcat. Place the following Dockerfile in a file named UserPermissionDenied.df:

```
FROM busybox:latest
USER 1000:1000
ENTRYPOINT ["nc"]
CMD ["-l", "-p", "80", "0.0.0.0"]
```

Build the Dockerfile and run the resulting image in a container. In this case the user (UID 1000) will lack the required privileges, and the command will fail:

```
docker build \
    -t dockerinaction/ch8_perm_denied \
    -f UserPermissionDenied.df \
    .
docker run dockerinaction/ch8_perm_denied
# Output:
# nc: bind: Permission denied
```

In cases like these, you may see no benefit in changing the default user. Instead, any startup scripts that you build should take on the responsibility of dropping permissions as soon as possible. The last question is which user should be dropped into?

Docker currently lacks support for the Linux USR namespace. This means that UID 1000 in the container is UID 1000 on the host machine. All other aspects apart from the UID and GID are segregated, just as they would be between computers. For example, UID 1000 on your laptop might be your username, but the username associated with UID 1000 inside a BusyBox container is default.

Ultimately, until Docker adopts the USR namespace, it will be difficult for image authors to know which UID/GID is appropriate to use. The only thing we can be sure of is that it's inappropriate to use common or system-level UID/GIDs where doing so can be avoided. With that in mind, it's still burdensome to use raw UID/GID numbers. Doing so makes scripts and Dockerfiles less readable. For that reason, it's typical for image authors to include RUN instructions that create users and groups used by the image. The following is the second instruction in a Postgres Dockerfile:

```
# add our user and group first to make sure their IDs get assigned
# consistently, regardless of whatever dependencies get added
RUN groupadd -r postgres && useradd -r -g postgres postgres
```

This instruction simply creates a postgres user and group with automatically assigned UID and GID. The instruction is placed early in the Dockerfile so that it will always be cached between rebuilds, and the IDs remain consistent regardless of other users that are added as part of the build. This user and group could then be used in a USER instruction. That would make for a safer default. But Postgres containers require elevated privileges during startup. Instead, this particular image uses a su or sudo-like program called gosu to start the Postgres process as the postgres user. Doing so makes sure that the process runs without administrative access in the container.

User permissions are one of the more nuanced aspects of building Docker images. The general rule you should follow is that if the image you're building is designed to run some specific application code, then the default execution should drop user permissions as soon as possible.

A properly functioning system should be reasonably secure with reasonable defaults in place. Remember, though, an application or arbitrary code is rarely perfect and could be intentionally malicious. For that reason, you should take additional steps to reduce the attack surface of your images.

8.5.3   *SUID and SGID permissions*

The last hardening action to cover is the mitigation of SUID or SGID permissions. The well-known file system permissions (read, write, execute) are only a portion of the set defined by Linux. In addition to those, two are of particular interest: SUID and SGID.

These two are similar in nature. An executable file with the SUID bit set will always execute as its owner. Consider a program like /usr/bin/passwd, which is owned by the root user and has the SUID permission set. If a non-root user like bob executes passwd, he will execute that program as the root user. You can see this in action by building an image from the following Dockerfile:

```
FROM ubuntu:latest
# Set the SUID bit on whoami
RUN chmod u+s /usr/bin/whoami
# Create an example user and set it as the default
RUN adduser --system --no-create-home --disabled-password --disabled-login \
    --shell /bin/sh example
USER example
# Set the default to compare the container user and
# the effective user for whoami
CMD  printf "Container running as:           %s\n" $(id -u -n) && \
     printf "Effectively running whoami as: %s\n" $(whoami)
```

Once you've created the Dockerfile, you need to build an image and run the default command in a container:

```
docker build -t dockerinaction/ch8_whoami .
docker run dockerinaction/ch8_whoami
```

Doing so prints results like these to the terminal:

```
Container running as:          example
Effectively running whoami as: root
```

The output of the default command shows that even though you've executed the whoami command as the example user, it's running from the context of the root user. The SGID works similarly. The difference is that the execution will be from the owning group's context, not the owning user.

Running a quick search on your base image will give you an idea of how many and which files have these permissions:

```
docker run --rm debian:wheezy find / -perm +6000 -type f
```

It will display a list like this:

```
/sbin/unix_chkpwd
/bin/ping6
/bin/su
/bin/ping
/bin/umount
/bin/mount
/usr/bin/chage
```

```
/usr/bin/passwd
/usr/bin/gpasswd
/usr/bin/chfn
/usr/bin/newgrp
/usr/bin/wall
/usr/bin/expiry
/usr/bin/chsh
/usr/lib/pt_chown
```

This command will find all of the SGID files:

```
docker run --rm debian:wheezy find / -perm +2000 -type f
```

The resulting list is much shorter:

```
/sbin/unix_chkpwd
/usr/bin/chage
/usr/bin/wall
/usr/bin/expiry
```

Each of the listed files in this particular image has the SUID or SGID permission, and a bug in any of them could be used to compromise the root account inside a container. The good news is that files that have either of these permissions set are typically useful during image builds but rarely required for application use cases. If your image is going to be running software that's arbitrary or externally sourced, it's a best practice to mitigate this risk of escalation.

Fix this problem and either delete all these files or unset their SUID and SGID permissions. Taking either action would reduce the image's attack surface. The following Dockerfile instruction will unset the SUID and GUID permissions on all files currently in the image:

```
RUN for i in $(find / -type f \( -perm +6000 -o -perm +2000 \)); \
    do chmod ug-s $i; done
```

Hardening images will help users build hardened containers. Although it's true that no hardening measures will protect users from intentionally building weak containers, those measures will help the more unsuspecting and most common type of user.

8.6   *Summary*

Most Docker images are built automatically from Dockerfiles. This chapter covers the build automation provided by Docker and Dockerfile best practices. Before moving on, make sure that you've understood these key points:

- Docker provides an automated image builder that reads instructions from Dockerfiles.
- Each Dockerfile instruction results in the creation of a single image layer.
- Merge instructions whenever possible to minimize the size of images and layer count.

- Dockerfiles include instructions to set image metadata like the default user, exposed ports, default command, and entrypoint.
- Other Dockerfile instructions copy files from the local file system or remote location into the produced images.
- Downstream builds inherit build triggers that are set with ONBUILD instructions in an upstream Dockerfile.
- Startup scripts should be used to validate the execution context of a container before launching the primary application.
- A valid execution context should have appropriate environment variables set, network dependencies available, and an appropriate user configuration.
- Init programs can be used to launch multiple processes, monitor those processes, reap orphaned child processes, and forward signals to child processes.
- Images should be hardened by building from content addressable image identifiers, creating a non-root default user, and disabling or removing any executable with SUID or SGID permissions.

Public and private
software distribution

> **This chapter covers**
> - Choosing a project distribution method
> - Using hosted infrastructure
> - Running and using your own registry
> - Understanding manual image distribution workflows
> - Distributing image sources

You have your own images from software you've written, customized, or just pulled from the internet. But what good is an image if nobody can install it? Docker is different from other container management tools because it provides image distribution features.

There are several ways to get your images out to the world. This chapter explores those distribution paradigms and provides a framework for making or choosing one or more for your own projects.

Hosted registries offer both public and private repositories with automated build tools. Running a private registry lets you hide and customize your image distribution infrastructure. Heavier customization of a distribution workflow might require you to abandon the Docker image distribution facilities and build your own. Some systems might abandon the image as the distribution unit altogether and distribute image sources.

This chapter will teach you how to select and use a method for distributing your images to the world or just at work.

9.1 Choosing a distribution method

The most difficult thing about choosing a distribution method is choosing the appropriate method for your situation. To help with this problem, each method presented in this chapter is examined on the same set of selection criteria.

The first thing to recognize about distributing software with Docker is that there's no universal solution. Distribution requirements vary for many reasons, and several methods are available. Every method has Docker tools at its core, so it's always possible to migrate from one to another with minimal effort. The best way to start is by examining the full spectrum of options at a high level.

9.1.1 A distribution spectrum

The image distribution spectrum is a balance between flexibility and complexity. The methods that provide the most flexibility can be the most complicated to use, whereas those that are the simplest to use are generally the most restrictive. Figure 9.1 shows the full spectrum.

The methods included in the spectrum range from hosted registries like Docker Hub to totally custom distribution architectures or source-distribution methods. Some of these subjects will be covered in more detail than others. Particular focus is placed on private registries because they provide the most balance between the two concerns.

Having a spectrum of choices illustrates your range of options, but you need a consistent set of selection criteria in order to determine which you should use.

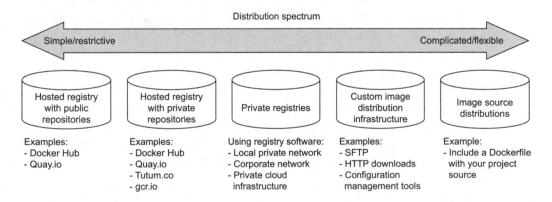

Figure 9.1 The image distribution spectrum

9.1.2 Selection criteria

Choosing the best distribution method for your needs may seem daunting with this many options. In situations like these you should take the time to understand the options, identify criteria for making a selection, and avoid the urge to make a quick decision or settle.

The following identified selection criteria are based on differences across the spectrum and on common business concerns. When making a decision, consider how important each of these is in your situation:

- Cost
- Visibility
- Transport speed or bandwidth overhead
- Longevity control
- Availability control
- Access control
- Artifact integrity
- Artifact confidentiality
- Requisite expertise

How each distribution method stacks up against these criteria is covered in the relevant sections over the rest of this chapter.

COST

Cost is the most obvious criterion, and the distribution spectrum ranges in cost from free to very expensive and "it's complicated." Lower cost is generally better, but cost is typically the most flexible criterion. For example, most people will trade cost for artifact confidentiality if the situation calls for it.

VISIBILITY

Visibility is the next most obvious criterion for a distribution method. Secret projects or internal tools should be difficult if not impossible for unauthorized people to discover. In another case, public works or open source projects should be as visible as possible to promote adoption.

TRANSPORTATION

Transportation speed and bandwidth overhead are the next most flexible criteria. File sizes and image installation speed will vary between methods that leverage image layers, concurrent downloads, and prebuilt images and those that use flat image files or rely on deployment time image builds. High transportation speeds or low installation latency is critical for systems that use just-in-time deployment to service synchronous requests. The opposite is true in development environments or asynchronous processing systems.

LONGEVITY

Longevity control is a business concern more than a technical concern. Hosted distribution methods are subject to other people's or companies' business concerns. An executive faced with the option of using a hosted registry might ask, "What happens if they go out of business or pivot away from repository hosting?" The question reduces to, "Will the business needs of the third party change before ours?" If this is a concern for you, then longevity control is important. Docker makes it simple to switch between methods, and other criteria like requisite expertise or cost may actually trump this concern. For those reasons, longevity control is another of the more flexible criteria.

AVAILABILITY

Availability control is the ability to control the resolution of availability issues with your repositories. Hosted solutions provide no availability control. Businesses typically provide some service-level agreement on availability if you're a paying customer, but there's nothing you can do to directly resolve an issue. On the other end of the spectrum, private registries or custom solutions put both the control and responsibility in your hands.

ACCESS CONTROL

Access control protects your images from modification or access by unauthorized parties. There are varying degrees of access control. Some systems provide only access control of modifications to a specific repository, whereas others provide course control of entire registries. Still other systems may include pay walls or digital rights management controls. Projects typically have specific access control needs dictated by the product or business. This makes access control requirements one of the least flexible and most important to consider.

INTEGRITY

Artifact integrity and confidentiality both fall in the less-flexible and more-technical end of the spectrum. Artifact integrity is trustworthiness and consistency of your files and images. Violations of integrity may include man-in-the-middle attacks, where an attacker intercepts your image downloads and replaces the content with their own. They might also include malicious or hacked registries that lie about the payloads they return.

CONFIDENTIALITY

Artifact confidentiality is a common requirement for companies developing trade secrets or proprietary software. For example, if you use Docker to distribute cryptographic material, then confidentiality will be a major concern. Artifact integrity and confidentiality features vary across the spectrum. Overall, the out-of-the-box distribution security features won't provide the tightest confidentiality or integrity. If that's one of your needs, an information security professional will need to implement and review a solution.

The last thing to consider when choosing a distribution method is the level of expertise required. Using hosted methods can be very simple and requires little more than a mechanical understanding of the tools. Building custom image or image source distribution pipelines requires expertise with a suite of related technologies. If you don't have that expertise or don't have access to someone who does, using more complicated solutions will be a challenge. In that case, you may be able to reconcile the gap at additional cost.

With this strong set of selection criteria, you can begin learning about and evaluating different distribution methods. The best place to start is on the far left of the spectrum with hosted registries.

9.2 Publishing with hosted registries

As a reminder, Docker registries are services that make repositories accessible to Docker pull commands. A registry hosts repositories. The simplest way to distribute your images is by using hosted registries.

A hosted registry is a Docker registry service that's owned and operated by a third-party vendor. Docker Hub, Quay.io, Tutum.co, and Google Container Registry are all examples of hosted registry providers. By default, Docker publishes to Docker Hub. Docker Hub and most other hosted registries provide both public and private registries, as shown in figure 9.2.

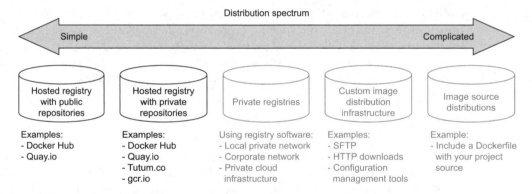

Figure 9.2   **The simplest side of the distribution spectrum and the topic of this section**

The example images used in this book are distributed with public repositories hosted on Docker Hub and Quay.io. By the end of this section you'll understand how to publish your own images using hosted registries and how hosted registries measure up to the selection criteria.

9.2.1 Publishing with public repositories: Hello World via Docker Hub

The simplest way to get started with public repositories on hosted registries is to push a repository that you own to Docker Hub. To do so, all you need is a Docker Hub account and an image to publish. If you haven't done so already, sign up for a Docker Hub account now.

Once you have your account, you need to create an image to publish. Create a new Dockerfile named HelloWorld.df and add the following instructions:

```
FROM busybox:latest          ◀─┐ From HelloWorld.df
CMD echo Hello World
```

Chapter 8 covers Dockerfile instructions. As a reminder, the FROM instruction tells the Docker image builder which existing image to start the new image from. The CMD instruction sets the default command for the new image. Containers created from this image will display "Hello World" and exit. Build your new image with the following command:

```
docker build \
    -t <insert Docker Hub username>/hello-dockerfile \      ◄── Insert your username
    -f HelloWorld.df \
    .
```

Be sure to substitute your Docker Hub username in that command. Authorization to access and modify repositories is based on the username portion of the repository name on Docker Hub. If you create a repository with a username other than your own, you won't be able to publish it.

Publishing images on Docker Hub with the docker command-line tool requires that you establish an authenticated session with that client. You can do that with the login command:

```
docker login
```

This command will prompt you for your username, email address, and password. Each of those can be passed to the command as arguments using the --username, --email, and --password flags. When you log in, the docker client maintains a map of your credentials for the different registries that you authenticate with in a file. It will specifically store your username and an authentication token, not your password.

You will be able to push your repository to the hosted registry once you've logged in. Use the docker push command to do so:

```
docker push <insert Docker Hub username>/hello-dockerfile      ◄── Insert your username
```

Running that command should create output like the following:

```
The push refers to a repository
[dockerinaction/hello-dockerfile] (len: 1)
7f6d4eb1f937: Image already exists
8c2e06607696: Image successfully pushed
6ce2e90b0bc7: Image successfully pushed
cf2616975b4a: Image successfully pushed
Digest:
  sha256:ef18de4b0ddf9ebd1cf5805fae1743181cbf3642f942cae8de7c5d4e375b1f20
```

The command output includes upload statuses and the resulting repository content digest. The push operation will create the repository on the remote registry, upload each of the new layers, and then create the appropriate tags.

Your public repository will be available to the world as soon as the push operation is completed. Verify that this is the case by searching for your username and your new repository. For example, use the following command to find the example owned by the dockerinaction user:

```
docker search dockerinaction/hello-dockerfile
```

Replace the dockerinaction username with your own to find your new repository on Docker Hub. You can also log in to the Docker Hub website and view your repositories to find and modify your new repository.

Having distributed your first image with Docker Hub, you should consider how this method measures up to the selection criteria; see table 9.1.

Table 9.1 Performance of public hosted repositories

Criteria	Rating	Notes
Cost	Best	Public repositories on hosted registries are almost always free. That price is difficult to beat. These are especially helpful when you're getting started with Docker or publishing open source software.
Visibility	Best	Hosted registries are well-known hubs for software distribution. A public repository on a hosted registry is an obvious distribution choice if you want your project to be well known and visible to the public.
Transport speed/size	Better	Hosted registries like Docker Hub are layer-aware and will work with Docker clients to transfer only the layers that the client doesn't already have. Further, pull operations that require multiple repositories to be transferred will perform those transfers in parallel. For those reasons, distributing an image from a hosted repository is fast, and the payloads are minimal.
Availability control	Worst	You have no availability control over hosted registries.
Longevity control	Good	You have no longevity control over hosted registries. But registries will all conform to the Docker registry API, and migrating from one host to another should be a low-cost exercise.
Access control	Better	Public repositories are open to the public for read access. Write access is still controlled by whatever mechanisms the host has put in place. Write access to public repositories on Docker Hub is controlled two ways. First, repositories owned by an individual may be written to only by that individual account. Second, repositories owned by organizations may be written to by any user who is part of that organization.
Artifact integrity	Best	The most recent version of the Docker registry API provides content-addressable images. These let you request an image with a specific cryptographic signature. The Docker client will validate the integrity of the returned image by recalculating the signature and comparing it to the one requested. Older versions of Docker that are unaware of the V2 registry API don't support this feature. In those cases and for other cases where signatures are unknown, a high degree of trust is put into the authorization and at-rest security features provided by the host.
Secrecy	Worst	Hosted registries and public repositories are never appropriate for storing and distributing cleartext secrets or sensitive code. Anyone can access these secrets.
Requisite experience	Best	Using public repositories on hosted registries requires only that you be minimally familiar with Docker and capable of setting up an account through a website. This solution is within reach for any Docker user.

Public repositories on hosted registries are the best choice for owners of open source projects or people who are just getting started with Docker. People should still be skeptical of software that they download and run from the internet, and so public repositories that don't expose their sources can be difficult for some users to trust. Hosted (trusted) builds solve this problem to a certain extent.

9.2.2 *Publishing public projects with automated builds*

A few different hosted registries offer automated builds. Automated builds are images that are built by the registry provider using image sources that you've made available. Image consumers have a higher degree of trust for these builds because the registry owner is building the images from source that can be reviewed.

Distributing your work with automated builds requires two components: a hosted image repository and a hosted Git repository where your image sources are published. Git is a popular distributed version-control system. A Git repository stores the change history for your project. Although distributed version-control systems like Git don't have architectural centralization, a few popular companies provide Git repository hosting. Docker Hub integrates with both Github.com and Bitbucket.org for automated builds.

Both of these hosted Git repository tools provide something called webhooks. In this context, a *webhook* is a way for your Git repository to notify your image repository that a change has been made to the source. When Docker Hub receives a webhook for your Git repository, it will start an automated build for your Docker Hub repository. This automation is shown in figure 9.3.

The automated build process pulls the sources for your project including a Dockerfile from your registered Git repository. The Docker Hub build fleet will use a `docker build` command to build a new image from those sources, tag it in accordance with the repository configuration, and then push it into your Docker Hub repository.

CREATING A DOCKER HUB AUTOMATED BUILD

The following example will walk you through the steps required to set up your own Docker Hub repository as an automated build. This example uses Git. Whole books

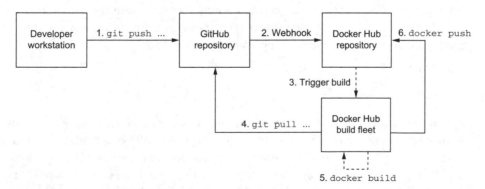

Figure 9.3   The Docker Hub automated build workflow

have been written about Git, and so we can't cover it in detail here. Git ships with several operating systems today, but if it isn't installed on your computer or you need general help, check the website at https://git-scm.com. For the purposes of this example, you need accounts on both Docker Hub and Github.com.

Log in to your Github.com account and create a new repository. Name it hello-docker and make sure that the repository is public. Don't initialize the repository with a license or a .gitignore file. Once the repository has been created on GitHub, go back to your terminal and create a new working directory named hello-docker.

Create a new file named Dockerfile and include the following lines:

```
FROM busybox:latest
CMD echo Hello World
```

This Dockerfile will produce a simple Hello World image. The first thing you need to do to get this built into a new repository at Docker Hub is add it to your Git repository. The following Git commands will create a local repository, add the Dockerfile to the repository, commit the change, and push your changes to your repository on GitHub. Be sure to replace <your username> with your GitHub username:

```
git init
git config --global user.email "you@example.com"      ← Use your email address
git config --global user.name "Your Name"
git remote add origin \
     https://github.com/<your username>/hello-docker.git   ← Use your GitHub username
```

Use your full name

Don't add or commit your files to your repository yet. Before you push your work to GitHub, you should create a new automated build and repository on Docker Hub. You must perform this step through the website at https://hub.docker.com. Once you log in, click the Create button in the header and select Automated Build from the drop-down menu. The website will walk you through setting up the automated build.

The steps include authenticating with GitHub and granting Docker Hub limited access to your account. That access is required so that Docker Hub can find your repositories and register appropriate webhooks for you. Next, you'll be prompted for the GitHub repository that you'd like to use for the automated build. Select the hello-docker repository that you just created. Once you complete the creation wizard, you should be directed to your repository page. Now go back to your terminal to add and push your work to your GitHub repository.

```
git add Dockerfile
git commit -m "first commit"
git push -u origin master
```

When you execute the last command, you may be prompted for your Github.com login credentials. After you present them, your work will be uploaded to GitHub, and you can view your Dockerfile online. Now that your image source is available online at GitHub, a build should have been triggered for your Docker Hub repository. Head back to the repository page and click the Build Details tab. You should see a build listed that was triggered from your latest push to the GitHub repository. Once that is complete, head back to the command line to search for your repository:

```
docker search <your username>/hello-docker
```
◄── **Insert your Docker Hub username**

Automated builds are preferred by image consumers and simplify image maintenance for most cases. There will be times when you don't want to make your source available to the general public. The good news is that most hosted repository providers offer private repositories.

9.2.3 *Private hosted repositories*

Private repositories are similar to public repositories from an operational and product perspective. Most registry providers offer both options, and any differences in provisioning through their websites will be minimal. Because the Docker registry API makes no distinction between the two types of repositories, registry providers that offer both generally require you to provision private registries through their website, app, or API.

The tools for working with private repositories are identical to those for working with public repositories, with one exception. Before you can use docker pull or docker run to install an image from a private repository, you need to have authenticated with the registry where the repository is hosted. To do so, you will use the docker login command just as you would if you were using docker push to upload an image.

The following commands prompt you to authenticate with the registries provided by Docker Hub, quay.io, and tutum.co. After creating accounts and authenticating, you'll have full access to your public and private repositories on all three registries. The login subcommand takes an optional server argument:

```
docker login
# Username: dockerinaction
# Password:
# Email: book@dockerinaction.com
# WARNING: login credentials saved in /Users/xxx/.dockercfg.
# Login Succeeded

docker login tutum.co
# Username: dockerinaction
# Password:
# Email: book@dockerinaction.com
# WARNING: login credentials saved in /Users/xxx/.dockercfg.
# Login Succeeded

docker login quay.io
# Username: dockerinaction
# Password:
# Email: book@dockerinaction.com
# WARNING: login credentials saved in /Users/xxx/.dockercfg.
# Login Succeeded
```

Before you decide that private hosted repositories are the distribution solution for you, consider how they might fulfill your selection criteria; see table 9.2

Table 9.2   Performance of private hosted repositories

Criteria	Rating	Notes
Cost	Best	The cost of private repositories typically scales with the number of repositories that you need. Plans usually range from a few dollars per month for 5 repositories up to around $50 for 50 repositories. Price pressure of storage and monthly virtual server hosting is a driving factor here. Users or organizations that require more than 50 repositories may find it more appropriate to run their own private registry.
Visibility	Best	Private repositories are by definition private. These are typically excluded from indexes and should require authentication before a registry acknowledges the repository's existence. Private repositories are poor candidates for publicizing availability of some software or distributing open source images. Instead they're great tools for small private projects or organizations that don't want to incur the overhead associated with running their own registry.
Transport speed/size	Better	Any hosted registry like Docker Hub will minimize the bandwidth used to transfer an image and enable clients to transfer an image's layers in parallel. Ignoring potential latency introduced by transferring files over the internet, hosted registries should always perform well against other non-registry solutions.
Availability control	Worst	No hosted registry provides any availability control. Unlike public repositories, however, using private repositories will make you a paying customer. Paying customers may have stronger SLA guarantees or access to support personnel.
Longevity control	Good	You have no longevity control over hosted registries. But registries will all conform to the Docker registry API, and migrating from one host to another should be a low-cost exercise.
Access control	Better	Both read and write access to private repositories is restricted to users with authorization.
Artifact integrity	Best	It's reasonable to expect all hosted registries to support the V2 registry API and content-addressable images.
Secrecy	Worst	Despite the privacy provided by these repositories, these are never suitable for storing clear-text secrets or trade-secret code. Although the registries require user authentication and authorization to requested resources, there are several potential problems with these mechanisms. The provider may use weak credential storage, have weak or lost certificates, or leave your artifacts unencrypted at rest. Finally, your secret material should not be accessible to employees of the registry provider.
Requisite experience	Best	Just like public repositories, using private repositories on hosted registries requires only that you be minimally familiar with Docker and capable of setting up an account through a website. This solution is within reach for any Docker user.

Individuals and small teams will find the most utility in private hosted repositories. Their low cost and basic authorization features are friendly to low-budget projects or private projects with minimal security requirements. Large companies or projects that need a higher degree of secrecy and have a suitable budget may find their needs better met by running their own private registry.

9.3 *Introducing private registries*

When you have a hard requirement on availability control, longevity control, or secrecy, then running a private registry may be your best option. In doing so, you gain control without sacrificing interoperability with Docker pull and push mechanisms or adding to the learning curve for your environment. People can interact with a private registry exactly as they would with a hosted registry.

The Docker registry software (called Distribution) is open source software and distributed under the Apache 2 license. The availability of this software and permissive license keep the engineering cost of running your own registry low. It's available through Docker Hub and is simple to use for non-production purposes. Figure 9.4 illustrates that private registries fall in the middle of the distribution spectrum.

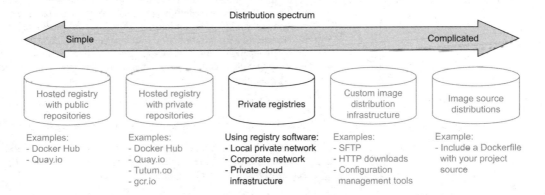

Figure 9.4   Private registries in the image distribution spectrum

Running a private registry is a great distribution method if you have special infrastructure use cases like the following:

- Regional image caches
- Team-specific image distribution for locality or visibility
- Environment or deployment stage-specific image pools
- Corporate processes for approving images
- Longevity control of external images

Before deciding that this is the best choice for you, consider the costs detailed in the selection criteria, shown in table 9.3.

Table 9.3 Performance of private registries

Criteria	Rating	Notes
Cost	Good	At a minimum, a private registry adds to hardware overhead (virtual or otherwise), support expense, and risk of failure. But the community has already invested the bulk of the engineering effort required to deploy a private registry by building the open source software. Cost will scale on different dimensions than hosted registries. Whereas the cost of hosted repositories scales with raw repository count, the cost of private registries scales with transaction rates and storage usage. If you build a system with high transaction rates, you'll need to scale up the number of registry hosts so that you can handle the demand. Likewise, registries that serve some number of small images will have lower storage costs than those serving the same number of large images.
Visibility	Good	Private registries are as visible as you decide to make them. But even a registry that you own and open up to the world will be less visible than advertised popular registries like Docker Hub.
Transport speed/size	Best	Latency between any client and any registry will vary based on the distance between those two nodes on the network, the speed of the network, and the congestion on the registry. Private registries may be faster or slower than hosted registries due to variance in any of those variables. But private registries will appeal most to people and organizations that are doing so for internal infrastructure. Eliminating a dependency on the internet or inter-datacenter networking will have a proportional improvement on latency. Because this solution is using a Docker registry, it will share the same parallelism gains as hosted registry solutions.
Availability control	Best	You have full control over availability as the registry owner.
Longevity control	Best	You have full control over solution longevity as the registry owner.
Access control	Good	The registry software doesn't include any authentication or authorization features out of the box. But implementing those features can be achieved with a minimal engineering exercise.
Artifact integrity	Best	Version 2 of the registry API supports content-addressable images, and the open source software supports a pluggable storage back end. For additional integrity protections, you can force the use of TLS over the network and use back-end storage with encryption at rest.
Secrecy	Good	Private registries are the first solution on the spectrum appropriate for storage of trade secrets or secret material. You control the authentication and authorization mechanisms. You also control the network and in-transit security mechanisms. Most importantly, you control the at-rest storage. It's in your power to ensure that the system is configured in such a way that your secrets stay secret.
Requisite experience	Good	Getting started and running a local registry requires only basic Docker experience. But running and maintaining a highly available production private registry requires experience with several technologies. The specific set depends on what features you want to take advantage of. Generally, you'll want to be familiar with NGINX to build a proxy, LDAP or Kerberos to provide authentication, and Redis for caching.

The biggest trade-off going from hosted registries to private registries is gaining flexibility and control while requiring greater depth and breadth of engineering experience to build and maintain the solution. The remainder of this section covers what you need to implement all but the most complicated registry deployment designs and highlights opportunities for customization in your environment.

9.3.1 Using the registry image

Whatever your reasons for doing so, getting started with the Docker registry software is easy. The Distribution software is available on Docker Hub in a repository named registry. Starting a local registry in a container can be done with a single command:

```
docker run -d -p 5000:5000 \
        -v "$(pwd)"/data:/tmp/registry-dev \
        --restart=always --name local-registry registry:2
```

The image that's distributed through Docker Hub is configured for insecure access from the machine running a client's Docker daemon. When you've started the registry, you can use it like any other registry with docker pull, run, tag, and push commands. In this case, the registry location is localhost:5000. The architecture of your system should now match that described in figure 9.5.

Companies that want tight version control on their external image dependencies will pull images from external sources like Docker Hub and copy them into their own

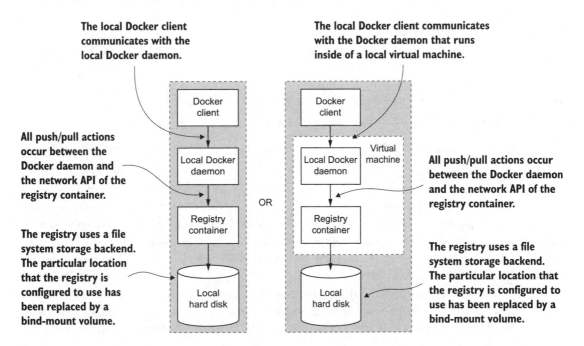

Figure 9.5 Interactions between the docker **client, daemon, local registry container, and local storage**

registry. To get an idea of what it's like working with your registry, consider a workflow for copying images from Docker Hub into your new registry:

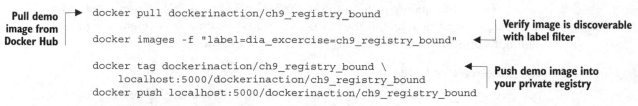

Pull demo image from Docker Hub

```
docker pull dockerinaction/ch9_registry_bound

docker images -f "label=dia_excercise=ch9_registry_bound"

docker tag dockerinaction/ch9_registry_bound \
    localhost:5000/dockerinaction/ch9_registry_bound
docker push localhost:5000/dockerinaction/ch9_registry_bound
```

Verify image is discoverable with label filter

Push demo image into your private registry

In running these four commands, you copy an example repository from Docker Hub into your local repository. If you execute these commands from the same location as where you started the registry, you'll find that the newly created data subdirectory contains new registry data.

9.3.2   *Consuming images from your registry*

The tight integration you get with the Docker ecosystem can make it feel like you're working with software that's already installed on your computer. When internet latency has been eliminated, such as when you're working with a local registry, it can feel even less like you're working with distributed components. For that reason, the exercise of pushing data into a local repository isn't very exciting on its own.

The next set of commands should impress on you that you're working with a real registry. These commands will remove the example repositories from the local cache for your Docker daemon, demonstrate that they're gone, and then reinstall them from your personal registry:

```
docker rmi \
    dockerinaction/ch9_registry_bound \
    localhost:5000/dockerinaction/ch9_registry_bound
```

Remove tagged reference

Pull from registry again

```
docker images -f "label=dia_excercise=ch9_registry_bound"

docker pull localhost:5000/dockerinaction/ch9_registry_bound

docker images -f "label=dia_excercise=ch9_registry_bound"

docker rm -vf local-registry
```

Demonstrate that image is back

Clean up local registry

You can work with this registry locally as much as you want, but the insecure default configuration will prevent remote Docker clients from using your registry (unless they specifically allow insecure access). This is one of the few issues that you'll need to address before deploying a registry in a production environment. Chapter 10 covers the registry software in depth.

This is the most flexible distribution method that involves Docker registries. If you need greater control over the transport, storage, and artifact management, you should consider working directly with images in a manual distribution system.

9.4   *Manual image publishing and distribution*

Images are files, and you can distribute them as you would any other file. It's common to see software available for download on websites, File Transport Protocol (FTP) servers, corporate storage networks, or via peer-to-peer networks. You could use any of these distribution channels for image distribution. You can even use email or USB keys in cases where you know your image recipients.

When you work with images as files, you use Docker only to manage local images and create files. All other concerns are left for you to implement. That void of functionality makes manual image publishing and distribution the second-most flexible but complicated distribution method. This section covers custom image distribution infrastructure, shown on the spectrum in figure 9.6.

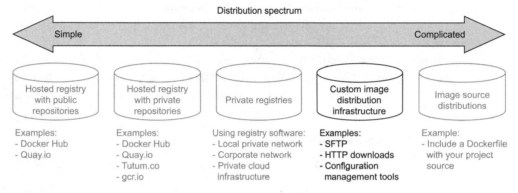

Figure 9.6   Docker image distribution over custom infrastructure

We've already covered all the methods for working with images as files. Chapter 3 covers loading images into Docker and saving images to your hard drive. Chapter 7 covers exporting and importing full file systems as flattened images. These techniques are the foundation for building distribution workflows like the one shown in figure 9.7.

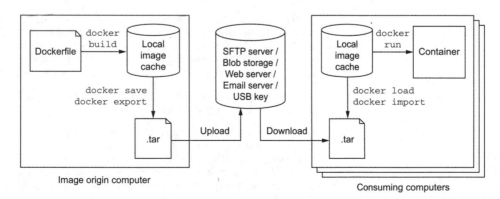

Figure 9.7   A typical manual distribution workflow with producer, transport, and consumers

The workflow illustrated in figure 9.7 is a generalization of how you'd use Docker to create an image and prepare it for distribution. You should be familiar with using `docker build` to create an image and `docker save` or `docker export` to create an image file. You can perform each of these operations with a single command.

You can use any file transport once you have an image in file form. One custom component not show in figure 9.7 is the mechanism that uploads an image to the transport. That mechanism may be a folder that is watched by a file-sharing tool like Dropbox. It could also be a piece of custom code that runs periodically, or in response to a new file, and uses FTP or HTTP to push the file to a remote server. Whatever the mechanism, this general component will require some effort to integrate.

The figure also shows how a client would ingest the image and use it to build a container after the image has been distributed. Similar to image origins, clients require some process or mechanism to acquire the image from a remote source. Once clients have the image file, they can use the `docker load` or `import` commands to complete the transfer.

It doesn't make sense to measure manual image distribution against individual selection criteria. Using a non-Docker distribution channel gives you full control. It will be up to you to determine how your options measure against the criteria shown in table 9.4.

Table 9.4   Performance of custom image distribution infrastructure.

Criteria	Rating	Notes
Cost	Good	Distribution costs are driven by bandwidth, storage, and hardware needs. Hosted distribution solutions like cloud storage will bundle these costs and generally scale down price per unit as your usage increases. But hosted solutions bundle in the cost of personnel and several other benefits that you may not need, driving up the price compared to a mechanism that you own.
Visibility	Good	Like private registries, most manual distribution methods are special and take more effort to advertise than well-known registries. Examples might include using popular websites or other well-known file distribution hubs.
Transport speed/size	Good	Whereas transport speed depends on the transport, file sizes are dependent on your choice of using layered images or flattened images. Remember, layered images maintain the history of the image, container-creation metadata, and old files that might have been deleted or overridden. Flattened images contain only the current set of files on the file system.
Availability control	Best	If availability control is an important factor for your case, you can use a transport mechanism that you own.
Longevity control	Bad	Using proprietary protocols, tools, or other technology that is neither open nor under your control will impact longevity control. For example, distributing image files with a hosted file-sharing service like Dropbox will give you no longevity control. On the other hand, swapping USB drives with your friend will last as long as the two of you decide to use USB drives.

Table 9.4 Performance of custom image distribution infrastructure.

Criteria	Rating	Notes
Access control	Bad	You could use a transport with the access control features you need or use file encryption. If you built a system that encrypted your image files with a specific key, you could be sure that only a person or people with the correct key could access the image.
Artifact integrity	Bad	Integrity validation is a more expensive feature to implement for broad distribution. At a minimum, you'd need a trusted communication channel for advertising cryptographic file signatures.
Secrecy	Good	You can implement content secrecy with cheap encryption tools. If you need meta-secrecy (where the exchange itself is secret) as well as content secrecy, then you should avoid hosted tools and make sure that the transport that you use provides secrecy (HTTPS, SFTP, SSH, or offline).
Requisite experience	Good	Hosted tools will typically be designed for ease of use and require a lesser degree of experience to integrate with your workflow. But you can use simple tools that you own as easily in most cases.

All the same criteria apply to manual distribution, but it's difficult to discuss them without the context of a specific transportation method.

9.4.1 A sample distribution infrastructure using the File Transfer Protocol

Building a fully functioning example will help you understand exactly what goes into a manual distribution infrastructure. This section will help you build an infrastructure with the File Transfer Protocol.

FTP is less popular than it used to be. The protocol provides no secrecy and requires credentials to be transmitted over the wire for authentication. But the software is freely available and clients have been written for most platforms. That makes FTP a great tool for building your own distribution infrastructure. Figure 9.8 illustrates what you'll build.

The example in this section uses two existing images. The first, dockerinaction/ch9_ftpd, is a specialization of the centos:6 image where vsftpd (an FTP daemon) has been installed and configured for anonymous write access. The second image, dockerinaction/ch9_ftp_client, is a specialization of a popular minimal Alpine Linux image. An FTP client named LFTP has been installed and set as the entrypoint for the image.

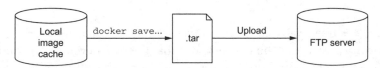

Figure 9.8 An FTP publishing infrastructure

To prepare for the experiment, pull a known image from Docker Hub that you want
to distribute. In the example, the `registry:2` image is used:

```
docker pull registry:2
```

Once you have an image to distribute, you can begin. The first step is building your
image distribution infrastructure. In this case, that means running an FTP server:

```
docker run -d --name ftp-transport -p 21:12 dockerinaction/ch9_ftpd
```

This command will start an FTP server that accepts FTP connections on TCP port 21
(the default port). Don't use this image in any production capacity. The server is configured to allow anonymous connections write access under the pub/incoming folder.
Your distribution infrastructure will use that folder as an image distribution point.

The next thing you need to do is export an image to the file format. You can use
the following command to do so:

```
docker save -o ./registry.2.tar registry:2
```

Running this command will export the `registry:2` image as a structured image file in
your current directory. The file will retain all the metadata and history associated with
the image. At this point, you could inject all sorts of phases like checksum generation
or file encryption. This infrastructure has no such requirements, and you should
move along to distribution.

The `dockerinaction/ch9_ftp_client` image has an FTP client installed and can
be used to upload your new image file to your FTP server. Remember, you started the
FTP server in a container named `ftp-transport`. If you're running the container on
your computer, you can use container linking to reference the FTP server from the client; otherwise, you'll want to use host name injection (see chapter 5), a DNS name of
the server, or an IP address:

```
docker run --rm --link ftp-transport:ftp_server \
    -v "$(pwd)":/data \
    dockerinaction/ch9_ftp_client \
    -e 'cd pub/incoming; put registry.2.tar; exit' ftp_server
```

This command creates a container with a volume bound to your local directory and
linked with your FTP server container. The command will use LFTP to upload a file
named registry.2.tar to the server located at ftp_server. You can verify that you
uploaded the image by listing the contents of the FTP server's folder:

```
docker run --rm --link ftp-transport:ftp_server \
   -v "$(pwd)":/data \
    dockerinaction/ch9_ftp_client \
    -e "cd pub/incoming; ls; exit" ftp_server
```

The registry image is now available for download to any FTP client that knows about
the server and can access it over the network. But that file may never be overridden in
the current FTP server configuration. You'd need to come up with your own versioning scheme if you were going to use a similar tool in production.

Advertising the availability of the image in this scenario requires clients to periodically poll the server using the last command you ran. You could alternatively build some website or send an email notifying clients about the image, but that all happens outside the standard FTP transfer workflow.

Before moving on to evaluating this distribution method against the selection criteria, consume the registry image from your FTP server to get an idea of how clients would need to integrate.

First, eliminate the registry image from your local image cache and the file from your local directory:

```
rm registry.2.tar
docker rmi registry:2
```
> **Need to remove any registry containers first**

Then download the image file from your FTP server:

```
docker run --rm --link ftp-transport:ftp_server \
    -v "$(pwd)":/data \
    dockerinaction/ch9_ftp_client \
    -e 'cd pub/incoming; get registry.2.tar; exit' ftp_server
```

At this point you should once again have the registry.2.tar file in your local directory. You can reload that image into your local cache with the docker load command:

```
docker load -i registry.2.tar
```

This is a minimal example of how a manual image publishing and distribution infrastructure might be built. With just a bit of extension you could build a production-quality, FTP-based distribution hub. In its current configuration this example matches against the selection criteria, as shown in table 9.5.

Table 9.5 Performance of a sample FTP-based distribution infrastructure

Criteria	Rating	Notes
Cost	Good	This is a low-cost transport. All the related software is free. Bandwidth and storage costs should scale llnearly with the number of images hosted and the number of clients.
Visibility	Worst	The FTP server is running in an unadvertised location with a non-standard integration workflow. The visibility of this configuration is very low.
Transport speed/size	Bad	In this example, all the transport happened between containers on the same computer, so all the commands finished quickly. If a client connects to your FTP service over the network, then speeds are directly impacted by your upload speeds. This distribution method will download redundant artifacts and won't download components of the image in parallel. Overall, this method isn't bandwidth-efficient.
Availability control	Best	You have full availability control of the FTP server. If it becomes unavailable, you're the only person who can restore service.

Table 9.5　Performance of a sample FTP-based distribution infrastructure

Criteria	Rating	Notes
Longevity control	Best	You can use the FTP server created for this example as long as you want.
Access control	Worst	This configuration provides no access control.
Artifact integrity	Worst	The network transportation layer does provide file integrity between endpoints. But it's susceptible to interception attacks, and there are no integrity protections between file creation and upload or between download and import.
Secrecy	Worst	This configuration provides no secrecy.
Requisite experience	Good	All requisite experience for implementing this solution has been provided here. If you're interested in extending the example for production, you'll need to familiarize yourself with `vsftpd` configuration options and `SFTP`

In short, there's almost no real scenario where this transport configuration is appropriate. But it helps illustrate the different concerns and basic workflows that you can create when you work with image as files. The only more flexible and potentially complicated image publishing and distribution method involves distributing image sources.

9.5　*Image source distribution workflows*

When you distribute image sources instead of images, you cut out all the Docker distribution workflow and rely solely on the Docker image builder. As with manual image publishing and distribution, source-distribution workflows should be evaluated against the selection criteria in the context of a particular implementation.

Using a hosted source control system like Git on GitHub will have very different traits from using a file backup tool like `rsync`. In a way, source-distribution workflows have a superset of the concerns of manual image publishing and distribution workflows. You'll have to build your workflow but without the help of the `docker save`, `load`, `export`, or `import` commands. Producers need to determine how they will package their sources, and consumers need to understand how those sources are packaged as well as how to build an image from them. That expanded interface makes source-distribution workflows the most flexible and potentially complicated distribution method. Figure 9.9 shows image source distribution on the most complicated end of the spectrum.

Image source distribution is one of the most common methods, despite having the most potential for complication. The reason is that the expanded interface has been standardized by popular version-control software.

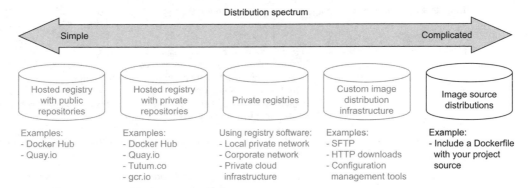

Figure 9.9   Using existing infrastructure to distribute image sources

9.5.1   *Distributing a project with Dockerfile on GitHub*

Using Dockerfile and GitHub to distribute image sources is almost identical to setting up automated builds on hosted Docker image repositories. All the steps for using Git to integrate your local Git repository with a repository on GitHub are the same. The only difference comes in that you don't create a Docker Hub account or repository. Instead, your image consumers will clone your GitHub repository directly and use docker build to build your image locally.

Supposing a producer had an existing project, Dockerfile, and GitHub repository, their distribution workflow would look like this:

```
git init
git config --global user.email "you@example.com"
git config --global user.name "Your Name"
git add Dockerfile
# git add *whatever other files you need for the image*
git commit -m "first commit"
git remote add origin https://github.com/<your username>/<your repo>.git
git push -u origin master
```

Meanwhile, a consumer would use a general command set that looks like this:

```
git clone https://github.com/<your username>/<your repo>.git
cd <your-repo>
docker build -t <your username>/<your repo> .
```

These are all steps that a regular Git or GitHub user is familiar with, as shown in table 9.6.

Table 9.6   Performance of image source distribution via GitHub

Criteria	Rating	Notes
Cost	Best	There's no cost if you're using a public GitHub repository.
Visibility	Best	GitHub is a highly visible location for open source tools. It provides excellent social and search components, making project discovery simple.

Table 9.6   Performance of image source distribution via GitHub

Criteria	Rating	Notes
Transport speed/size	Good	By distributing image sources, you can leverage other registries for base layers. Doing so will reduce the transportation and storage burden. GitHub also provides a content delivery network (CDN). That CDN is used to make sure clients around the world can access projects on GitHub with low network latency.
Availability control	Worst	Relying on GitHub or other hosted version-control providers eliminates any availability control.
Longevity control	Bad	Although Git is a popular tool and should be around for a while, you forego any longevity control by integrating with GitHub or other hosted version-control providers.
Access control	Good	GitHub or other hosted version-control providers do provide access control tools for private repositories.
Artifact integrity	Good	This solution provides no integrity for the images produced as part of the build process, or of the sources after they have been cloned to the client machine. But integrity is the whole point of version-control systems. Any integrity problems should be apparent and easily recoverable through standard Git processes.
Secrecy	Worst	Public projects provide no source secrecy.
Requisite Experience	Good	Image producers and consumers need to be familiar with Dockerfile, the Docker builder, and the Git tooling.

Image source distribution is divorced from all Docker distribution tools. By relying only on the image builder, you're free to adopt any distribution toolset available. If you're locked into a particular toolset for distribution or source control, this may be the only option that meets your criteria.

9.6   Summary

This chapter covers various software distribution mechanisms and the value contributed by Docker in each. A reader that has recently implemented a distribution channel, or is currently doing so, might take away additional insights into their solution. Others will learn more about available choices. In either case, it is important to make sure that you have gained the following insights before moving on:

- Having a spectrum of choices illustrates your range of options.
- You should always use a consistent set of selection criteria in order to evaluate your distribution options and determine which method you should use.
- Hosted public repositories provide excellent project visibility, are free, and require very little experience to adopt.
- Consumers will have a higher degree of trust in images generated by automated builds because a trusted third party builds them.

- Hosted private repositories are cost-effective for small teams and provide satisfactory access control.
- Running your own registry enables you to build infrastructure suitable for special use cases without abandoning the Docker distribution facilities.
- Distributing images as files can be accomplished with any file-sharing system.
- Image source distribution is flexible but only as complicated as you make it. Using popular source-distribution tools and patterns will keep things simple.

Running
customized registries

10

This chapter covers

- Working directly with the Registry API
- Building a central registry
- Registry authentication tools
- Configuring a registry for scale
- Integrating through notifications

Chapter 9 covers several methods of distributing Docker images, one of them involving running a Docker registry. A Docker registry is a flexible image distribution component that's useful on its own or as part of larger complex systems. For that reason, understanding how to configure your own registry will help you get the most out of Docker.

Someone developing software that integrates with a Docker registry may want to run a local instance to develop against. They might also use it as a staging environment for their project. A development team might deploy their own central registry to share their work and streamline integrations. A company may run one or more centralized registries that are backed by durable artifact storage. These could be used to control external image dependencies or for managing deployment artifacts.

Figure 10.1 illustrates these configurations. This chapter covers all these use cases, scaling approaches, and an introduction to the Registry API itself. By the end of this chapter you will be able to launch an appropriately configured registry for any use case.

Any program that implements the Registry API is a registry. This chapter uses the Distribution (docker/distribution) project. The project is available on Docker Hub in the registry repository.

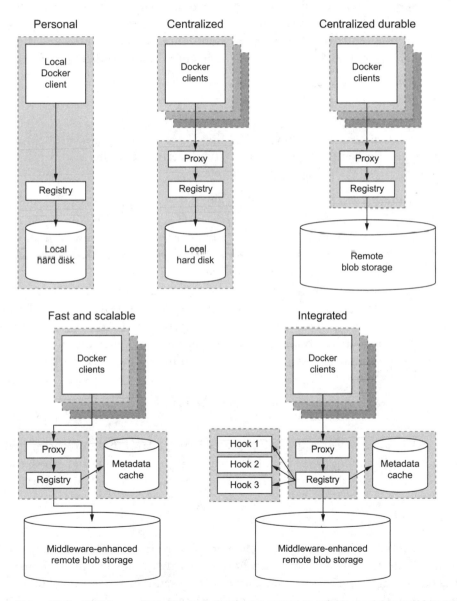

Figure 10.1   Registry configurations ranging from personal to reliable, scalable, and integrated

10.1   *Running a personal registry*

Launching a personal registry is great if you're just getting started or using your own for development purposes. That material is introduced in chapter 9, but this section demonstrates how to use the Registry API to access your new registry.

10.1.1   *Reintroducing the Image*

Over the course of this chapter you'll launch and relaunch containers providing a registry several times. In each instance you're going to use specializations of the Distribution project as provided by the registry:2 repository.

A personal registry rarely requires customization. In such a use case, you can use the official image. Pull the image and launch a personal registry to get started:

```
docker run -d --name personal_registry \
   -p 5000:5000 --restart=always \
   registry:2
```

> **TIP** At the time of this writing, the latest tag refers to the last version of the registry as implementing the V1 Registry API. The examples in this chapter require the V2 API unless otherwise noted.

The Distribution project runs on port 5000, but clients make no assumptions about locations and attempt connecting to port 80 (HTTP) by default. You could map port 80 on your host to port 5000 on the container, but in this case you should map port 5000 directly. Anytime you connect to the registry, you'll need to explicitly state the port where the registry is running.

The container you started from the registry image will store the repository data that you send to it in a managed volume mounted at /var/lib/registry. This means you don't have to worry about the data being stored on the main layered file system.

An empty registry is a bit boring, so tag and push an image into it before moving on. Use the registry image itself, but in order to differentiate the example, use a different repository name:

```
docker tag registry:2 localhost:5000/distribution:2
docker push localhost:5000/distribution:2
```

The push command will output a line for each image layer that's uploaded to the registry and finally output the digest of the image. If you want, you can remove the local tag for localhost:5000/distribution:2 and then try pulling from your registry:

```
docker rmi localhost:5000/distribution:2
docker pull localhost:5000/distribution:2
```

All these commands are covered in chapter 2 and chapter 7. The difference is that in those chapters you're working with hosted registries. This example highlights that your knowledge, scripts, and automation infrastructure are portable between hosted solutions and your custom infrastructure when run your own registry. Using the command-line tools like this is great for scripts and users, but you'll want to use the API directly if you're developing software to integrate with a registry.

10.1.2 *Introducing the V2 API*

The V2 Registry API is RESTful. If you're unfamiliar with RESTful APIs, it's enough to know that a RESTful API is a patterned use of Hypertext Transfer Protocol (HTTP) and its primitives to access and manipulate remote resources. There are several excellent online resources and books on the subject. In the case of a Docker registry, those resources are tags, manifests, blobs, and blob uploads. You can find the full Registry specification at https://docs.docker.com/registry/spec/api/.

Because RESTful APIs use HTTP, you might take some time to familiarize yourself with the details of that protocol. The examples in this chapter are complete, and you won't need any deep knowledge of HTTP in order to follow along, but you'll get much more from the experience if you're comfortable with what's happening behind the scenes.

In order to exercise any RESTful service you'll need an HTTP client. The truly savvy reader may know how to use a raw TCP connection to issue HTTP requests, but most prefer not to bother with the low-level details of the protocol. Although web browsers are capable of making HTTP requests, command-line tools will give you the power to fully exercise a RESTful API.

The examples in this chapter use the cURL command-line tool. Because this is a book about Docker, you should use cURL from inside a container. Using cURL in this way will also work for both Docker native and Boot2Docker users. Prepare an image for this purpose (and practice your Dockerfile skills):

```
FROM gliderlabs/alpine:latest          ◄── From curl.df
LABEL source=dockerinaction
LABEL category=utility
RUN apk --update add curl
ENTRYPOINT ["curl"]
CMD ["--help"]

docker build -t dockerinaction/curl -f curl.df .
```

With your new dockerinaction/curl image, you can issue the cURL commands in the examples without worrying about whether cURL is installed or what version is installed on your computer. Celebrate your new image and get started with the Registry API by making a simple request to your running registry:

```
docker run --rm --net host dockerinaction/curl -Is
    http://localhost:5000/v2/          ◄── Note the /v2/
```

That request will result in the following output:

```
HTTP/1.1 200 OK
Content-Length: 2
Content-Type: application/json; charset=utf-8
Docker-Distribution-Api-Version: registry/2.0
```

This command is used to validate that the registry is running the V2 Registry API and returns the specific API version in the HTTP response headers. The last component of that request, /v2/, is a prefix for every resource on the V2 API.

If you accidentally issued this request to a registry that was running the V1 API, the output would look something like this:

```
HTTP/1.1 404 NOT FOUND
Server: gunicorn/19.1.1
Connection: keep-alive
Content-Type: text/html
Content-Length: 233
```

HTTP DETAIL   This command used an HTTP HEAD request to retrieve only the response headers. A successful GET request for this resource will return the same headers and response body with an empty document.

Now that you've used cURL to validate that the registry is indeed using the V2 API, you should do something a bit more interesting. The next command will retrieve the list of tags in the distribution repository on your registry:

```
docker run --rm -u 1000:1000 --net host \
    dockerinaction/curl -s http://localhost:5000/v2/distribution/tags/list
```

Running that command should display a result like the following:

```
{"name":"distribution","tags":["2"]}
```

Here you can see that the registry responded to your request with a JSON document that lists the tags in your distribution repository. In this case there's only one, 2. A JSON document is a structured document of key-value pairs. It uses braces to represent objects (which contain another set of key-value pairs), square brackets to represent lists, and quoted strings to label elements and represent string values.

Run this example again, but this time add another tag to your repository to yield a more interesting result:

```
docker tag \
    localhost:5000/distribution:2 \
    localhost:5000/distribution:two                    ◀─┘ Creative tag name

docker push localhost:5000/distribution:two

docker run --rm \
    -u 1000:1000 \                              ┌─ Run without
    --net host \                         ◀──────┘  network namespace
    dockerinaction/curl \
    -s http://localhost:5000/v2/distribution/tags/list
```

Run as unprivileged user ─┐ (pointing to -u 1000:1000)

The curl command will return output like the following:

```
{"name":"distribution","tags":["2","two"]}
```

In the output you can clearly see that the repository contains both the tags that you've defined. Each distinct tag that's pushed to this repository on your registry will be listed here.

You can use the personal registry that you created in this section for any testing or personal productivity needs you might have. But the uses are somewhat limited without any changes to the configuration. Even if you have no plans for deploying a centralized registry, you may benefit from some customization to adopt the registry's notifications feature discussed in section 10.5. You'll need to know how to customize the registry image before you can make those changes.

10.1.3 *Customizing the Image*

The remainder of this chapter explains how to build upon the registry image to grow out of the personal registry and into more advanced use cases. You'll need to know a bit more about the registry image itself before you can do that.

This chapter will specialize the registry image with Dockerfiles. If you're unfamiliar with Dockerfile syntax and haven't read chapter 8, then you should do so now or review the online documentation at https://docs.docker.com/reference/builder.

The first things you need to know about the image are the key components:

- The base image for `registry` is Debian and it has updated dependencies.
- The main program is named `registry` and is available on the `PATH`.
- The default configuration file is config.yml.

Different project maintainers will all have different ideas about the best base image. In the case of Docker, Debian is a frequent choice. Debian has a minimal footprint for a fully featured distribution and takes only approximately 125 MB on your hard drive. It also ships with a popular package manager, so installing or upgrading dependencies should never be an issue.

The main program is named `registry` and is set as the entrypoint for the image. This means that when you start a container from this image, you can omit any command arguments to take the default behavior or add your own arguments directly to the trailing portion of the `docker run` command.

Like all Docker projects, the Distribution project aims to provide a sensible default configuration. That default configuration is located in a file named config.yml. As the name implies, the configuration is written in YAML. If you're not familiar with YAML, there's no reason to worry. YAML is designed to maximize human readability. If you're interested, you'll find several YAML resources at http://yaml.org.

This configuration file is the real star of this chapter. There are several ways that you might inject your own configuration in the image. You might modify the included file directly. A bind-mount volume could be used to override the file with one that you've been writing. In this case, you'll copy in your own file to another location and set a new default command for your new image.

The configuration file contains nine top-level sections. Each defines a major functional component of the registry:

- version—This is a required field and specifies the configuration version (not software version).
- log—The configuration in this section controls the logging output produced by the Distribution project.
- storage—The storage configuration controls where and how images are stored and maintained.
- auth—This configuration controls in-registry authentication mechanisms.
- middleware—The middleware configuration is optional. It's used to configure the storage, registry, or repository middleware in use.
- reporting—Certain reporting tools have been integrated with the Distribution project. These include Bugsnag and NewRelic. This section configures each of those toolsets.
- http—This section specifies how Distribution should make itself available on the network.
- notifications—Webhook-style integration with other projects is configured in the notifications section.
- redis—Finally, configuration for a Redis cache is provided in the redis section.

With these components in mind, you should be ready to build advanced registry use cases by customizing the registry image. Remember, the Distribution project is rapidly evolving. If you hit a snag with the instructions in this book, you can always consult the online documentation for reference or check out the project itself at https://github.com/docker/distribution.

10.2   *Enhancements for centralized registries*

Launching a local copy of the registry image with no modifications works well for personal purposes or testing. When more than one person needs access to the same registry it is called a centralized registry. This section explains how to implement a centralized registry by customizing the official registry image. Figure 10.2 shows the changes involved in growing from a personal registry into a centralized registry.

For more than one person to access the registry, it will need to be available on a network. You can accomplish that easily enough by mapping the registry container to port 80 on the network interface of the computer it's running on (docker run ... -p 80:5000 ...). Introducing a dependency on the network introduces a whole set of new vulnerabilities. From snooping to corrupting image transfers, man-in-the-middle attacks can create several problems. Adding transport layer security will protect your system from these and other attacks.

Once clients can access the registry, you'll want to make sure that only the right users can access it. This is called authentication (covered in section 10.2.3).

The most unavoidable issue that any service owner encounters is client compatibility. With multiple clients connecting to your registry, you need to consider what

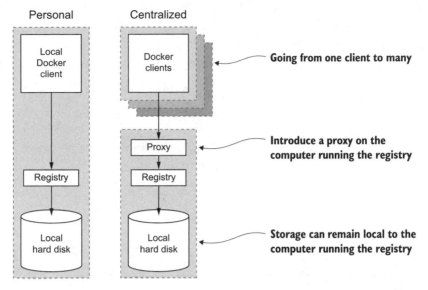

Figure 10.2 Personal versus centralized Docker registry system architecture

versions of Docker they're using. Supporting multiple client versions can be tricky. Section 10.2.4 demonstrates one way to handle the problem.

Before moving on to the next registry type, section 10.2.5 covers best practices for production registry configurations. These include hardening and preventive maintenance steps.

Most of these concerns are focused on interactions with clients. Although the Distribution software has some tools to meet the new needs, adding a proxy to the system introduces the required flexibility to implement all these enhancements.

10.2.1 Creating a reverse proxy

Creating a reverse proxy is a quick task when you use the right base image and Dockerfile to make your customizations. Figure 10.3 illustrates the relationship between the reverse proxy and your registry.

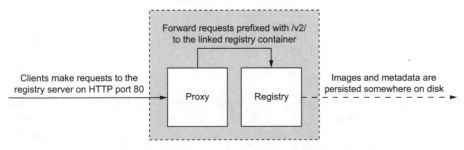

Figure 10.3 Inserting a reverse proxy between clients and a registry

Your reverse proxy configuration will involve two containers. The first will run the NGINX reverse proxy. The second will run your registry. The reverse proxy container will be linked to the registry container on the host alias, `registry`. Get started by creating a new file named basic-proxy.conf and include the following configuration:

```
upstream docker-registry {                    ◀┐  From basic-proxy.conf
  server registry:5000;
}

server {                                        ┌─  Container port
  listen 80;                                  ◀┘   requirement
  # Use the localhost name for testing purposes
  server_name localhost;
  # A real deployment would use the real hostname where it is deployed
  # server_name mytotallyawesomeregistry.com;

  client_max_body_size 0;
  chunked_transfer_encoding on;

  # We're going to forward all traffic bound for the registry    ┌─ Note /v2/
  location /v2/ {                                               ◀┘  prefix
    proxy_pass                          http://docker-registry;
    proxy_set_header   Host             $http_host;
    proxy_set_header   X-Real-IP        $remote_addr;
    proxy_set_header   X-Forwarded-For  $proxy_add_x_forwarded_for;
    proxy_set_header   X-Forwarded-Proto $scheme;
    proxy_read_timeout                  900;
  }
}
```

Annotations in the margin:
- **Link alias requirement** → `server registry:5000;`
- **Resolves to the upstream** → `proxy_pass http://docker-registry;`

As stated earlier in the book, NGINX is a sophisticated piece of software. Whole books have been dedicated to its use, and so I won't do it the disservice of attempting to explain it here. The bits of this configuration that you should understand are annotated. This configuration will forward all traffic on port 80 for the HTTP host localhost and with the path prefix /v2/ on to http://registry:5000. This configuration will be the base for other modifications you make to your reverse proxy going forward.

Once you have your reverse proxy configuration, you'll want to build a new image. A minimal Dockerfile should suffice. It should start from the latest NGINX image and include your new configuration. The base NGINX image takes care of all the standard things like exposing ports. Create a new file named basic-proxy.df and paste in the following Dockerfile:

```
FROM nginx:latest                          ◀┐  From basic-proxy.df
LABEL source=dockerinaction
LABEL category=infrastructure
COPY ./basic-proxy.conf /etc/nginx/conf.d/default.conf
```

> **TIP** In production, you really should include an environment validation script (see section 8.4.1) just to make sure that the containers have been linked correctly. But because you're using an NGINX upstream directive, it will verify that the host can be resolved for you.

At this point you should be ready to build your image. Use the following `docker build` command to do so:

```
docker build -t dockerinaction/basic_proxy -f basic-proxy.df .
```

Now you're ready to put it all together. Your personal registry should already be running from the example in section 10.1.1. Use it again here because it should already be primed with some content. The following commands will create your new reverse proxy and test the connection:

```
docker run -d --name basic_proxy -p 80:80 \          ◀── Start reverse proxy
    --link personal_registry:registry \
    dockerinaction/basic_proxy

docker run --rm -u 1000:1000 --net host \            ◀── Run cURL to query your
    dockerinaction/curl \                                registry through the proxy
    -s http://localhost:80/v2/distribution/tags/list
```

Link to registry

A few things are happening quickly, so before you move on, take some time to make sure you understand what's going on here.

You created a personal registry earlier. It's running in a container named `personal_registry` and has exposed port 5000. You also added a few tagged images to a repository named distribution hosted by your personal registry. The first command in this set creates a new container running a reverse proxy that listens on port 80. The reverse proxy container is linked to your registry. Any traffic that the proxy receives on port 80 that's also requesting a path prefixed with /v2/ will be forwarded to port 5000 on your registry container.

Finally, you run a `curl` command from the same host where your Docker daemon is running. That command makes a request to port 80 on the localhost (in this case you need that host name). The request is proxied to your registry (because the path starts with /v2/), and the registry responds with a list of tags contained in the distribution repository.

> **NOTE** This end-to-end test is very similar to what would happen if your proxy and registry were deployed to a different host with some known name. Comments in the basic-proxy.conf file explain how to set the host name for production deployments.

The reverse proxy that you're building here doesn't add anything to your system except another hop in the network and a hardened HTTP interface. The next three sections explain how to modify this basic configuration to add TLS, authentication, and multi-version client support.

10.2.2 *Configuring HTTPS (TLS) on the reverse proxy*

Transport layer security (TLS) provides endpoint identification, message integrity, and message privacy. It's implemented at a layer below HTTP and is what provides the *S* in HTTPS. Using TLS to secure your registry is more than a best practice. The Docker daemon won't connect to a registry without TLS unless that registry is running on local-host. That makes these steps mandatory for anyone running a centralized registry.

What about SSH tunnels?

Readers who have experience with TLS may already know that the power the public key infrastructure provides comes with expense and complexity. A cheap and arguably less complex way to secure your registry's network traffic is to enable connections only through Secure Shell (SSH).

SSH uses similar security techniques as TLS but lacks the third-party trust mechanism that makes TLS scale to large numbers of users. But SSH does provide a protocol for tunneling network traffic.

To secure your registry with SSH, you'd install an SSH server (OpenSSH) on the same machine as the registry. With the SSH server in place, map the registry only to the loopback interface (localhost) on the machine. Doing so will restrict inbound registry traffic to what comes through the SSH server.

When clients want to use your registry in this configuration, they'll create an SSH tunnel. That tunnel binds a local TCP port and forwards traffic to it over an SSH connection between your computer and the remote SSH server and out to some destination host and port. To put this in context, clients create a tunnel that allows them to treat your registry as if it were running locally. A client would use a command line like this to create the tunnel:

```
ssh -f -i my_key user@ssh-host -L 4000:localhost:5000 -N
```

With the tunnel created, the client would use the registry as if it were running locally on port 4000.

Using SSH tunnels might work if you're running a centralized registry for a small team. A prerequisite to their use is user account management and authentication (so you can solve the authentication issue at the same time). But the practice doesn't scale well because of account management overhead and generally requires a higher degree of user sophistication than HTTPS.

An HTTPS endpoint is different from the HTTP endpoint in three ways. First, it should listen on TCP port 443. Second, it requires signed certificate and private key files. Last, the host name of the server and the proxy configuration must match the one used to create the certificate. In this example, you're going to create a self-signed certificate for the localhost name. Such a certificate won't work well for a real registry, but there are many guides available to help you replace that certificate with one issued by a certificate authority. Figure 10.4 illustrates the new HTTPS protection in relation to your proxy and registry.

The first step in making this design a reality is to generate a private and public key pair and a self-signed certificate. Without Docker you'd need to install OpenSSL and

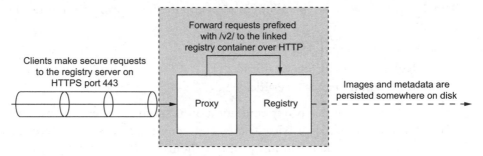

Figure 10.4   Adding an HTTPS (TLS) endpoint to the proxy

run three complicated commands. With Docker (and a public image created by CenturyLink) you can do the whole thing with one command:

```
docker run --rm -e COMMON_NAME=localhost -e KEY_NAME=localhost \
    -v "$(pwd)":/certs centurylink/openssl
```

This command will generate a 4096-bit RSA key pair and store the private key file and self-signed certificate in your current working directory. The image is publicly available and maintained with an automated build on Docker Hub. It's fully auditable, so the more paranoid are free to validate (or re-create) the image as needed. Of the three files that are created, you'll use two. The third is a certificate-signing request (CSR) and can be removed.

The next step is to create your proxy configuration file. Create a new file named tls-proxy.conf and copy in the following configuration. Again, relevant lines are annotated:

```
upstream docker-registry {                      ◄── From tls-proxy.conf
  server registry:5000;
}

server {
  listen 443 ssl;
  server_name localhost                          ◄── Named localhost

  client_max_body_size 0;
  chunked_transfer_encoding on;

  ssl_certificate /etc/nginx/conf.d/localhost.crt;     ◄── Note SSL configuration
  ssl_certificate_key /etc/nginx/conf.d/localhost.key;

  location /v2/ {
    proxy_pass                         http://docker-registry;
    proxy_set_header  Host             $http_host;
    proxy_set_header  X-Real-IP        $remote_addr;
    proxy_set_header  X-Forwarded-For  $proxy_add_x_forwarded_for;
    proxy_set_header  X-Forwarded-Proto $scheme;
    proxy_read_timeout                 900;
  }
}
```

Note use of port 443 and "ssl" ──► (annotation for `listen 443 ssl;`)

The differences between this configuration and the basic proxy configuration include the following:

- Listening on port 443
- Registration of an SSL certificate
- Registration of an SSL certificate key

You should note that this proxy configuration is set to use the same registry on port 5000. Running multiple proxies against the same registry is no different from the registry's perspective than running multiple clients.

The last step before you put it all together is the creation of a Dockerfile. This time, in addition to copying the proxy configuration, you'll also need to copy the certificate and key file into the image. The following Dockerfile uses the multisource form of the COPY directive. Doing so eliminates the need for multiple layers that you might otherwise create as the result of multiple COPY directives. Create a new file named tls-proxy.df and insert the following lines:

```
FROM nginx:latest
LABEL source=dockerinaction
LABEL category=infrastructure
COPY ["./tls-proxy.conf", \
      "./localhost.crt", \         ◄─┐ Copy new certificate
      "./localhost.key", \      ◄─┐ Copy private key
      "/etc/nginx/conf.d/"]
```

Build your new image with the following docker build command:

```
docker build -t dockerinaction/tls_proxy -f tls-proxy.df .
```

Now put it all together by starting your proxy and testing it with curl:

```
docker run -d --name tls-proxy -p 443:443  \  ◄─┐ Note port 443
    --link personal_registry:registry \
    dockerinaction/tls_proxy
```

Note link ─┐ (points to --link line)

```
docker run --rm \
    --net host \
    dockerinaction/curl -ks \      ◄─┐ Note "k" flag
    https://localhost:443/v2/distribution/tags/list   ◄─┐ Note "https" and "443"
```

This command should list both tags for the distribution repository in your personal registry:

```
{"name":"distribution","tags":["2","two"]}
```

The curl command in this example uses the -k option. That option will instruct curl to ignore any certificate errors with the request endpoint. It's required in this case because you're using a self-signed certificate. Aside from that nuance, you're successfully making a request to your registry over HTTPS.

10.2.3 *Adding an authentication layer*

There are three mechanisms for authentication included with the Distribution project itself. These are appropriately named silly, token, and htpasswd. As an alternative to configuring authentication directly on the Distribution project, you can configure various authentication mechanisms in the reverse proxy layer (see section 10.2.2).

The first, silly, is completely insecure and should be ignored. It exists for development purposes only and may be removed in later versions of the software.

The second, token, uses JSON web token (JWT) and is the same mechanism that's used to authenticate with Docker Hub. It's a sophisticated approach to authentication that enables the registry to validate that a caller has authenticated with a third-party service without any back-end communication. The key detail to take away from this is that users don't authenticate with your registry directly. Using this mechanism requires that you deploy a separate authentication service.

There are a few open source JWT authentication services available but none that can be recommended for production use. Until the JWT ecosystem matures, the best course of action is to use the third authentication mechanism, htpasswd.

htpasswd is named for an open source program that ships with the Apache Web Server utilities. htpasswd is used to generate encoded username and password pairs where the password has been encrypted with the bcrypt algorithm. When you adopt the htpasswd authentication form, you should be aware that passwords are sent from the client to your registry unencrypted. This is called HTTP basic authentication. Because HTTP basic sends passwords over the network, it's critical that you use this authentication form in tandem with HTTPS.

There are two ways to add htpasswd authentication to your registry: at the reverse proxy layer and on the registry itself. In either case, you'll need to create a password file with htpasswd. If you don't have htpasswd installed, you can do so using Docker. Create an image from the following Dockerfile (named htpasswd.df) and build command:

```
FROM debian:jessie
LABEL source=dockerinaction
LABEL category=utility
RUN apt-get update && \
    apt-get install -y apache2-utils
ENTRYPOINT ["htpasswd"]
```

Build your image once you have the Dockerfile:

```
docker build -t htpasswd -f htpasswd.df .
```

With your new image available, you can create a new entry for a password file like so:

```
docker run -it --rm htpasswd -nB <USERNAME>
```

It's important to replace <USERNAME> with the username you want to create and use the -nB flags for htpasswd. Doing so will display the output in your terminal and use the bcrypt algorithm. The program will prompt you for your password twice and then generate the password file entry. Copy the result into a file named registry.password. The result should look something like this:

```
registryuser:$2y$05$mfQjXkprC94Tjk4IQz4vOOK6q5VxUhsxC6zajd35ys1O2J2x1aLbK
```

Once you have a password file, you can implement HTTP Basic authentication in NGINX by simply adding two lines to the configuration file presented in section 10.2.2. Create tls-authproxy.conf and add these lines:

```
# filename: tls-auth-proxy.conf
upstream docker-registry {
  server registry:5000;
}

server {
  listen 443 ssl;
  server_name localhost

  client_max_body_size 0;
  chunked_transfer_encoding on;

  # SSL
  ssl_certificate /etc/nginx/conf.d/localhost.crt;
  ssl_certificate_key /etc/nginx/conf.d/localhost.key;

  location /v2/ {
    auth_basic "registry.localhost";                           ◀── Authentication realm
    auth_basic_user_file /etc/nginx/conf.d/registry.password;  ◀── Password file

    proxy_pass                          http://docker-registry;
    proxy_set_header   Host             $http_host;
    proxy_set_header   X-Real-IP        $remote_addr;
    proxy_set_header   X-Forwarded-For  $proxy_add_x_forwarded_for;
    proxy_set_header   X-Forwarded-Proto $scheme;
    proxy_read_timeout                  900;
  }
}
```

Now create a new Dockerfile named tls-auth-proxy.df:

```
FROM nginx:latest
LABEL source=dockerinaction
LABEL category=infrastructure
COPY ["./tls-auth-proxy.conf", \
      "./localhost.crt", \
      "./localhost.key", \
      "./registry.password", \
      "/etc/nginx/conf.d/"]
```

With that change, you could use the rest of the instructions in section 10.2.2 to rebuild your registry to process HTTP basic authentication. Rather than repeat that work, it's more worthwhile to configure Distribution to use TLS and HTTP basic.

Adding TLS and basic authentication directly to your registry is useful if you want to tighten security on your personal registry. In production it's likely more suitable to terminate the TLS connection at your proxy layer.

The following configuration file (named tls-auth-registry.yml) adds TLS and HTTP basic authentication to an otherwise default Distribution container:

```
version: 0.1
log:
    level: debug
    fields:
        service: registry
        environment: development
storage:
    filesystem:
        rootdirectory: /var/lib/registry
    cache:
        layerinfo: inmemory
    maintenance:
        uploadpurging:
            enabled: false
http:
    addr: :5000
    secret: asecretforlocaldevelopment
    tls:
        certificate: /localhost.crt        TLS configuration
        key: /localhost.key
    debug:
        addr: localhost:5001
auth:
    htpasswd:
        realm: registry.localhost          Authentication configuration
        path: /registry.password
```

The annotated text shows both sections of the configuration that have been changed. The first is the http section. A subsection has been added named tls. The tls section has two properties, certificate and key. The values of these properties are paths to the certificate and key file that you generated in section 10.2.2. You'll need to either copy these files into the image or use volumes to mount them into the container at runtime. It's always a bad idea to copy key files into an image for anything other than testing purposes.

The second new section is auth. As you can see, the new htpasswd section uses two properties. The first, realm, simply defines the HTTP authentication realm. It's just a string. The second, path, is the location of the registry.password file that you created with htpasswd. Put all these things together with a quick Dockerfile (named tls-auth-registry.df):

```
# Filename: tls-auth-registry.df
FROM registry:2
LABEL source=dockerinaction
LABEL category=infrastructure
# Set the default argument to specify the config file to use
```

```
# Setting it early will enable layer caching if the
# tls-auth-registry.yml changes.
CMD ["/tls-auth-registry.yml"]
COPY ["./tls-auth-registry.yml", \
      "./localhost.crt", \
      "./localhost.key", \
      "./registry.password", \
      "/"]
```

Again, copying your key file into the image for production is a bad idea. Use volumes instead. The previous Dockerfile copies all your specialization material into the root directory for demonstration purposes. Build and launch the new secured registry with docker build and docker run:

```
docker build -t dockerinaction/secure_registry -f tls-auth-registry.df  .

docker run -d --name secure_registry \
    -p 5443:5000 --restart=always \
    dockerinaction/secure_registry
```

If you secure the registry itself with TLS, you may encounter problems when you install a reverse proxy. The reason is that application-level proxy software (like NGINX or Apache httpd) operates at the HTTP level. It needs to inspect request traffic in order to know how it needs to be routed or to route traffic from a specific client consistently to the same upstream host. Such a proxy would see encrypted traffic only if the TLS session was terminated by the registry. A functioning solution would either terminate the TLS session at the proxy layer (as you did earlier) or use a proxy (load-balancer) that operates at a lower network layer (like layer 4). For more information about network layers, look up information on the OSI model.

One example where your proxy would need to inspect the request content in order to route correctly is if you need to support multiple client versions. The Registry API changed with the release of Docker 1.6. If you want to support both Registry APIs, then you'll need to implement an API-aware proxy layer.

10.2.4 *Client compatibility*

The registry protocol changed dramatically between version 1 and version 2. Docker clients older than version 1.6 can't talk to version 2 registries. Distinguishing between version 1- and version 2-compatible clients and subsequently directing requests to compatible registry services are simple with our proxy in place.

For the sake of clarity, the examples in this section omit any HTTPS or authentication. But you're encouraged to combine the relevant features to build a proxy to suit your needs. Figure 10.5 shows the proxy and routing configuration that you'll build to support multiple client versions.

Like the previous proxies that you've built, this modification requires three steps:

- Create an NGINX configuration file (dual-client-proxy.conf).
- Create a brief Dockerfile (dual-client-proxy.df).
- Build the new image.

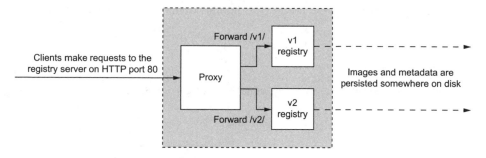

Figure 10.5   Routing clients based on requested Registry API version

Start by placing the new proxy configuration in a file named dual-client-proxy.conf and include the following:

```
upstream docker-registry-v2 {
  server registry2:5000;                          V2 registry upstream
}
upstream docker-registry-v1 {
  server registry1:5000;                          VI registry upstream
}

server {
  listen 80;
  server_name localhost;

  client_max_body_size 0;
  chunked_transfer_encoding on;

  location /v1/ {                          ◄─┐ VI URL prefix
    proxy_pass                               http://docker-registry-v1;
    proxy_set_header  Host                   $http_host;
    proxy_set_header  X-Real-IP              $remote_addr;
    proxy_set_header  X-Forwarded-For        $proxy_add_x_forwarded_for;
    proxy_set_header  X-Forwarded-Proto      $scheme;
    proxy_read_timeout                       900;
  }

  location /v2/ {                          ◄─┐ V2 URL prefix
    proxy_pass                               http://docker-registry-v2;
    proxy_set_header  Host                   $http_host;
    proxy_set_header  X-Real-IP              $remote_addr;
    proxy_set_header  X-Forwarded-For        $proxy_add_x_forwarded_for;
    proxy_set_header  X-Forwarded-Proto      $scheme;
    proxy_read_timeout                       900;
  }
}
```

VI upstream routing → (location /v1/)

V2 upstream routing → (location /v2/)

The only notable difference from the basic proxy configuration is the inclusion of a second upstream server and a second location specification for URLs starting with

/v1/. Next, create a new Dockerfile named dual-client-proxy.df and include the following directives:

```
FROM nginx:latest
LABEL source=dockerinaction
LABEL category=infrastructure
COPY ./dual-client-proxy.conf /etc/nginx/conf.d/default.conf
```

Last, create your new image:

```
docker build -t dual_client_proxy -f dual-client-proxy.df .
```

Before you can start a proxy that forwards traffic for both v1 and v2 Registry API requests, you'll need to have a v1 registry running. The following command will pull the 0.9.1 registry software and start it in a container:

```
docker run -d --name registry_v1 registry:0.9.1
```

With both versions of the registry running, you can finally create your dual-API support proxy. The following commands will create the proxy and link it to both registries and then test the v1 and v2 APIs:

```
docker run -d --name dual_client_proxy \
    -p 80:80 \
    --link personal_registry:registry2 \
    --link registry_v1:registry1 \
    dual_client_proxy

docker run --rm -u 1000:1000 \                    ◀─┐ Test v1 from host
    --net host \
    dockerinaction/curl -s http://localhost:80/v1/_ping

docker run --rm -u 1000:1000 \                    ◀─┐ Test v2 from host
    --net host \
    dockerinaction/curl -Is http://localhost:80/v2/
```

As time goes on, fewer and fewer clients will require v1 registry support. But it's always possible that another API change could happen in the future. Proxies are the best way to handle those situations.

10.2.5 *Before going to production*

Production configurations should typically differ from development or test configurations in a few specific ways. The most prominent difference is related to secret materials management, followed by log tuning, debug endpoints, and reliable storage.

Secrets such as private keys should never be committed to an image. It's easy to move or manipulate images in such a way that secrets can be revealed. Instead, any system that is serious about the security of secrets should only store secrets in read-protected memory or something more robust like a software vault or hardware security module.

The Distribution project makes use of a few different secrets:

- TLS private key
- SMTP username and password

- Redis secret
- Various remote storage account ID and key pairs
- Client state signature key

It's important that these not be committed to your production registry configuration or included with any image that you might create. Instead, consider injecting secret files by bind-mounting volumes that are on mounted tmpfs or RAMDisk devices and setting limited file permissions. Secrets that are sourced directly from the configuration file can be injected using environment variables.

Environment variables prefixed with REGISTRY_ will be used as overrides to the configuration loaded by the Distribution project. Configuration variables are fully qualified and underscore-delimited for indentation levels. For example, the client state secret in the configuration file at

```
http:
    secret: somedefaultsecret
```

can be overridden using an environment variable named REGISTRY_HTTP_SECRET. If you want to start a container running the Distribution project in production, you should inject that secret using the -e flag on the docker run command:

```
docker run -d -e REGISTRY_HTTP_SECRET=<MY_SECRET> registry:2
```

There are a growing number of centralized secret management and secret distribution projects. You should invest some time in selecting one for your production infrastructure.

In production a logging configuration that's set too sensitive can overwhelm disk or log-handling infrastructure. Dial down the log level by setting an environment variable. Set REGISTRY_LOG_LEVEL to error or warn:

```
docker run -d -e REGISTRY_LOG_LEVEL=error registry:2
```

The next production configuration difference is simple. Disable the debug endpoint. This can be accomplished with environment variable configuration overriding. Setting REGISTRY_HTTP_DEBUG to an empty string will ensure Distribution doesn't start a debug endpoint:

```
docker run -d -e REGISTRY_HTTP_DEBUG='' registry:2
```

When you deploy a registry to a production environment, you'll likely need to move storage off the local file system. The biggest issue with local file system storage is specialization. Every image stored in a registry that uses local storage specializes the computer where it's running. That specialization reduces the durability of the registry. If the hard drive storing the registry data crashes or that one machine becomes inoperable, then you may experience data loss or at best reduced availability.

Using local storage in production is appropriate when volatility is acceptable or for use cases involving reproducible images. Aside from those specific cases, you need data durability, and so you'll need a durable storage back end.

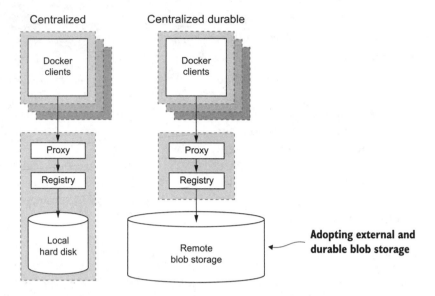

Figure 10.6   How to improve the durability of a centralized registry

10.3 *Durable blob storage*

Blob is short for *binary large object*. A registry deals in image layers (blobs) and meta-data. The term is relevant because there are several popular blob storage services and projects. To adopt durable blob storage, you'll need to make a change to your registry's configuration file and build a new image. Figure 10.6 shows how to grow from a centralized to a durable centralized registry.

The Distribution project currently supports popular blob storage back ends in addition to the local file system. The section of the configuration file that deals with storage is appropriately named `storage`. That mapping has four conflicting properties that define the storage back end. Only one of these properties should be present in a valid registry configuration:

- `filesystem`
- `azure`
- `s3`
- `rados`

The `filesystem` property is used by the default configuration and has only a single property, `rootdirectory`, that specifies the base directory to use for local storage. For example, the following is a sample from the default configuration:

```
storage:
    filesystem:
        rootdirectory: /var/lib/registry
```

The other storage properties configure the Distribution project for integration with various distributed blob storage services and are covered over the remainder of this section, starting with Azure.

10.3.1 *Hosted remote storage with Microsoft's Azure*

Azure is the name of Microsoft's cloud services product family. One service in that family is a blob storage service named Storage. If you have an Azure account, you can use the Storage service for your registry blob storage. You can learn more about the service on the website: http://azure.microsoft.com/services/storage/.

In order to adopt Azure for your blob storage, you need to use the azure property and set three subproperties: accountname, accountkey, and container. In this context, container refers to an Azure Storage container, not a Linux container.

A minimal Azure configuration file might be named azure-config.yml and include the following configuration:

```
# Filename: azure-config.yml
version: 0.1
log:
    level: debug
    fields:
        service: registry
        environment: development
storage:
    azure:                                    ◄──┐ Azure-specific fields
        accountname: <your account name>
        accountkey: <your base64 encoded account key>
        container: <your container>
        realm: core.windows.net
    cache:
        layerinfo: inmemory
    maintenance:
        uploadpurging:
            enabled: false
http:
    addr: :5000
    secret: asecretforlocaldevelopment
    debug:
        addr: localhost:5001
```

Replace the text in angle brackets with configuration for your account. The realm property should be set to the realm where you want to store your images. See the official Azure Storage documentation for details. realm is not a required property and will default to core.windows.net.

You can pack the new configuration into a layer over the original registry image with the following Dockerfile. You could name it azure-config.df:

```
# Filename: azure-config.df
FROM registry:2
LABEL source=dockerinaction
LABEL category=infrastructure
```

```
# Set the default argument to specify the config file to use
# Setting it early will enable layer caching if the
# azure-config.yml changes.
CMD ["/azure-config.yml"]
COPY ["./azure-config.yml","/azure-config.yml"]
```

And you can build it with the following docker build command:

```
docker build -t dockerinaction/azure-registry -f azure-config.df .
```

With an Azure Storage back end, you can build a durable registry that scales in terms of expense instead of technical complexity. That trade-off is one of the strong points of hosted remote blob storage. If you're interested in using a hosted solution, you might consider the more mature AWS Simple Storage Service.

10.3.2 Hosted remote storage with Amazon's Simple Storage Service

Simple Storage Service (S3) from AWS offers several features in addition to blob storage. You can configure blobs to be encrypted at rest, versioned, access audited, or made available through AWS's content delivery network (see section 10.4.2).

Use the s3 storage property to adopt S3 as your hosted remote blob store. There are four required subproperties: accesskey, secretkey, region, and bucket. These are required to authenticate your account and set the location where blob reads and writes will happen. Other subproperties specify how the Distribution project should use the blob store. These include encrypt, secure, v4auth, chunksize, and rootdirectory.

Setting the encrypt property to true will enable data at rest encryption for the data your registry saves to S3. This is a free feature that enhances the security of your service.

The secure property controls the use of HTTPS for communication with S3. The default is false and will result in the use of HTTP. If you're storing private image material, you should set this to true.

The v4auth property tells the registry to use version 4 of the AWS authentication protocol. In general this should be set to true but defaults to false.

Files greater than 5 GB must be split into smaller files and reassembled on the service side in S3. But chunked uploads are available to files smaller than 5 GB and should be considered for files greater than 100 MB. File chunks can be uploaded in parallel, and individual chunk upload failures can be retired individually. The Distribution project and its S3 client perform file chunking automatically, but the chunksize property sets the size beyond which files should be chunked. The minimum chunk size is 5 MB.

Finally, the rootdirectory property sets the directory within your S3 bucket where the registry data should be rooted. This is helpful if you want to run multiple registries from the same bucket:

```
# Filename: s3-config.yml
version: 0.1
```

```
log:
    level: debug
    fields:
        service: registry
        environment: development
storage:
    cache:
        layerinfo: inmemory
    s3:                                    ◄─┐ S3 configuration
        accesskey: <your awsaccesskey>
        secretkey: <your awssecretkey>
        region: <your bucket region>
        bucket: <your bucketname>
        encrypt: true
        secure: true
        v4auth: true
        chunksize: 5242880
        rootdirectory: /s3/object/name/prefix
    maintenance:
        uploadpurging:
            enabled: false
http:
    addr: :5000
    secret: asecretforlocaldevelopment
    debug:
        addr: localhost:5001
```

If you've created a configuration file named s3-config.yml and provided your account
access key, secret, bucket name, and region, you can pack the updated registry configuration into a new image just like you did for Azure with the following Dockerfile:

```
# Filename: s3-config.df
FROM registry:2
LABEL source=dockerinaction
LABEL category=infrastructure
# Set the default argument to specify the config file to use
# Setting it early will enable layer caching if the
# s3-config.yml changes.
CMD ["/s3-config.yml"]
COPY ["./s3-config.yml","/s3-config.yml"]
```

And you can build it with the following docker build command:

```
docker build -t dockerinaction/s3-registry -f s3-config.df .
```

Both S3 and Azure are offered under a use-based cost model. There's no up-front cost
to get started, and many smaller registries will be able to operate within the free tier of
either service.

   If you aren't interested in a hosted data service and don't hesitate in the face of
some technical complexity, then you might alternatively consider running a Ceph
storage cluster and the RADOS blob storage back end.

10.3.3 *Internal remote storage with RADOS (Ceph)*

Reliable Autonomic Distributed Object Store (RADOS) is provided by a software project named Ceph (http://ceph.com). Ceph is the software that you'd use to build your own Azure Storage or AWS S3-like distributed blob storage service. If you have a budget, time, and a bit of expertise, you can deploy your own Ceph cluster and save money over the long term. More than money, running your own blob storage puts you in control of your data.

If you decide to go that route, you can use the `rados` storage property to integrate with your own storage:

```
version: 0.1
log:
    level: debug
    fields:
        service: registry
        environment: development
storage:
    cache:
        layerinfo: inmemory
storage:
    rados:               ◀──┐  RADOS configuration
        poolname: radospool
        username: radosuser
        chunksize: 4194304
    maintenance:
        uploadpurging:
            enabled: false
http:
    addr: :5000
    secret: asecretforlocaldevelopment
    debug:
        addr: localhost:5001
```

The three subproperties are `poolname`, `username`, and `chunksize`. The `username` property should be self-explanatory, but `poolname` and `chunksize` are interesting.

Ceph stores blobs in pools. A *pool* is configured with certain redundancy, distribution, and behavior. The pool a blob is stored in will dictate how that blob is stored across your Ceph storage cluster. The `poolname` property tells Distribution which pool to use for blob storage.

Ceph chunks are similar to but not the same as S3 chunks. Chunks are important to Ceph's internal data representation. An overview of the Ceph architecture can be found here: http://ceph.com/docs/master/architecture/. The default chunk size is 4 MB, but if you need to override that value, you can do so with the `chunksize` property.

Adopting a distributed blob storage system is an important part of building a durable registry. If you intend on exposing your registry to the world, you will need enhancements for fast and scalable registries. The next section explains how to implement those enhancements.

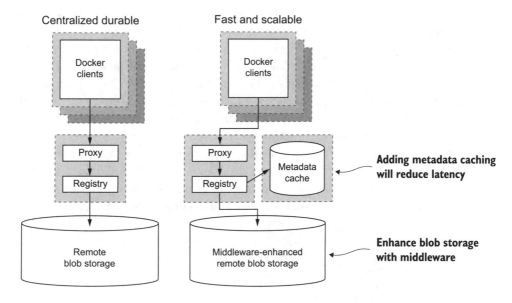

Figure 10.7　The fast and scalable architecture introduces a metadata cache and middleware.

10.4　*Scaling access and latency improvements*

With the reverse proxy and a durable storage back end in place, you should be able to scale your registry horizontally. But doing so introduces additional latency overhead. If you need to scale your registry to serve thousands of transactions per second, then you'll need to implement a caching strategy. You may even consider using a content delivery network like Amazon CloudFront.

As illustrated in figure 10.7, this section introduces two new components that will help you achieve low-latency response times.

Most readers won't buy additional machines for the sole purpose of running the exercises, so these examples will let you use separate containers instead of separate machines. If you're reading along while implementing your multi-machine registry and need information about linking software between hosts, consult chapter 5.

10.4.1　*Integrating a metadata cache*

When you need low-latency data retrieval, a cache is the first tool to reach for. The Distribution project can cache repository metadata using either an in-memory map or Redis. Redis (http://redis.io) is a popular, open source, key-value cache and data-structure server.

The in-memory map option is appropriate for smaller registries or development purposes, but using a dedicated caching project like Redis will help improve the reliability of your cache and reduce average latencies.

The Distribution configuration for metadata caching is set with the `cache` subproperty of the `storage` property. Cache has one subproperty named `blobdescriptor` with two potential values, `inmemory` and `redis`. If you're using `inmemory`, then setting that value is the only configuration required, but if you're using Redis, you need to provide additional connection pool configuration.

The top-level `redis` property has only one requisite subproperty, `addr`. The `addr` property specifies the location of the Redis server to use for the cache. The server can be running on the same computer or a different one, but if you use the localhost name here, it must be running in the same container or another container with a joined network. Using a known host alias gives you the flexibility to delegate that linkage to a runtime configuration. In the following configuration sample, the registry will attempt to connect to a Redis server at redis-host on port 6379:

```
# Filename: redis-config.yml
version: 0.1
log:
    level: debug
    fields:
        service: registry
        environment: development
http:
    addr: :5000
    secret: asecretforlocaldevelopment
    debug:
        addr: localhost:5001
storage:
    cache:                              ⟵┐ Cache configuration
        blobdescriptor: redis
    s3:
        accesskey: <your awsaccesskey>
        secretkey: <your awssecretkey>
        region: <your bucket region>
        bucket: <your bucketname>
        encrypt: true
        secure: true
        v4auth: true
        chunksize: 5242880
        rootdirectory: /s3/object/name/prefix
    maintenance:
        uploadpurging:
            enabled: false
redis:                                  ⟵┐ Redis-specific details
    addr: redis-host:6379
    password: asecret
    dialtimeout: 10ms
    readtimeout: 10ms
    writetimeout: 10ms
    pool:
        maxidle: 16
        maxactive: 64
        idletimeout: 300s
```

The `redis` configuration in this example sets several optional properties. The `password` property defines the password that will be passed to the Redis `AUTH` command on connection. The `dialtimeout`, `readtimeout`, and `writetimeout` properties specify timeout values for connecting to, reading from, or writing to the Redis server. The last property, `pool`, has three subproperties that define the attributes for the connection pool.

The minimum pool size is specified with the `maxidle` property. The maximum pool size is set with the `maxactive` property. Finally, the time from the last use of an active connection to the moment it's a candidate to be flipped into an idle state is specified with the `idletimeout` property. Any connections that are flipped to idle when the current number of idle connections has reached the maximum will be closed.

Use dummy values in place of secrets in order to produce environment-agnostic images. Properties like `password` should be overridden at runtime using environment variables.

The cache configuration will help reduce latency associated with serving registry metadata, but serving image blobs remains inefficient. By integrating with remote blob storage like S3, a registry becomes a streaming bottleneck during image transfer. Streaming connections are tricky because the connections tend to be long-lived relative to metadata queries. Things are made even trickier when long-lived connections are made through the same load-balancing infrastructure as short-lived connections.

You can try out this configuration yourself by building a registry with this configuration and linking in a Redis container:

```
docker run -d --name redis redis
docker build -t dockerinaction/redis-registry -f redis-config.df .
docker run -d --name redis-registry \
    --link redis:redis-host -p 5001:5000 \
    dockerinaction/redis-registry
```

The next section explains how you can use a content delivery network (CDN) and registry middleware to streamline blob downloads.

10.4.2 *Streamline blob transfer with storage middleware*

Middleware, in the Distribution project, acts like advice or decorators for a registry, repository, or storage driver. At present, Distribution ships with a single storage middleware. It integrates your registry and S3 storage back end with AWS CloudFront. CloudFront is a content delivery network.

CDNs are designed for geographically aware network access to files. This makes CloudFront a perfect solution to the remaining scale issue caused by adopting durable and distributed blob storage.

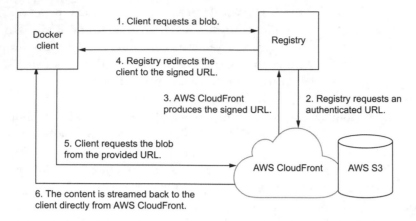

Figure 10.8   Offloading streaming blob traffic with AWS CloudFront storage middleware

Downloading a file is streamlined with the CloudFront middleware enabled and S3 in use for your storage back end. Figure 10.8 illustrates how data flows through the integrated configuration.

Rather than streaming blobs from S3 back to your registry and subsequently back to the requesting client, integration with CloudFront lets you redirect clients to authenticated CloudFront URLs directly. This eliminates network overhead associated with image download for your local network. It also offloads long-lived connections to the appropriately designed CloudFront service.

Enabling the CloudFront middleware is as simple as adding the appropriate configuration. The following sample is complete with S3, Redis, and CloudFront:

```
# Filename: scalable-config.conf
version: 0.1
log:
    level: debug
    fields:
        service: registry
        environment: development
http:
    addr: :5000
    secret: asecretforlocaldevelopment
    debug:
        addr: localhost:5001
storage:
    cache:
        blobdescriptor: redis
    s3:
        accesskey: <your awsaccesskey>
        secretkey: <your awssecretkey>
        region: <your bucket region>
        bucket: <your bucketname>
```

```
            encrypt: true
            secure: true
            v4auth: true
            chunksize: 5242880
            rootdirectory: /s3/object/name/prefix
      maintenance:
          uploadpurging:
                enabled: false
redis:
    addr: redis-host:6379
    password: asecret
    dialtimeout: 10ms
    readtimeout: 10ms
    writetimeout: 10ms
    pool:
        maxidle: 16
        maxactive: 64
        idletimeout: 300s                    ◄─┐  Middleware configuration
middleware:
    storage:
        - name: cloudfront
          options:
              baseurl: <https://my.cloudfronted.domain.com/>
              privatekey: </path/to/pem>
              keypairid: <cloudfrontkeypairid>
              duration: 3000
```

The `middleware` property and `storage` subproperty are a bit different from other configurations you've seen so far. The `storage` subproperty contains a list of named storage middleware, each with its own set of options specific to the middleware.

In this sample, you're using the middleware named `cloudfront` and setting its `baseurl`, `privatekey` path, `keypairid` name, and the `duration` over which the authenticated URLs are valid. Consult the CloudFront user documentation (http://aws.amazon.com/cloudfront) for the correct settings for your account.

Once you've added a configuration specific to your AWS account and CloudFront distribution, you can bundle the configuration with a Dockerfile and deploy any number of high-performance registry containers. With the proper hardware and configuration you could scale to thousands of image pulls or pushes per second.

All that activity generates useful data. A component like your registry should be integrated with the rest of your systems to react to events or centrally collect data. The Distribution project makes these integrations possible with notifications.

10.5 *Integrating through notifications*

Launching your own registry can help you build your own distribution infrastructure, but to do so you need to integrate it with other tools. Notifications are a simple webhook-style integration tool. When you provide an endpoint definition in the registry configuration file, the registry will make an HTTP request and upload a

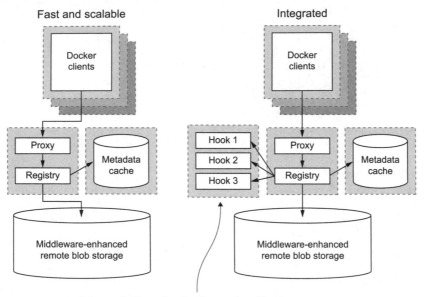

Adopt a dedicated cache fleet and notifications

Figure 10.9   Notifications, reporting, and a dedicated metadata cache

JSON-encoded event for each push or pull event on the registry. Figure 10.9 shows how notifications integrate your system architecture.

When Distribute is configured to send notifications, any valid push or pull event triggers the delivery of JSON documents describing the event to configured endpoints. This is the primary integration mechanism for the Distribute project.

Notifications can be used to collect usage metrics, trigger deployments, trigger image rebuilds, send email, or do anything else you can think of. You might use a notification integration to post messages to your IRC channel, regenerate user documentation, or trigger an indexing service to scan the repository. In this example, the last of the chapter, you'll integrate the Distribution project with the Elasticsearch project (https://github.com/elastic/elasticsearch) and a web interface to create a fully searchable database of registry events.

Elasticsearch is a scalable document index and database. It provides all the functionality required to run your own search engine. Calaca is a popular open source web interface for Elasticsearch. In this example, you'll run each of these in its own container, a small pump implemented with Node.js, and a Distribution registry configured to send notifications to the pump. Figure 10.10 shows the integration you will build in this example.

To build this system, you'll use the official Elasticsearch image from Docker Hub and two images provided for this example. All this material is open source, so if you're

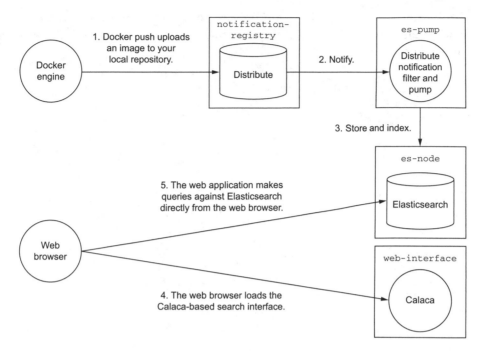

Figure 10.10 Integrating Distribute with Elasticsearch

interested in the mechanics at work, please inspect the repositories. Details of the integration and Distribution configuration will be covered here. Prepare for the example by pulling the required images from Docker Hub:

```
docker pull elasticsearch:1.6
docker pull dockerinaction/ch10_calaca
docker pull dockerinaction/ch10_pump
```

Briefly, the `dockerinaction/ch10_calaca` image contains a basic Calaca release that has been configured to use an Elasticsearch node running on localhost. The name is important in this case to comply with cross-origin resource sharing (CORS) rules. The `dockerinaction/ch10_pump` image contains a small Node.js service. The service listens for notifications and forwards notifications that contain pull or push actions on repository manifests. This represents a small subset of the types of notifications sent by the registry.

Every valid action on a registry results in a notification, including the following:

- Repository manifest uploads and downloads
- Blob metadata requests, uploads, and downloads

Notifications are delivered as JSON objects. Each notification contains a list of events. Each event contains properties that describe the event. The following stub shows the available properties:

```
{ "events": [{
  "id": "921a9db6-1703-4fe4-9dda-ea71ad0014f1",
  "timestamp": ...
  "action": "push",
  "target": {
    "mediaType": ...
    "length": ...
    "digest": ...
    "repository": ...
    "url": ...
  },
  "request": {
    "id": ...
    "addr": ...
    "host": ...
    "method": ...
    "useragent": ...
  },
  "actor": {},
  "source": {
    "addr": ...
    "instanceID": ...
  }
}]}
```

The service in `dockerinaction/ch10_pump` inspects each element in the event list and then forwards appropriate events to the Elasticsearch node.

Now that you have an idea of how the pump works, start up the Elasticsearch and pump containers:

```
docker run -d --name elasticsearch -p 9200:9200 \
    elasticsearch:1.6 -Des.http.cors.enabled=true

docker run -d --name es-pump -p 8000 \
    --link elasticsearch:esnode \
    dockerinaction/ch10_pump
```

Containers created from the Elasticsearch image can be customized without creating a whole image by passing environment variables to the Elasticsearch program itself. In the previous command, you enable CORS headers so that you can integrate this container with Calaca. With these components in place, any number of Distribution instances might send notifications to the `es-pump` container. All the relevant data will be stored in Elasticsearch.

Next, create a container to run the Calaca web interface:

```
docker run -d --name calaca -p 3000:3000 \
    dockerinaction/ch10_calaca
```

Notice that the container running Calaca doesn't need a link to the Elasticsearch container. Calaca uses a direct connection from your web browser to the Elasticsearch node. In this case, the provided image is configured to use the Elasticsearch node running on localhost. If you're running VirtualBox, the next step can be tricky.

VirtualBox users have not technically bound their `elasticsearch` container's port to localhost. Instead it's bound to the IP address of their VirtualBox virtual machine. You can solve this problem with the VBoxManage program included with VirtualBox. Use the program to create port-forwarding rules between your host network and the default virtual machine. You can create the rules you need with two commands:

```
VBoxManage controlvm "$(docker-machine active)" natpf1 \
    "tcp-port9200,tcp,,9200,,9200"
VBoxManage controlvm "$(docker-machine active)" natpf1 \
    "tcp-port3000,tcp,,3000,,3000"
```

These commands create two rules: forward port 9200 on localhost to port 9200 of the default virtual machine, and do the same for port 3000. Now VirtualBox users can interact with these ports in the same way that native Docker users can.

At this point, you should be ready to configure and launch a new registry. For this example, start from the default registry configuration and simply add a `notifications` section. Create a new file and copy in the following configuration:

```
# Filename: hooks-config.yml
version: 0.1
log:
    level: debug
    formatter: text
    fields:
        service: registry
        environment: staging
storage:
    filesystem:
        rootdirectory: /var/lib/registry
    maintenance:
        uploadpurging:
            enabled: true
            age: 168h
            interval: 24h
            dryrun: false
http:
    addr: 0.0.0.0:5000
    secret: asecretforlocaldevelopment
    debug:
        addr: localhost:5001          ◄──┘ Notification configuration
notifications:
    endpoints:
        - name: webhookmonitor
          disabled: false
          url: http://webhookmonitor:8000/
          timeout: 500
          threshold: 5
          backoff: 1000
```

The last section, notifications, specifies a list of endpoints to notify. The configuration of each endpoint includes a name, URL, attempt timeout, attempt threshold, and backoff time. You can also disable individual endpoints without removing the configuration by setting the disabled attribute to false. In this case, you've defined a single endpoint at webhookmonitor on port 8000. If you were deploying this to a distributed environment, webhookmonitor might be set to resolve to a different host. In this example, webhookmonitor is an alias for the container running the pump.

Once you've saved the configuration file, you can start the new registry container and see notifications in action. The following command will create a registry. It uses the base image, injects the configuration using a bind-mount volume, and sets the configuration file to use with the last argument. The command creates a link to the pump and assigns it to the webhookmonitor alias. Finally, it binds the registry to port 5555 on localhost (or the Boot2Docker IP address):

```
docker run -d --name ch10-hooks-registry -p 5555:5000 \
    --link es-pump:webhookmonitor \
    -v "$(pwd)"/hooks-config.yml:/hooks-config.yml \
    registry:2 /hooks-config.yml
```

With that last component running, you're ready to test the system. Test the Calaca container first. Open a web browser and navigate to http://localhost:3000/. When you do, you should see a simple web page titled calaca and a large search box. Nothing that you search for will have any results at this point because no notifications would have been sent to Elasticsearch yet. Push and pull images from your repository to see Elasticsearch and notifications at work.

Tag and push one of your existing images into your new registry to trigger notifications. You might consider using the dockerinaction/curl image that you created earlier in the chapter. It's a small image, and the test will be fast:

```
docker tag dockerinaction/curl localhost:5555/dockerinaction/curl
docker push localhost:5555/dockerinaction/curl
```

If you named the cURL image something different, you'll need to use that name instead of the one provided here. Otherwise, you should be ready to search. Head back to Calaca in your web browser and type curl in the search box.

As you finish typing curl, a single search result should appear. The results listed here correspond to registry events. Any valid push or pull will trigger the creation of one such event in Elasticsearch. Calaca has been configured to display the repository name, the event type, the timestamp on the event, and finally the raw notification. If you push the same repository again, then there should be two events. If you pull the repository instead, there will be a third event for the curl search term, but the type will be pull. Try it yourself:

```
docker pull localhost:5555/dockerinaction/curl
```

The raw notifications are included in the search results to help you get creative with searching the events. Elasticsearch indexes the whole document, so any field on the event is a potential search term. Try using this example to build interesting queries:

- Search for `pull` or `push` to see all pull or push events.
- Search for a particular repository prefix to get a list of all events for that prefix.
- Track activity on specific image digests.
- Discover clients by requesting an IP address.
- Discover all repositories accessed by a client.

This long example should reinforce the potential of a Distribution-based registry as a key component in your release or deployment workflow. The example should also serve as a reminder of how Docker can reduce the barrier to working with any containerized technology.

The most complex part of setting up this example was creating containers, linking containers, and injecting configuration with volumes. In chapter 11 you'll learn how to set up and iterate on this example using a simple YAML file and a single command.

10.6 *Summary*

This chapter dives deep into building Docker registries from the Distribution project. This information is important both for readers who intend to deploy their own registries and for readers who want to develop a deeper understanding of the primary image distribution channel. The specific material covered is summarized in the following points:

- A Docker registry is defined by the API it exposes. The Distribution project is an open source implementation of the Registry API v2.
- Running your own registry is as simple as starting a container from the `registry:2` image.
- The Distribution project is configured with a YAML file.
- Implementing a centralized registry with several clients typically requires implementing a reverse proxy, adopting TLS, and adding an authentication mechanism.
- Authentication can be offloaded to a reverse proxy or implemented by the registry itself.
- Although other authentication mechanisms are available, HTTP basic authentication is the simplest to configure and the most popular.
- Reverse proxy layers can help ease Registry API changes for mixed client versions.
- Inject secrets in production configurations with bind-mount volumes and environment variable configuration overrides. Do not commit secrets to images.
- Centralized registries should consider adopting remote blob storage like Azure, S3, or Ceph.

- Distribution can be configured to scale by creating a metadata cache (Redis-based) or adopting the Amazon Web Services CloudFront storage middleware.
- It's simple to integrate Distribution with the rest of your deployment, distribution, and data infrastructure using notifications.
- Notifications push event data to configured endpoints in JSON form.

Part 3

Multi-Container and Multi-Host Environments

If part 1 is focused on the isolation provided by containers, this part is focused on their composition. Most valuable systems are composed of two or more components. Simple management of multiple components is more important than ever due to the rise of large-scale server software, service-oriented-architectures, microservices, and now the Internet-of-Things. In building these systems, we've adopted tools like cluster computing, orchestration, and service discovery. These are difficult and nuanced problems in themselves. This final part of *Docker in Action* will introduce three other Docker tools and demonstrate how to use Docker in the wild.

Declarative environments with Docker Compose

11

This chapter covers

- Using Docker Compose
- Manipulating environments and iterating on projects
- Scaling services and cleaning up
- Building declarative environments

Have you ever joined a team with an existing project and struggled to get your development environment set up or IDE configured? If someone asked you to provision a test environment for their project, could you enumerate all the questions you'd need to ask to get the job done? Can you imagine how painful it is for development teams and system administrators to resynchronize when environments change? All of these are common and high-effort tasks. They can be time-intensive while adding little value to a project. In the worst case, they give rise to policies or procedures that limit developer flexibility, slow the iteration cycle, and bring paths of least resistance to the forefront of technical decision making.

This chapter introduces you to Docker Compose (also called Compose) and how you can use it to solve these common problems.

11.1   *Docker Compose: up and running on day one*

Compose is a tool for defining, launching, and managing services, where a *service* is defined as one or more replicas of a Docker container. Services and systems of services are defined in YAML files (http://yaml.org) and managed with the command-line program docker-compose. With Compose you can use simple commands to accomplish these tasks:

- Build Docker images
- Launch containerized applications as services
- Launch full systems of services
- Manage the state of individual services in a system
- Scale services up or down
- View logs for the collection of containers making a service

Compose lets you stop focusing on individual containers and instead describe full environments and service component interactions. A Compose file might describe four or five unique services that are interrelated but should maintain isolation and may scale independently. This level of interaction covers most of the everyday use cases for system management. For that reason, most interactions with Docker will be through Compose.

By this point you've almost certainly installed Docker, but you may not have installed Compose. You can find up-to-date installation instructions for your environment at https://docs.docker.com/compose/install/. Official support for Windows has not been implemented at the time of this writing. But many users have successfully installed Compose on Windows through pip (a Python package manager). Check the official site for up-to-date information. You may be pleasantly surprised to find that Compose is a single binary file and that installation instructions are quite simple. Take the time to install Compose now.

The best way to develop an appreciation for any tool is to use it. The rest of this section will get you started with a few situational examples.

11.1.1   *Onboarding with a simple development environment*

Suppose you've started a new job as a software developer with a forward-looking team that owns a mature project. If you've been in a similar situation before, you may anticipate that you're going to spend a few days installing and configuring your IDE and getting an operational development environment running on your workstation. But on your first day at this job, your peers give you three simple instructions to get started:

1 Install Docker.
2 Install Docker Compose.
3 Install and use Git to clone the development environment.

Rather than ask you to clone a development environment here, I'll have you create a new directory named wp-example and copy the following docker-compose.yml file into that directory:

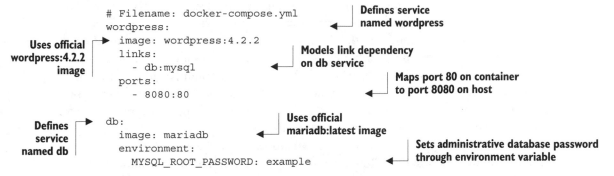

As you may be able to tell from examining the file, you're going to launch a Word-Press service and an independent database. This is an iteration of a basic example from chapter 2. Change to the directory where you created the docker-compose.yml file and start it all up with the following command:

```
docker-compose up
```

This should result in output similar to the following:

```
Creating wpexample_db_1...
Creating wpexample_wordpress_1...
...
```

You should be able to open http://localhost:8080/ (or replace "localhost" with your virtual machine's IP address) in a web browser and discover a fresh WordPress installation. This example is fairly simple but does describe a multi-service architecture. Imagine a typical three- or four-tier web application that consists of a web server, application code, a database, and maybe a cache. Launching a local copy of such an environment might typically take a few days—longer if the person doing the work is less familiar with some of the components. With Compose, it's as simple as acquiring the docker-compose.yml file and running `docker-compose up`.

When you've finished having fun with your WordPress instance, you should clean up. You can shut down the whole environment by pressing Ctrl-C (or Control-C). Before you remove all the containers that were created, take a moment to list them with both the `docker` and `docker-compose` commands:

```
docker ps
docker-compose ps
```

Using `docker` displays a list of two (or more) containers in the standard fashion. But listing the containers with `docker-compose` includes only the list of containers that are defined by the docker-compose.yml in the current directory. This form is more refined and succinct. Filtering the list in this way also helps you focus on the containers that make up the environment you're currently working on. Before moving on, take the time to clean up your environment.

Compose has an rm command that's very similar to the docker rm command. The difference is that docker-compose rm will remove all services or a specific service defined by the environment. Another minor difference is that the -f option doesn't force the removal of running containers. Instead, it suppresses a verification stage.

So, the first step in cleaning up is to stop the environment. You can use either docker-compose stop or docker-compose kill for this purpose. Using stop is preferred to kill for reasons explained in part 1. Like other Compose commands, these can be passed a service name to target for shutdown.

Once you've stopped the services, clean up with the docker-compose rm command. Remember, if you omit the -v option, volumes may become orphaned:

```
docker-compose rm -v
```

Compose will display a list of the containers that are going to be removed and prompt you for verification. Press the Y key to proceed. With the removal of these containers, you're ready to learn how Compose manages state and tips for avoiding orphan services while iterating.

This WordPress sample is trivial. Next, you'll see how you might use Compose to model a much more complicated environment.

11.1.2 A complicated architecture: distribution and Elasticsearch integration

At the end of chapter 10, you create a much more complicated example. You launch four related components that together provide a Docker registry that's configured to pump event data into an Elasticsearch instance and provide a web interface for searching those events. See figure 11.1.

Setting up the example required image builds and careful accounting while linking containers together. You can quickly re-create the example by cloning an existing environment from version control and launching it with Compose:

```
git clone https://github.com/dockerinaction/ch11_notifications.git
cd ch11_notifications
docker-compose up -d
```

When you run the last command, Docker will spring to life building various images and starting containers. It differs from the first example in that you use the -d option. This option launches the containers in detached mode. It operates exactly like the -d option on the docker run command. When the containers are detached, the log output of each of the containers will not be streamed to your terminal.

If you need to access that data, you could use the docker logs command for a specific container, but that does not scale well if you're running several containers. Instead, use the docker-compose logs command to get the aggregated log stream for

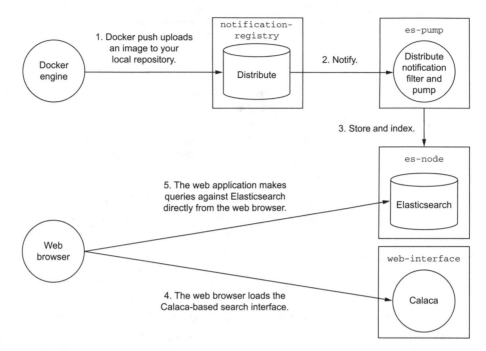

Figure 11.1 The data flow through the four containers that make up the notification registry example

all the containers or some subset of the services managed by Compose. For example, if you want to see all the logs for all the services, run this:

```
docker-compose logs
```

This command will automatically follow the logs, so when you've finished, press Ctrl-C or Control-C to quit. If you want to see only one or more services, then name those services:

```
docker-compose logs pump elasticsearch
```

In this example, you launched the complete environment with a single command and viewed the output with a single command. Being able to operate at such a high level is nice, but the more powerful fact is that you're also in possession of the various sources and can iterate locally with the same ease.

Suppose you have another service that you'd like to bind on port 3000. This would conflict with the calaca service in this example. Making the change is as simple as changing ch11_notifications/docker-compose.yml and running docker-compose up again. Take a look at the file:

```
registry:
  build: ./registry
  ports:
```

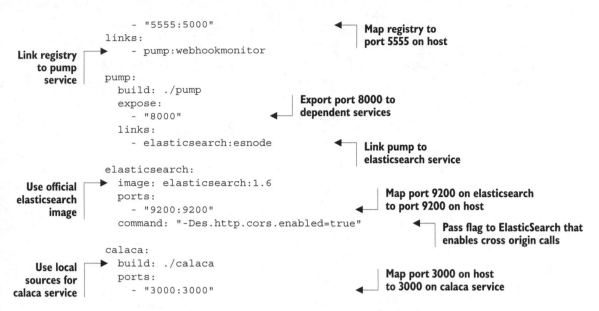

Change the last line where it reads 3000:3000 to 3001:3000 and save the file. With the change made, you can rebuild the environment by simply running docker-compose up -d again. When you do, it will stop the currently running containers, remove those containers, create new containers, and reattach any volumes that may have been mounted on the previous generation of the environment. When possible, Compose will limit the scope of restarted containers to those that have been changed.

If the sources for your services change, you can rebuild one or all of your services with a single command. To rebuild all the services in your environment, run the following:

```
docker-compose build
```

If you only need to rebuild one or some subset of your services, then simply name the service. This command will rebuild both the calaca and pump services:

```
docker-compose build calaca pump
```

At this point, stop and remove the containers you created for these services:

```
docker-compose rm -vf
```

By working with these examples, you've touched on the bulk of the development workflow. There are a few surprises: Docker Compose lets the person or people who define the environment worry about the details of working with Docker and frees users or developers to focus on the contained applications.

11.2 *Iterating within an environment*

Learning how Compose fits into your workflow requires a rich example. This section uses an environment similar to one you might find in a real API product. You'll work

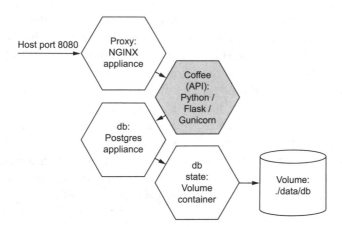

Figure 11.2 Services and service dependencies of the example environment in this chapter

through scenarios and manage the full life cycle for many services. One scenario will guide you through scaling independent services, and another will teach you about state management. Try not to focus too much on how the environment is implemented. The next section covers that.

The environment you're onboarding with in this section is an API for working with coffee shop metadata. It's the "brain child of a hot new startup catering to local entrepreneurs and freelancers." At least it is for the purpose of the example. The environment structure is illustrated in figure 11.2.

Download this example from the GitHub repository:

```
git clone https://github.com/dockerinaction/ch11_coffee_api.git
```

When you run this command, Git will download the most recent copy of the example and place it in a new directory named ch11_coffee_api under your current directory. When you're ready, change into that directory to start working with the environment.

11.2.1 Build, start, and rebuild services

With the sources and environment description copied from version control, start the development workflow by building any artifacts that are declared in the environment. You can do that with the following command:

```
docker-compose build
```

The output from the `build` command will include several lines indicating that specific services have been skipped because they use an image. This environment is made up of four components. Of those, only one requires a build step: the Coffee API. You should see from the output that when Compose built this service, it triggered a Dockerfile build and created an image. The build step runs a `docker build` command for the referenced services.

The Coffee API's source and Dockerfile are contained in the coffee folder. It's a simple Flask-based Python application that listens on port 3000. The other services in the environment are out-of-the-box components sourced from images on Docker Hub.

With the environment built, check out the resulting images that have been loaded into Docker. Run `docker images` and look for an image named ch11coffeeapi_coffee. Compose uses labels and prefixed names to identify images and containers that were created for a given environment. In this case the image produced for the `coffee` service is prefixed with ch11coffeeapi_ because that's the derived name for the environment. The name comes from the directory where the docker-compose.yml file is located.

You've built a local artifact for the Coffee API, but the environment may reference images that aren't present on your system. You can pull all those with a single Compose command:

```
docker-compose pull
```

This command will pull the most recent images for the tags referenced in the environment. At this point, all the required artifacts should be available on your machine. Now you can start services. Start with the `db` service and pay special attention to the logs:

```
docker-compose up -d db
```

Notice that before Compose started the `db` service, it started the `dbstate` service. This happens because Compose is aware of all the defined services in the environment, and the `db` service has a dependency on the `dbstate` service. When Compose starts any particular service, it will start all the services in the dependency change for that service. This means that as you iterate, and you only need to start or restart a portion of your environment, Compose will ensure that it comes up with all dependencies attached.

Now that you've seen that Compose is aware of service dependencies, start up the whole environment:

```
docker-compose up
```

When you use an unqualified `docker-compose up` command, Compose will create or re-create every service in the environment and start them all. If Compose detects any services that haven't been built or services that use missing images, it will trigger a build or fetch the appropriate image (just like `docker run`). In this case, you may have noticed that this command re-created the `db` service even though it was already running. This is done to ensure that everything has been brought up in a functioning state. But if you know that the dependencies of a particular service are operating correctly, you can start or restart a service without its dependencies. To do so, include the `--no-dep` flag.

Suppose, for example, that you made a minor adjustment to the configuration for the proxy service (contained in `docker-compose.yml`) and wanted to restart the proxy only. You might simply run the following:

```
docker-compose up --no-dep -d proxy
```

This command will stop any proxy containers that might be running, remove those containers, and then create and start a new container for the proxy service. Every other service in the system will remain unaffected. If you had omitted the `--no-dep` flag, then every service would have been re-created and restarted because every service in this environment is either a direct or transitive dependency of proxy.

The `--no-dep` flag can come in handy when you're starting systems where components have long-running startup procedures and you're experiencing race conditions. In those cases, you might start those first to let them initialize before starting the rest of the services.

With the environment running, you can try experimenting with and iterating on the project. Load up http://localhost:8080/api/coffeeshops (or use your virtual machine IP address) in a web browser. If everything is working properly, you should see a JSON document that looks something like this:

```
{
  "coffeeshops": []
}
```

This endpoint lists all coffee shops in the system. You can see that the list is empty. Next, add some content to become a bit more familiar with the API you're working on. Use the following cURL command to add content to your database:

```
curl -H "Content-Type: application/json" \
    -X POST \
    -d '{"name":"Albina Press", "address": " 5012 Southeast Hawthorne
        Boulevard, Portland, OR", "zipcode": 97215, "price": 2,
        "max_seats": 40, "power": true, "wifi": true}' \
    http://localhost:8080/api/coffeeshops/
```

You may need to substitute your virtual machine IP address for "localhost." The new coffee shop should be in your database now. You can test by reloading /api/coffeeshops/ in your browser. The result should look like the following response:

```
{
  "coffeeshops": [
    {
      "address": " 5012 Southeast Hawthorne Boulevard, Portland, OR",
      "id": 35,
      "max_seats": 40,
      "name": "Albina Press",
      "power": true,
      "price": 2,
      "wifi": true,
      "zipcode": 97215
    }
  ]
}
```

Now, as is common in the development life cycle, you should add a feature to the Coffee API. The current implementation only lets you create and list coffee shops. It would be nice to add a basic ping handler for health checks from a load balancer. Open http://localhost:8080/api/ping (or use your virtual machine IP address) in a web browser to see how the current application responds.

You're going to add a handler for this path and have the application return the host name where the API is running. Open ./coffee/api/api.py in your favorite editor and add the following code to the end of the file:

```
@api.route('/ping')
def ping():
    return os.getenv('HOSTNAME')
```

If you're having problems with the next step in the example, or if you're not in the mood to edit files, you can check out a feature branch on the repository where the changes have already been made:

```
git checkout feature-ping
```

Once you've made the change and saved the file (or checked out the updated branch), rebuild and re-create the service with the following commands:

```
docker-compose build coffee
docker-compose up -d
```

The first command will run a `docker build` command for the Coffee API again and generate an updated image. The second command will re-create the environment. There's no need to worry about the coffee shop data you created. The managed volume that was created to store the database will be detached and reattached seamlessly to the new database container. When the command is finished, refresh the web page that you loaded for /api/ping earlier. It should display an ID of a familiar style. This is the container ID that's running the Coffee API. Remember, Docker injects the container ID into the `HOSTNAME` environment variable.

In this section you cloned a mature project and were able to start iterating on its functionality with a minimal learning curve. Next you'll scale, stop, and tear down services.

11.2.2 *Scale and remove services*

One of the most impressive and useful features of Compose is the ability to scale a service up and down. When you do, Compose creates more replicas of the containers providing the service. Fantastically, these replicas are automatically cleaned up when you scale down. But as you might expect, containers that are running when you stop an environment will remain until the environment is rebuilt or cleaned up. In this section you'll learn how to scale up, scale down, and clean up your services.

Continuing with the Coffee API example, you should have the environment running. You can check with the `docker-compose  ps` command introduced earlier. Remember, Compose commands should be executed from the directory where your docker-compose.yml file is located. If the environment isn't running (proxy, coffee, and db services running), then bring it up with `docker-compose up -d`.

Suppose you were managing a test or production environment and needed to increase the parallelism of the `coffee` service. To do so, you'd only need to point your machine at your target environment (as you'll see in chapter 12) and run a single command. In the parameters of this example, you're working with your development environment. Before scaling up, get a list of the containers providing the `coffee` service:

```
docker-compose ps coffee
```

The output should look something like the following:

```
       Name              Command         State          Ports
------------------------------------------------------------------------
ch11coffeeapi_coffee_1   ./entrypoint.sh    Up    0.0.0.0:32807->3000/tcp
```

Notice the far-right column, which details the host-to-container port mapping for the single container running the service. You can access the Coffee API served by this container directly (without going through the proxy) by using this public port (in this case, 32807). The port number will be different on your computer. If you load the ping handler for this container, you'll see the container ID running the service. Now that you've established a baseline for your system, scale up the `coffee` service with the following command:

```
docker-compose scale coffee=5
```

The command will log each container that it creates. Use the `docker-compose ps` command again to see all the containers running the `coffee` service:

```
       Name              Command         State          Ports
------------------------------------------------------------------------
ch11coffeeapi_coffee_1   ./entrypoint.sh    Up    0.0.0.0:32807->3000/tcp
ch11coffeeapi_coffee_2   ./entrypoint.sh    Up    0.0.0.0:32808->3000/tcp
ch11coffeeapi_coffee_3   ./entrypoint.sh    Up    0.0.0.0:32809->3000/tcp
ch11coffeeapi_coffee_4   ./entrypoint.sh    Up    0.0.0.0:32810->3000/tcp
ch11coffeeapi_coffee_5   ./entrypoint.sh    Up    0.0.0.0:32811->3000/tcp
```

As you can see, there are now five containers running the Coffee API. These are all identical with the exception of their container IDs and names. These containers even use identical host port mappings. The reason this example works is that the Coffee API's internal port 3000 has been mapped to the host's ephemeral port (port 0). When you bind to port 0, the OS will select an available port in a predefined range. If instead it were always bound to port 3000 on the host, then only one container could be running at a time.

Test the ping handler on a few different containers (using the dedicated port for the container) before moving on. This example project is used throughout the remainder of the book. At this point, however, there's not much else to do but scale back down to a single instance. Issue a similar command to scale down:

```
docker-compose scale coffee=1
```
◄─┐ **Note the 1 here**

The logs from the command indicate which instances are being stopped and removed. Use the `docker-compose ps` command again to verify the state of your environment:

```
        Name                    Command         State            Ports
------------------------------------------------------------------------
ch11coffeeapi_coffee_1      ./entrypoint.sh      Up       0.0.0.0:32807->3000/tcp
```

Before moving on to learning about persistent state, clean up the environment so you can start fresh with `docker-compose rm`.

11.2.3 *Iteration and persistent state*

You've already learned the basics of environment state management with Compose. At the end of the last section you stopped and removed all the services and any managed volumes. Before that you also used Compose to re-create the environment, effectively removing and rebuilding all the containers. This section is focused on the nuances of the workflow and edge cases that can have some undesired effects.

First, a note about managed volumes. Volumes are a major concern of state management. Fortunately, Compose makes working with managed volumes trivial in iterative environments (see figure 11.3). When a service is rebuilt, the attached managed volumes are not removed. Instead they are reattached to the replacing containers for that service. This means that you're free to iterate without losing your data. Managed volumes are finally cleaned up when the last container is removed using `docker-compose rm` and the -v flag.

The bigger issue with state management and Compose is environment state. In highly iterative environments you'll be changing several things, including the environment configuration. Certain types of changes can create problems.

For example, if you rename or remove a service definition in your docker-compose.yml, then you lose the ability to manage it with Compose. Tying this back to the Coffee API example, the `coffee` service was named `api` during development. The environment was in a constant state of flux, and at some point when the `api` service was running, the service was renamed to `coffee`. When that happened, Compose was

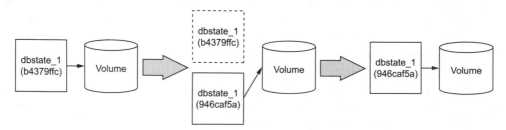

Figure 11.3   A volume container will have the same managed volume reattached after being re-created.

no longer aware of the `api` service. Rebuilds and relaunches worked only on the new `coffee` service, and the `api` service was orphaned.

You can discover this state when you use `docker ps` to list the running containers and notice that containers for old versions of the service are running when none should be. Recovery is simple enough. You can either use `docker` commands to directly clean up the environment or add the orphan service definition back to the docker-compose.yml and clean up with Compose.

11.2.4 Linking problems and the network

The last thing to note about using Compose to manage systems of services is remembering the impact of container-linking limitations.

In the Coffee API sample project, the proxy service has a link dependency on the `coffee` service. Remember that Docker builds container links by creating firewall rules and injecting service discovery information into the dependent container's environment variables and /etc/hosts file.

In highly iterative environments, a user may be tempted to relaunch only a specific service. That can cause problems if another service is dependent on it. For example, if you were to bring up the Coffee API environment and then selectively relaunch the `coffee` service, the `proxy` service would no longer be able to reach its upstream dependency. When containers are re-created or restarted, they come back with different IP addresses. That change makes the information that was injected into the `proxy` service stale.

It may seem burdensome at times, but the best way to deal with this issue in environments without dynamic service discovery is to relaunch whole environments, at a minimum targeting services that don't act as upstream dependencies. This is not an issue in robust systems that use a dynamic service discovery mechanism or overlay network. Multi-host networking is briefly discussed in chapter 12.

So far, you've used Compose in the context of an existing project. When starting from scratch, you have a few more things to consider.

11.3 Starting a new project: Compose YAML in three samples

Defining an environment is no trivial task, requiring insight and forethought. As project requirements, traffic shape, technology, financial constraints, and local expertise change, so will the environment for your project. For that reason, maintaining clear separation of concerns between the environment and your project is critical. Failing to do so often means that iterating on your environment requires iterating on the code that runs there. This section demonstrates how the features of the Compose YAML can help you build the environments you need.

The remainder of this section will examine portions of the docker-compose.yml file included with the Coffee API sample. Relevant excerpts are included in the text.

11.3.1 *Prelaunch builds, the environment, metadata, and networking*

Begin by examining the coffee service. This service uses a Compose managed build, environment variable injection, linked dependencies, and a special networking configuration. The service definition for coffee follows:

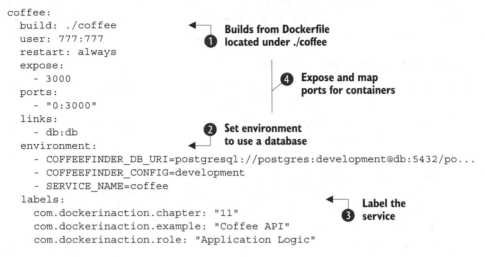

```
coffee:
  build: ./coffee          ◄──┐   Builds from Dockerfile
  user: 777:777              ❶   located under ./coffee
  restart: always
  expose:
    - 3000                         ❹ Expose and map
  ports:                              ports for containers
    - "0:3000"
  links:
    - db:db               ❷ Set environment
  environment:              to use a database
    - COFFEEFINDER_DB_URI=postgresql://postgres:development@db:5432/po...
    - COFFEEFINDER_CONFIG=development
    - SERVICE_NAME=coffee
  labels:                          ◄──┐  Label the
    com.dockerinaction.chapter: "11"  ❸  service
    com.dockerinaction.example: "Coffee API"
    com.dockerinaction.role: "Application Logic"
```

When you have an environment that's closely tied to specific image sources, you might want to automate the build phase of those services with Compose. In the Coffee API sample project this is done for the coffee service. But the use case extends beyond typical development environment needs.

If your environments use data-packed volume containers to inject environment configuration, you might consider using a Compose managed build phase for each environment. Whatever the reason, these are available with a simple YAML key and structure. See ❶ in the preceding Compose file.

The value of the build key is the directory location of the Dockerfile to use for a build. You can use relative paths from the location of the YAML file. You can also provide an alternative Dockerfile name using the dockerfile key.

The Python-based application requires a few environment variables to be set so that it can integrate with a database. Environment variables can be set for a service with the environment key and a nested list or dictionary of key-value pairs. In ❷ the list form is used.

Alternatively you can provide one or many files containing environment variable definitions with the env_file key. Similar to environment variables, container metadata can be set with a nested list or dictionary for the labels key. The dictionary form is used at ❸.

Using detailed metadata can make working with your images and containers much easier, but remains an optional practice. Compose will use labels to store metadata for service accounting.

Last, ❹ shows where this service customizes networking by exposing a port, binding to a host port, and declaring a linked dependency.

The expose key accepts a list of container ports that should be exposed by firewall rules. The ports key accepts a list of strings that describe port mappings in the same format accepted by the -p option on the docker run command. The links command accepts a list of link definitions in the format accepted by the docker run --link flag. Working with these options should be familiar after reading chapter 5.

11.3.2 Known artifacts and bind-mount volumes

Two critical components in the Coffee API sample are provided by images downloaded from Docker Hub. These are the proxy service, which uses an official NGINX repository, and the db service, which uses the official Postgres repository. Official repositories are reasonably trustworthy, but it's a best practice to pull and inspect third-party images before deploying them in sensitive environments. Once you've established trust in an image, you should use content-addressable images to ensure no untrusted artifacts are deployed.

Services can be started from any image with the image key. Both the proxy and db services are image-based and use content-addressable images:

```
db:
  image: postgres@sha256:66ba100bc635be17...          ◄── Use content-addressable images
  volumes_from:                                             for trusted Postgres version
    - dbstate
  environment:
    - PGDATA=/var/lib/postgresql/data/pgdata
    - POSTGRES_PASSWORD=development
  labels:
    com.dockerinaction.chapter: "11"
    com.dockerinaction.example: "Coffee API"
    com.dockerinaction.role: "Database"
```

Use a data container pattern ← points to `volumes_from:`

```
proxy:
  image: nginx@sha256:a2b8bef333864317...          ◄── Use content-addressable image
  restart: always                                        for trusted NGINX version
  volumes:
    - ./proxy/app.conf:/etc/nginx/conf.d/app.conf
  ports:
    - "8080:8080"
  links:
    - coffee
  labels:
    com.dockerinaction.chapter: "11"
    com.dockerinaction.example: "Coffee API"
    com.dockerinaction.role: "Load Balancer"
```

Inject configuration via volume ← points to `volumes:`

The Coffee API project uses both a database and load balancer with only minimal configuration. The configuration that's provided comes in the form of volumes.

The proxy uses a volume to bind-mount a local configuration file into the NGINX dynamic configuration location. This is a simple way to inject configuration without the trouble of building completely new images.

The db service uses the `volumes_from` key to list services that define required volumes. In this case db declares a dependency on the `dbstate` service, a volume container service.

In general, the YAML keys are closely related to features exposed on the `docker run` command. You can find a full reference at https://docs.docker.com/compose/yml/.

11.3.3   *Volume containers and extended services*

Occasionally you'll encounter a common service archetype. Examples might include a NodeJS service, Java service, NGINX-based load balancer, or a volume container. In these cases, it may be appropriate to manifest those archetypes as parent services and extend and specialize those for particular instances.

The Coffee API sample project defines a volume container archetype named `data`. The archetype is a service like any other. In this case it specifies an image to start from, a command to run, a UID to run as, and label metadata:

```
data:
  image: gliderlabs/alpine
  command: echo Data Container
  user: 999:999
  labels:
    com.dockerinaction.chapter: "11"
    com.dockerinaction.example: "Coffee API"
    com.dockerinaction.role: "Volume Container"
```

Alone, the service does nothing except define sensible defaults for a volume container. Note that it doesn't define any volumes. That specialization is left to each volume container that extends the archetype:

```
dbstate:
  extends:
    file: docker-compose.yml        Reference to parent
    service: data                   service in another file
  volumes:
    - /var/lib/postgresql/data/pgdata
```

The `dbstate` service defined a volume container that extends the `data` service. Service extensions must specify both the file and service name being extended. The relevant keys are `extends` and nested `file` and `service`. Service extensions work in a similar fashion to Dockerfile builds. First the archetype container is built and then it is committed. The child is a new container built from the freshly generated layer. Just like a Dockerfile build, these child containers inherit all the parent's attributes including metadata.

The `dbstate` service defines the managed volume mounted at /var/lib/postgresql/data/pgdata with the `volumes` key. The `volumes` key accepts a list of volume specifications allowed by the `docker run -v` flag. See chapter 4 for information about volume types, volume containers, and volume nuances.

Docker Compose is a critical tool for anyone who has made Docker a core component of their infrastructure. With it, you'll be able to reduce iteration time, version control environments, and orchestrate ad hoc service interactions with declarative documents. Chapter 12 builds on Docker Compose use cases and introduces Docker Machine to help with forensic and automated testing.

11.4 Summary

This chapter focuses on an auxiliary Docker client named Docker Compose. Docker Compose provides features that relieve much of the tedium associated with command-line management of containers. The chapter covers the following:

- Docker Compose is a tool for defining, launching, and managing services, where a service is defined as one or more replicas of a Docker container.
- Compose uses environment definitions that are provided in YAML configuration files.
- Using the `docker-compose` command-line program, you can build images, launch and manage services, scale services, and view logs on any host running a Docker daemon.
- Compose commands for managing environments and iterating on projects are similar to `docker` command-line commands. Building, starting, stopping, removing, and listing services all have equivalent container-focused counterparts.
- With Docker Compose you can scale the number of containers running a service up and down with a single command.
- Declaring environment configuration with YAML enables environment versioning, sharing, iteration, and consistency.

Clusters with Machine
and Swarm

This chapter covers

- Creating virtual machines running Docker with Docker Machine
- Integrating with and managing remote Docker daemons
- An introduction to Docker Swarm clusters
- Provisioning whole Swarm clusters with Docker Machine
- Managing containers in a cluster
- Swarm solutions to container scheduling and service discovery

The bulk of this book is about interacting with Docker on a single machine. In the real world, you'll work with several machines at the same time. Docker is a great building block for creating large-scale server software. In such environments, you encounter all sort of new problems that aren't addressed by the Docker engine directly.

How can a user launch an environment where different services run on different hosts? How will services in such a distributed environment locate service

248

dependencies? How can a user quickly create and manage large sets of Docker hosts in a provider-agnostic way? How should services be scaled for availability and failover? With services spread all over a set of hosts, how will the system know to direct traffic from load balancers?

The isolation benefits that containers provide are localized to a given machine. But as the initial shipping container metaphor prophesied, the container abstraction makes all sorts of tooling possible. Chapter 11 talked about Docker Compose, a tool for defining services and environments. In this chapter, you'll read about Docker Machine and Docker Swarm. These tools address the problems that Docker users encounter when provisioning machines, orchestrating deployments, and running clustered server software.

Docker Engine and Docker Compose simplify the lives of developers and operations personnel by abstracting the host from contained software. Docker Machine and Docker Swarm help system administrators and infrastructure engineers extend those abstractions into clustered environments.

12.1 Introducing Docker Machine

The first step in learning about and solving distributed systems problems is building a distributed system. Docker Machine can create and tear down whole fleets of Docker-enabled hosts in a matter of seconds. Learning how to use this tool is essential for anyone who wants to learn how to use Docker in distributed cloud or local virtual environments.

Your choice of driver

Docker Machine ships with a number of drivers out of the box. Each driver integrates Docker Machine with a different virtual machine technology or cloud-based virtual computing provider. Every cloud platform has its advantages and disadvantages. There's no difference between a local host and a remote host from the perspective of a Docker client.

Using a local virtual machine driver like VirtualBox will minimize the cost of running the examples in this chapter, but you should consider choosing a driver for your preferred cloud provider instead. There is something powerful about knowing that the commands you'll issue here are actually managing real-world resources and that the examples you will deploy are going to be running on the internet. At that point, you're only a few domain-specific steps away from building real products.

If you do decide to use a cloud provider for these examples, you'll need to configure your environment with the provider-specific information (like access key and secret key) as well as substitute driver-specific flags in any commands in this chapter.

You can find detailed information about the driver-specific flags by running the `docker-machine help create` command or consulting online documentation.

12.1.1 *Building and managing Docker Machines*

Between the `docker` command line and Compose, you've been introduced to several commands. This section introduces commands for the `docker-machine` command-line program. Because these tools are all so similar in form and function, this section will make the introduction through a small set of examples. If you want to learn more about the `docker-machine` command line, you can always use the `help` command:

```
docker-machine help
```

The first and most important thing to know how to do with Docker Machine is how to create Docker hosts. The next three commands will create three hosts using the VirtualBox driver. Each command will create a new virtual machine on your computer:

```
docker-machine create --driver virtualbox host1
docker-machine create --driver virtualbox host2
docker-machine create --driver virtualbox host3
```

After you run these three commands (they can take a few minutes), you'll have three Docker hosts managed by Docker Machine. Docker Machine tracks these machines with a set of files in your home directory (under ~/.docker/machine/). They describe the hosts you have created, the certificate authority certificates used to establish secure communications with the hosts, and a disk image used for VirtualBox-based hosts.

Docker Machine can be used to list, inspect, and upgrade your fleet as well. Use the `ls` subcommand to get a list of managed machines:

```
docker-machine ls
```

That command will display results similar to the following:

```
NAME     ACTIVE    DRIVER       STATE     URL                           SWARM
host1              virtualbox   Running   tcp://192.168.99.100:2376
host2              virtualbox   Running   tcp://192.168.99.101:2376
host3              virtualbox   Running   tcp://192.168.99.102:2376
```

This command will list each machine, the driver it was created with, its state, and the URL where the Docker daemon can be reached. If you're using Docker Machine to run Docker locally, you'll have another entry in this list, and that entry will likely be marked as `active`. The active machine (indicated with an asterisk under the ACTIVE column) is the one that your environment is currently configured to communicate with. Any commands issued with the `docker` or `docker-compose` command-line interface will connect with the daemon on the active machine.

If you want to know more about a specific machine or look up a specific part of its configuration, you can use the `inspect` subcommand:

```
docker-machine inspect host1                                    ◀─┐ JSON document describing
docker-machine inspect --format "{{.Driver.IPAddress}}" host1    the machine
                                                               ◀─┐ Just the
                                                                  IP address
```

The `inspect` subcommand for `docker-machine` is very similar to the `docker inspect` command. You can even use the same Go template syntax (http://golang.org/pkg/text/template/) to transform the raw JSON document that describes the machine. This example used a template to retrieve the IP address of the machine. If you needed that in practice, you would use the `ip` subcommand:

```
docker-machine ip host1
```

Docker Machine lets you build a fleet with relative ease, and it's important that you can maintain that fleet with the same ease. Any managed machine can be upgraded with the `upgrade` subcommand:

```
docker-machine upgrade host3
```

This command will result in output like the following:

```
Stopping machine to do the upgrade...
Upgrading machine host3...
Downloading ...
Starting machine back up...
Starting VM...
```

The upgrade procedure stops the machine, downloads an updated version of the software, and restarts the machine. With this command, you can perform rolling upgrades to your fleet with minimal effort.

You will occasionally need to manipulate files on one of your machines or access the terminal on a machine directly. It could be that you need to retrieve or prepare the contents of a bind mount volume. Other times you may need to test the network from the host or customize the host configuration. In those cases, you can use the `ssh` and `scp` subcommands.

When you create or register a machine with Docker Machine, it creates or imports an SSH private key file. That private key can be used to authenticate as a privileged user on the machine over the SSH protocol. The `docker-machine ssh` command will authenticate with the target machine and bind your terminal to a shell on the machine.

For example, if you wanted to create a file on the machine named host1, you could issue the following commands:

```
docker-machine ssh host1        ◀─┐ Bind your terminal
                                    to shell on host1
touch dog.file
exit                            ◀─┐ Exit remote shell
                                    and stop command
```

It seems a bit silly to use a fully bound terminal to run a single command. If you don't need a fully interactive terminal, you can alternatively specify the command to run as an additional argument to the `ssh` subcommand. Run the following command to write the name of a dog to the file you just created:

```
docker-machine ssh host1 "echo spot > dog.file"
```

If you have files on one machine that you need to copy elsewhere, you can use the `scp` subcommand to do so securely. The `scp` subcommand takes two arguments: a source host and file and a destination host and file. Try it for yourself and copy the file you just created from host1 to host2, and then use the ssh subcommand to view it on host2:

```
docker-machine scp host1:dog.file host2:dog.file
docker-machine ssh host2 "cat dog.file"
```
⟵⌐ **Outputs: spot**

The SSH-related commands are critical for customizing configuration, retrieving volume contents, and performing other host-related maintenance. The rest of the commands that you need to build and maintain fleets are predictable.

The commands for starting, stopping (or killing), and removing a machine are just like equivalent commands for working with containers. The docker-machine command offers four subcommands: start, stop, kill, and rm:

```
docker-machine stop host2
docker-machine kill host3
docker-machine start host2
docker-machine rm host1 host2 host3
```

This section covered the bulk of the basic mechanics for building and maintaining a fleet with Docker Machine. The next section demonstrates how you can use Docker Machine to configure your client environment to work with those machines and how to access the machines directly.

12.1.2 *Configuring Docker clients to work with remote daemons*

Docker Machine accounts for and tracks the state of the machines that it manages. You can use Docker Machine to upgrade Docker on remote hosts, open SSH connections, and securely copy files between hosts. But Docker clients like the docker command-line interface or docker-compose are designed to connect to a single Docker host at a time. For that reason, one of the most important functions of Docker Machine is producing environment configuration for an active Docker host.

The relationship between Docker Machine, Docker clients, and the environment is illustrated in figure 12.1.

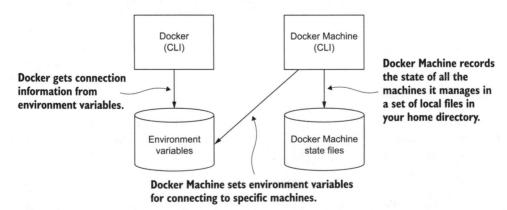

Figure 12.1 **The relationship between** docker, docker-machine, **and relevant state sources**

Get started learning how to manage your Docker environment by creating a couple new machines and activating one. Start by running `create`:

```
docker-machine create --driver virtualbox machine1
docker-machine create --driver virtualbox machine2
```

In order to activate this new machine, you must update your environment. Docker Machine includes a subcommand named `env`. The `env` subcommand attempts to automatically detect the user's shell and print commands to configure the environment to connect to a specific machine. If it can't automatically detect the user's shell, you can set the specific shell with the `--shell` flag:

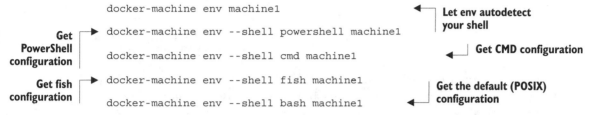

Each of these commands will print out the list of shell-specific commands that need to be run along with a comment on how to invoke `docker-machine` so that these are executed automatically. For example, to set machine1 as the active machine, you can execute the `docker-machine env` command in a POSIX shell:

```
eval "$(docker-machine env machine1)"
```

If you use Windows and run PowerShell, you would run a command like the following:

```
docker-machine env --shell=powershell machine1 | Invoke-Expression
```

You can validate that you've activated machine1 by running the `active` subcommand. Alternatively, you can check the `ACTIVE` column on the output from the `ls` subcommand:

```
docker-machine active
docker-machine ls
```

Any client that observes the environment configuration on your local computer will use the Docker Remote API provided at the specified URL for the active machine. When the active machine is changed, so will the targets of any Docker client commands be changed. The state of this environment is illustrated in figure 12.2.

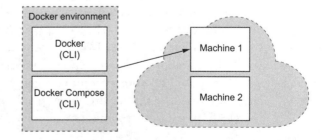

Figure 12.2 One of two machines created with Docker Machine has been activated in the local environment. Docker clients will use the Docker API provided by that machine.

Create a few containers and experience for yourself how simple and subtle it is to work with multiple machines. Start by pulling an image onto the active machine:

```
docker pull dockerinaction/ch12_painted
```

Images pulled onto an active machine will only be pulled onto that machine. This means that if you'll be using some common image across your fleet, you'll need to pull that image on each of those machines. This is important to understand if minimizing container startup time is important. In those cases, you'll want to pull on as many machines in parallel as possible and before container-creation time. Before you start a container with this image, change the active machine to machine2 and list the images:

```
eval "$(docker-machine env machine2)"
docker images
```
◀── **Replace with equivalent command appropriate for your shell**

The output from the images subcommand should be empty. This example helps illustrate the need to pull images on each machine independently. This machine, machine2, has never had any images installed.

Next, pull the image and run a container for dockerinaction/ch12_painted on machine2:

```
docker run -t dockerinaction/ch12_painted \
    Tiny turtles tenderly touch tough turnips.
```

Now compare the list of containers on machine1 with those on machine2:

```
docker ps -a
eval "$(docker-machine env machine1)"
docker ps -a
```
◀── **Replace with equivalent command appropriate for your shell**

Again, the list is empty because no containers have been created on machine1. This simple example should help illustrate how easy it is to work with multiple machines. It should also illustrate how confusing it can be to manually connect to, orchestrate, and schedule work across a sizable fleet of machines. Unless you specifically query for the active host, it's difficult to keep track of where your Docker clients are directed as the number of machines you use increases.

Orchestration can be simplified by taking advantage of Docker Compose, but Compose is like any other Docker client and will use only the Docker daemon that your environment has been configured to use. If you were to launch an environment with Compose and your current configuration where machine1 is active, all the services described by that environment would be created on machine1. Before moving on, clean up your environment by removing both machine1 and machine2:

```
docker-machine rm machine1 machine2
```

Docker Machine is a great tool for building and managing machines in a Docker-based fleet. Docker Compose provides orchestration for Docker container-based services. The main problems that remain are scheduling containers across a fleet of Docker machines and later discovering where those services have been deployed. Docker Swarm will provide the solutions.

12.2 *Introducing Docker Swarm*

Unless you've worked in a distributed systems environment before or built out dynamic deployment topologies, the problems that Docker Swarm solves will require some effort to understand. This section dives deeply into those and explains how Swarm addresses each from a high level.

When people encounter the first problem, they may ask themselves, "Which machine should I choose to run a given container?" Organizing the containers you need to run across a fleet of machines is not a trivial task. It used to be the case that we would deploy different pieces of software to different machines. Using the machine as a unit of deployment made automation simpler to reason about and implement, given existing tooling. When a machine is your unit of deployment, figuring out which machine should run a given program is not a question you need to answer. The answer is always "a new one." Now, with Linux containers for isolation and Docker for container tooling, the remaining major concerns are efficiency of resource usage, the performance characteristics of each machine's hardware, and network locality. Selecting a machine based on these concerns is called *scheduling*.

After someone figures out a solution to the first problem, they'll immediately ask, "Now that my service has been deployed somewhere in my network, how can other services find it?" When you delegate scheduling to an automated process, you can't know where services will be deployed beforehand. If you can't know where a service will be located, how can other services use it? Traditionally, server software uses DNS to resolve a known name to a set of network locations. DNS provides an appropriate lookup interface, but writing data is another problem altogether. Advertising the availability of a service at a specific location is called registration, and resolving the location of a named service is called service discovery.

In this chapter you learn how Swarm solves these problems by building a Swarm cluster with Docker Machine, exploring scheduling algorithms, and deploying the Coffee API example.

12.2.1 *Building a Swarm cluster with Docker Machine*

A Swarm cluster is made up of two types of machines. A machine running Swarm in management mode is called a manager. A machine that runs a Swarm agent is called a node.

In all other ways, Swarm managers and nodes are just like any other Docker machines. These programs require no special installation or privileged access to the

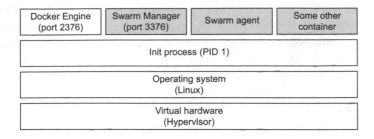

Figure 12.3   Swarm, Swarm Manager, and another program run in containers on an otherwise typical virtual machine running the Docker engine.

machines. They run in Docker containers. Figure 12.3 illustrates the computing stack of a typical Swarm manager machine. It is running the manager program, the Swarm agent, and another container.

Docker Machine can provision Swarm clusters as easily as standalone Docker machines. The only difference is a small set of additional command-line parameters that are included when you use the `create` subcommand.

The first, `--swarm`, indicates that the machine being created should run the Swarm agent software and join a cluster. Second, using the `--swarm-master` parameter will instruct Docker Machine to configure the new machine as a Swarm manager. Third, every type of machine in a Swarm cluster requires a way to locate and identify the cluster it's joining (or managing). The `--swarm-discovery` parameter takes an additional argument that specifies the unique identifier of the cluster. Figure 12.4 illustrates a small cluster of machines and a standalone machine for contrast.

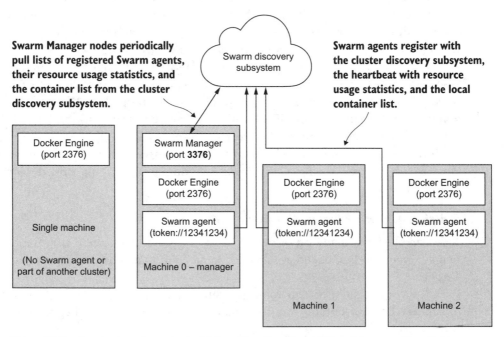

Figure 12.4   Swarm manager and agent interaction through a cluster discovery subsystem

In this illustration you can see that the Swarm agent on each node communicates with a Swarm discovery subsystem to advertise its membership in a cluster identified by token://12341234. Additionally, the single machine running the Swarm manager polls the Swarm discovery subsystem for an updated list of nodes in the cluster. Before diving into the Swarm discovery subsystem and other mechanics at work here, use Docker Machine to create a new Swarm cluster of your own. The next few commands will guide you through this process.

The first step in creating your own Swarm cluster is creating a cluster identifier. Like most subsystems abstracted by Docker, the Swarm discovery subsystem can be changed to fit your environment. By default, Swarm uses a free and hosted solution provided on Docker Hub. Run the following commands to create a new cluster identifier:

Create a new local Docker
```
docker-machine create --driver virtualbox local
eval "$(docker-machine env local)"     ◄── Replace with equivalent command
                                            appropriate for your shell
docker run --rm swarm create
```

The last command should output a hexadecimal identifier that looks like this:

```
b26688613694dbc9680cd149d389e279
```

Copy the resulting value and substitute that for <TOKEN> in the next three commands. The following set of commands will create a three-node Swarm cluster using virtual machines on your computer. Note that the first command uses the `--swarm-master` parameter to indicate that the machine being created should manage the new Swarm cluster:

```
docker-machine create \
    --driver virtualbox \
    --swarm \
    --swarm-discovery token://<TOKEN> \
    --swarm-master \           ◄─┐ Note this flag
    machine0-manager

docker-machine create \
    --driver virtualbox \
    --swarm \
    --swarm-discovery token://<TOKEN> \
    machine1

docker-machine create \
    --driver virtualbox \
    --swarm \
    --swarm-discovery token://<TOKEN> \
    machine2
```

These machines can be identified as part of a Swarm cluster in output from the `ls` subcommand of `docker-machine`. The name of the cluster manager is included in the column labeled `SWARM` for any node in a cluster:

```
NAME              ... URL                      SWARM
machine0-manager      tcp://192.168.99.106:2376 machine0-manager (manager)
machine1              tcp://192.168.99.107:2376 machine0-manager
machine2              tcp://192.168.99.108:2376 machine0-manager
```

A Docker client could be configured to work with any of these machines individually. They're all running the Docker daemon with an exposed TCP socket (like any other Docker machine). But when you configure your clients to use the Swarm endpoint on the master, you can start working with the cluster like one big machine.

12.2.2 *Swarm extends the Docker Remote API*

Docker Swarm manager endpoints expose the Swarm API. Swarm clients can use that API to control or inspect a cluster. More than that, though, the Swarm API is an extension to the Docker Remote API. This means that any Docker client can connect directly to a Swarm endpoint and treat a cluster as if it were a single machine.

Figure 12.5 illustrates how Swarm manager delegates work—specified by Docker clients—to nodes in the cluster.

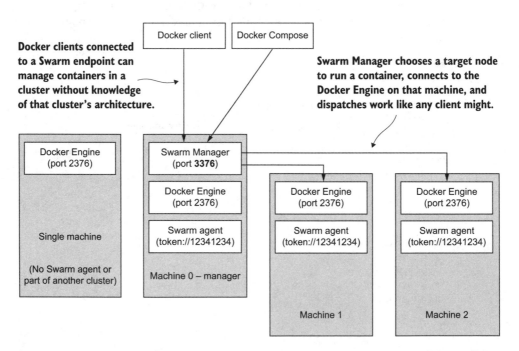

Figure 12.5   Deploying a container in a cluster requires no knowledge of the cluster because the Swarm API extends the Docker Remote API.

The implementation of the Docker Remote API provided by Swarm is very different from the Docker Engine. Depending on the specific feature, a single request from a client may impact one or many Swarm nodes.

Configure your environment to use the Swarm cluster that you created in the last section. To do so, add the `--swarm` parameter to the `docker-machine env` subcommand. If you're using a POSIX-compatible shell, run the following command:

```
eval "$(docker-machine env --swarm machine0-manager)"
```

If you're using PowerShell, the run the following:

```
docker-machine env --swarm machine0-master | Invoke-Expression
```

When your environment is configured to access a Swarm endpoint, the `docker` command-line interface will use Swarm features. For example, using the `docker info` command will report information for the whole cluster instead of details for one specific daemon:

```
docker info
```

That output will look similar to the following:

```
Containers: 4
Images: 3
Role: primary
Strategy: spread
Filters: affinity, health, constraint, port, dependency
Nodes: 3
 machine0-manager: 192.168.99.110:2376
  ? Containers: 2
  ? Reserved CPUs: 0 / 1
  ? Reserved Memory: 0 B / 1.022 GiB
  ? Labels: executiondriver=native-0.2, kernelversion=4.0.9-...
 machine1: 192.168.99.111:2376
  ? Containers: 1
  ? Reserved CPUs: 0 / 1
  ? Reserved Memory: 0 B / 1.022 GiB
  ? Labels: executiondriver=native-0.2, kernelversion=4.0.9-...
 machine2: 192.168.99.112:2376
  ? Containers: 1
  ? Reserved CPUs: 0 / 1
  ? Reserved Memory: 0 B / 1.022 GiB
  ? Labels: executiondriver=native-0.2, kernelversion=4.0.9-...
CPUs: 3
Total Memory: 3.065 GiB
Name: 942f56b2349a
```

Notice that this sample output includes a configuration summary for the cluster, a list of the nodes in the cluster, and a description of the resources available on each node. Before moving on, take a moment to reflect on what's happening here. This is the first evidence you've seen that the nodes in your cluster are advertising their endpoint and that the manager is discovering those nodes. Further, all this information is specific to a Swarm cluster, but you were able to retrieve it through the same `docker` command that you would use with a standalone machine. Next, create a container in your cluster:

```
docker run -t -d --name hello-swarm \
    dockerinaction/ch12_painted \
    Hello Swarm
```

This time you ran a ch12_painted container in detached mode. The output will be in the logs, and the container will not have been automatically removed. You can view the output of that container with the `logs` subcommand:

```
docker logs hello-swarm
```

```
 _    _        _  _          _____                                   
| |  | |      | || |        / ____|                                  
| |__| |  ___ | || |  ___  | (___   __      __   __ _   _ __  _ __ ___  
|  __  | / _ \| || | / _ \  \___ \  \ \ /\ / /  / _` | | '__|| '_ ` _ \ 
| |  | ||  __/| || || (_) | ____) |  \ V  V /  | (_| | | |   | | | | | |
|_|  |_| \___||_||_| \___/ |_____/    \_/\_/    \__,_| |_|   |_| |_| |_|
```

This command looks just like it would if you were accessing a standalone machine. In fact, the protocol is the same, so any Docker client that can fetch logs from a Docker Remote endpoint can retrieve logs from a Swarm endpoint. You can discover which machine has the container with the `ps` subcommand. Use filtering to grab the container named `hello-swarm`:

```
docker ps -a -f name=hello-swarm
```

Notice in the `NAMES` column that the container name is prefixed with one of the machine names in your cluster. This could be any of the nodes. If you create a similar container with a slightly different name like `hello-world2`, the cluster may schedule that container on a different host. Before you do that, though, take a moment to examine the cluster information again:

```
docker info
```

Notice the number of containers and images in the cluster:

```
Containers: 5
Images: 4
```

The `Containers` and `Images` numbers are a non-distinct sum for the cluster. Because you have three nodes in the cluster, you need three agent containers and one manager container. The remaining container is the `hello-swarm` container that you just created. The four images are made up of the three copies of the `swarm` image and one copy of `dockerinaction/ch12_painted`. The thing to notice here is that when you create a container with the `run` command, the required image will be pulled only on the host where the container is scheduled. That's why there's only one copy of the image instead of three.

If you want to make sure that the images you use are pulled on each of the machines in the cluster, you can use the `pull` subcommand. Doing so will eliminate any warm-up latency if a container is scheduled on a node that doesn't have the required image:

```
docker pull dockerinaction/ch12_painted
```

This command will launch a pull operation on each node:

```
machine0-manager: Pulling dockerinaction/ch12_painted:latest... :
    downloaded
machine1: Pulling dockerinaction/ch12_painted:latest... : downloaded
machine2: Pulling dockerinaction/ch12_painted:latest... : downloaded
```

Similarly, removing containers will remove the named container from whichever machine it is located on, and removing an image will remove it from all nodes in the cluster. Swarm hides all this complexity from the user and in doing so frees them to work on more interesting problems.

Not every decision can be made in a vacuum, though. Different algorithms for scheduling containers can have significant impact on the efficiency and performance characteristics of your cluster. Next, you'll learn about different algorithms and hints the user can provide to manipulate the Swarm scheduler.

12.3 Swarm scheduling

One of the most powerful arguments for adopting Linux containers as your unit of deployment is that you can make more efficient use of your hardware and cut hardware and power costs. Doing that requires intelligent placement of containers on your fleet.

Swarm provides three different scheduling algorithms. Each has its own advantages and disadvantages. The scheduling algorithm is set when you create a Swarm manager. A user can tune the scheduling algorithms for a given Swarm cluster by providing constraints for specific containers.

Constraints can be set for each container, but because the scheduling algorithm is set on the Swarm manager, you need to specify that setting when you create your cluster. The Docker Machine `create` subcommand provides the `--swarm-strategy` parameter for this purpose. The default selection is `spread`.

12.3.1 The Spread algorithm

A Swarm cluster that uses the Spread algorithm will try to schedule containers on under-used nodes and spread a workload over all nodes equally. The algorithm specifically ranks all the nodes in the fleet by their resource usage and then ranks those with the same resource rank according to the number of containers each is running. The machine with the most resources available and fewest containers will be selected to run a new container. Figure 12.6 illustrates how three equal-size containers might be scheduled in a cluster with three similar nodes.

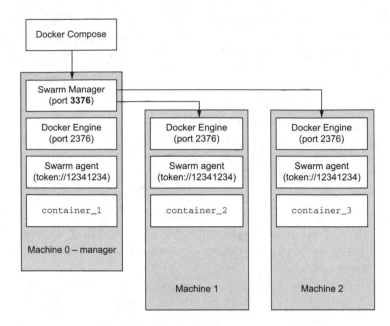

Figure 12.6   **The Spread algorithm spreads a workload evenly across the nodes in a cluster.**

You can see in figure 12.6 that each of the three scheduled containers was placed on a separate host. At this point, any of these three machines would be a candidate to run a fourth container. The chosen machine will be running two containers when that fourth container is scheduled. Scheduling a fifth container will cause the cluster to choose between the two machines that are running only a single container. The selection rank of a machine is determined by the number of containers it's running relative to all other machines in the cluster. Those machines running fewer containers will have a higher rank. In the event that two machines have the same rank, one will be chosen at random.

The Spread algorithm will try to use your whole fleet evenly. Doing so minimizes the potential impact of random machine failure and ties individual machine congestion with fleet congestion. Consider an application that runs a large, varying number of replica containers.

Create a new Compose environment description in `flock.json` and define a single service named `bird`. The `bird` service periodically paints `bird` on standard out:

```
bird:
  image: dockerinaction/ch12_painted
  command: bird
  restart: always
```

Watch Swarm distribute 10 copies of the `bird` service across the cluster when you use Compose to scale up:

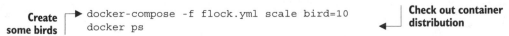

Create some birds
```
docker-compose -f flock.yml scale bird=10
docker ps
```
Check out container distribution

The output for the ps command will include 10 containers. The name of each container will be prefixed with the name of the machine where it has been deployed. These will have been evenly distributed across the nodes in the cluster. Use the following two commands to clean up the containers in this experiment:

```
docker-compose -f flock.yml kill
docker-compose -f flock.yml rm -vf
```

This algorithm works best in situations where resource reservations have been set on containers and there is a low degree of variance in those limits. As the resources required by containers and the resources provided by nodes diversify, the Spread algorithm can cause issues. Consider the distribution in figure 12.7.

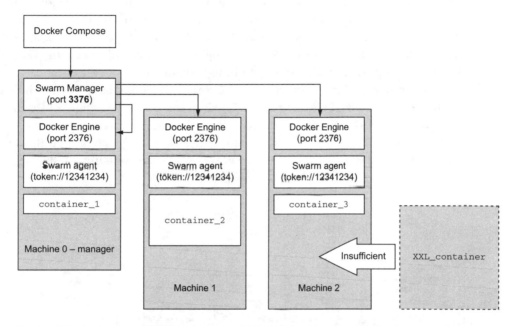

Figure 12.7   A new container is unable to be scheduled due to a poor distribution.

Figure 12.7 illustrates how introducing higher variance in the resources required by containers can cause poor performance of the Spread algorithm. In this scenario, the new container, XXL_container, can't be scheduled because no machine has sufficient resources. In retrospect, it's clear that the scheduler might have avoided this situation if it had scheduled container_3 on either Machine0 or Machine1. You can avoid this type of situation without changing the scheduling algorithm if you use filters.

12.3.2 *Fine-tune scheduling with filters*

Before the Swarm scheduler applies a scheduling algorithm, it gathers and filters a set of candidate nodes according to the Swarm configuration and the needs of the

container. Each candidate node will pass through each of the filters configured for
the cluster. The set of active filters used by a cluster can be discovered with the `docker`
`info` command. When a `docker` client is configured for a Swarm endpoint, output
from the `info` subcommand will include a line similar to the following:

```
Filters: affinity, health, constraint, port, dependency
```

A cluster with these filters enabled will reduce the set of candidate nodes to those that
have any affinity, constraint, dependency, or port required by the container being
scheduled and to those in which the node is healthy.

An affinity is a requirement for colocation with another container or image. A constraint is a requirement on some machine property like kernel version, storage driver,
network speed, disk type, and so on. Although you can use a set of predefined
machines for defining constraints, you can also create constraints on any label that
has been applied to a node's daemon. A dependency is a modeled container dependency such as a link or shared volume. Finally, a port filter will reduce the set of candidate nodes to those with the requested host port available.

The poor distribution described in figure 12.7 could have been avoided with
labeled nodes and a label constraint defined on the containers. Figure 12.8 illustrates
a better way to configure the system.

In figure 12.8, both Machine0 and Machine1 were created with the label
`size=small`, and Machine2 was labeled `size=xxl`. When containers 1–3 were created,

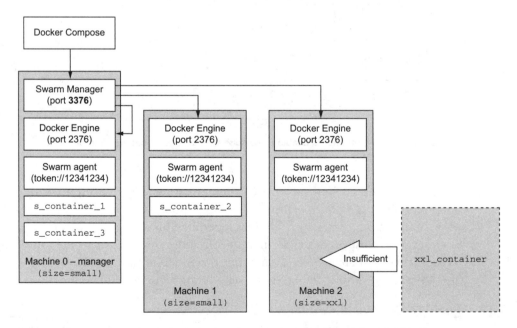

**Figure 12.8 Node labels and constrained containers prune the scheduling candidates to
appropriate nodes.**

they provided an environment variable that indicated a constraint on nodes labeled size=small. That constraint narrows the node candidate pool to Machine0 or Machine1. Those containers are spread across those nodes as in other examples. When the xxl_container is created with a constraint on nodes labeled size=xxl, the candidate pool is narrowed to a single node. As long as that one node is not filtered for any other reason, it will be scheduled on Machine2.

You can label the nodes that you create in your cluster by setting the --engine-label parameter of the docker-machine create command. For example, you'd use the following command to create a new node labeled with size=small in your cluster:

```
docker-machine create -d virtualbox \
    --swarm \
    --swarm-discovery token://<YOUR TOKEN> \
    --engine-label size=small \          ◄─┐ Apply an engine label
    little-machine

docker-machine create -d virtualbox \
    --swarm \
    --swarm-discovery token://<YOUR TOKEN> \
    --engine-label size=xxl \            ◄─┐ Apply an engine label
    big-machine
```

In addition to whatever labels you might apply to nodes, containers can specify constraints on standard properties that all nodes will specify by default:

- node—The name or ID of the node in the cluster
- storagedriver—The name of the storage driver used by the node
- executiondriver—The name of the execution driver used by the node
- kernelversion—The version of the Linux kernel powering the node
- operatingsystem—The operating system name on the node

Each node provides these values to the Swarm master. You can discover what each node in your cluster is reporting with the docker info subcommand.

Containers communicate their affinity and constraint requirements using environment variables. Each constraint or affinity rule is set using a separate environment variable. A rule that the xxl_container might have applied in the previous example would look like this:

```
docker run -d -e constraint:size==xxl \     ◄─┐ Constraint
    -m 4G \                                      environment variable
    -c 512 \
    postgres
```

Constraint rules are specified using the prefix constraint: on the environment variable. To set a container affinity rule, set an environment variable with a prefix of affinity: and an appropriate affinity definition. For example, if you want to schedule a container created from the nginx:latest image, but you want to make sure that the candidate node already has the image installed, you would set an environment variable like so:

```
docker run -d -e affinity:image==nginx \
    -p 80:80 \
    nginx
```
◄─── **Affinity environment variable**

Any node where the `nginx` image has been installed will be among the candidate node set. If, alternatively, you wanted to run a similar program, like `ha-proxy`, for comparison and needed to make sure that program runs on separate nodes, you could create a negated affinity:

```
docker run -d -e affinity:image!=nginx \
    -p 8080:8080 \
    haproxy
```
◄─── **Anti-affinity environment variable**

This command would eliminate any node that contains the `nginx` image from the candidate node set. The two rules you've seen so far use different rule operators, `==` and `!=`, but other components of the rule syntax make it highly expressive. An affinity or constraint rule is made of a key, an operator, and a value. Whereas keys must be known and fully qualified, values can have one of three forms:

- Fully qualified with alphanumeric characters, dots, hyphens, and underscores (for example, `my-favorite.image-1`)
- A pattern specified in glob syntax (for example, `my-favorite.image-*`)
- A full (Go-flavored) regular expression (for example, `/my-[a-z]+\.image-[0-9]+/`)

The last tool for creating effective rules is the soft operator. Add a tilde to the end of the operator when you want to make a scheduling suggestion instead of a rule. For example, if you wanted to suggest that Swarm schedule an NGINX container on a node where the image has already been installed but schedule it if the condition can't be met, then you would use a rule like the following:

```
docker run -d -e affinity:image==~nginx \
    -p 80:80 \
    nginx
```
◄─── **Suggested affinity environment variable**

Filters can be used to customize any of the scheduling algorithms. With foresight into your anticipated workload and the varying properties of your infrastructure, filters can be used to great effect.

The Spread algorithm's defining trait (even fleet usage by container volume) will always be applied to the filtered set of nodes, and so it will always conflict with one cloud feature. Automatically scaling the number of nodes in a cluster is feasible when only some nodes become unused. Until that condition is met, the underlying technology (be that Amazon Web Services EC2 or any other) will be unable to scale down your cluster. This results in low utilization of an oversized fleet. Adopting the BinPack scheduling algorithm can help in this case.

12.3.3 *Scheduling with BinPack and Random*

Two other scheduling algorithms you should understand are BinPack and Random. The BinPack scheduling algorithm prefers to make the most efficient use of each node before scheduling work on another. This algorithm uses the fewest number of nodes required to support the workload. Random provides a distribution that can be a compromise between Spread and BinPack. Each node in the candidate pool has an equal opportunity of being selected, but that doesn't guarantee that the distribution will realize evenly across that pool.

There are a few caveats worth reviewing before you adopt either algorithm over Spread. Figure 12.9 illustrates how the BinPack algorithm might schedule three containers.

BinPack can make informed decisions about packing efficiency only if it knows the resource requirements of the container being scheduled. For that reason, BinPack makes sense only if you're dedicated to creating resource reservations for the containers in your system. Using resource-isolation features such as memory limits, CPU weights, and block IO weights will isolate your containers from neighboring resource abuses. Although these limits don't create local reservations for resources, the Swarm scheduler will treat them as reservations to prevent overburdening any one host.

BinPack addresses the initial problem you encountered with the Spread algorithm. BinPack will reserve large blocks of resources on nodes by prioritizing efficient use of each node. The algorithm takes a greedy approach, selecting the busiest node with

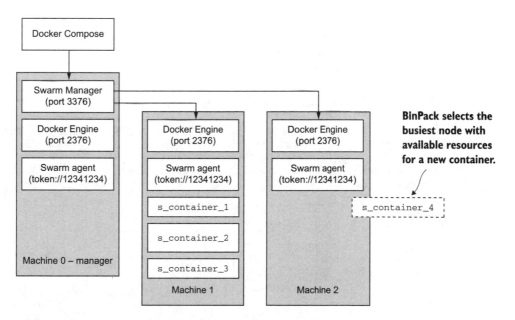

Figure 12.9 BinPack scheduling on a new node only when the busiest node has insufficient resources to take more work

the fewest resources that are still sufficient to meet the requirements of the container being scheduled. This is sometimes called a best fit.

BinPack is particularly useful if the containers in your system have high variance in resource requirements or if your project requires a minimal fleet and the option of automatically downsizing. Whereas the Spread algorithm makes the most sense in systems with a dedicated fleet, BinPack makes the most sense in a wholly virtual machine fleet with scale-on-demand features. This flexibility is gained at the cost of reliability.

BinPack creates a minimal number of maximally critical nodes. This distribution increases the likelihood of failure on the few busy nodes and increases the impact of any such failure. This may be an acceptable trade, but it's certainly one you should keep in mind when building critical systems.

The Random algorithm provides a compromise between Spread and BinPack. It relies on probability alone for selecting from the candidate nodes. In practice, this means it's possible for your fleet to simultaneously contain busy nodes and idle nodes. Figure 12.10 illustrates one possible distribution of three containers in a three-node candidate set.

This algorithm will probably distribute work fairly over a fleet and probably accommodate high variance in resource requirements in your container set. But *probably* means that you have no guarantees. It's possible that the cluster will contain hot spots or that it will be used inefficiently and lack large resource blocks to accommodate large containers. Entropy-focused engineers may gravitate toward this algorithm so that the greater system must account for these possibilities.

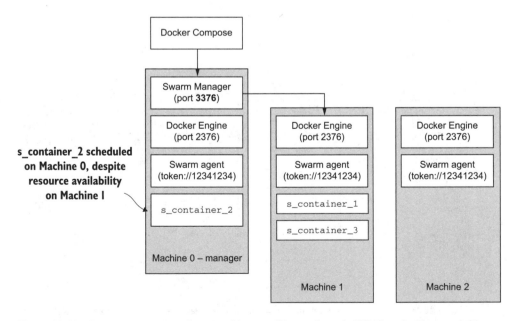

Figure 12.10   The Random scheduling algorithm considers only probability in selecting a machine.

As Swarm matures and more data from nodes becomes available, new scheduling algorithms may emerge. The project itself is young, but these three provide the fundamental building blocks for robust systems. Scheduling lets the system choose where your containers will run, and the last problem Swarm tackles is helping those containers locate each other with a service discovery abstraction.

12.4 Swarm service discovery

Any distributed system requires some mechanism to locate its pieces. If that distributed system is made up of several processes on the same machine, they need to agree on some named shared memory pool or queue. If the components are designed to interact over a network, they need to agree on names for each other and decide on a mechanism to resolve those names. Most of the time, networked applications rely on DNS for name-to-IP address resolution.

Docker uses container links to inject static configuration into a container's name-resolution system. In doing so, contained applications need not be aware that they're running in a container. But a stand-alone Docker engine has no visibility into services running on other hosts, and service discovery is limited to the containers running locally.

Alternatively, Docker allows a user to set the default DNS servers and search domains for each container or every container on a host. That DNS server can be any system that exposes a DNS interface. In the last few years, several such systems have emerged, and a rich ecosystem has evolved to solve service discovery in a multi-host environment.

As those systems evolved, Docker announced the Swarm project and a common interface for this type of system. The goal of the Swarm project is to provide a "batteries included" but optional solution for clustering containers. A major milestone for this project is abstracted service discovery in a multi-host environment. Delivering on that milestone requires the development of several technologies and enhancements to the Docker Engine.

As you reach the end of this book, remember that you're diving into the tail of an unfinished story. These are some of the most rapidly advancing features and tools in the system. You'll see each of these approaches to service discovery in the wild. Just as with most other pieces of the Docker toolset, you're free to adopt or ignore the parts that make sense in your situation. The remainder of this section should help you make an informed decision.

12.4.1 Swarm and single-host networking

The Docker Engine creates local networks behind a bridge network on every machine where it's installed. This topic is explored in depth in chapter 5. Situated as a container deployed on a Docker node, it's beyond the scope of a Swarm agent to restructure that network in reaction to the discovery of other Swarm nodes and containers in the cluster. For that reason, if a Swarm cluster is deployed on Docker machines that

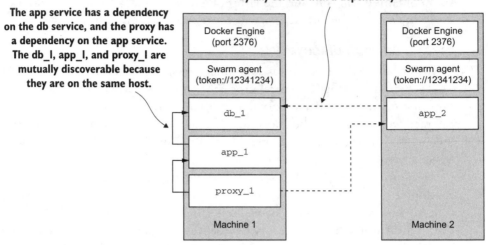

If a new instance of the app service were scheduled on Machine 2, then it would not be able to discover a container filling its dependency on the db service. It would further be undiscoverable by any service with a dependency on it.

The app service has a dependency on the db service, and the proxy has a dependency on the app service. The db_l, app_l, and proxy_l are mutually discoverable because they are on the same host.

Figure 12.11   A three-tiered application deployed in a cluster with single-host networking

operate single-host networks, then containers deployed with Swarm can only discover other containers running on the same host. Figure 12.11 illustrates how single-host networking limits the candidate set for a scheduler.

The dependency filter ensures that a container will never be scheduled on a host where one of its dependencies is undiscoverable. You can try this for yourself by deploying the Coffee API on your existing Swarm cluster.

First, use Git to clone the Compose environment description for a rich Coffee API example:

```
git clone git@github.com:dockerinaction/ch12_coffee_api.git
```

After you run that command, change into the new directory and make sure that your Docker environment is pointed at your Swarm cluster:

```
cd ch12_coffee_api
eval "$(docker-machine env machine0-manager)"
```

Once you've set up your environment, you're ready to launch the example using Docker Compose. The following command will start the environment in your Swarm cluster:

```
docker-compose up -d
```

Now use the docker CLI to view the distribution of the new containers on your cluster. The output will be very wide due to the machine named prefixing all the container names and aliases. For example, a container named "bob" running on machine1 will be displayed as "machine1/bob." You may want to redirect or copy the output to a file for review without wrapping lines:

```
docker ps
```

If you have the `less` command installed, you can use the `-S` parameter to chop the long lines and arrows to navigate:

```
docker ps | less -S
```
← **The less command may not be available on your system**

In examining the output, you'll notice that every container is running on the same machine even though your Swarm is configured to use the Spread algorithm. Once the first container that's a dependency of another was scheduled, the dependency filter excluded any other node from the candidate pool for the others.

Now that the environment is running, you should be able to query the service. Note the name of the machine where the environment has been deployed and substitute that name for <MACHINE> in the following cURL command:

```
curl http://$(docker-machine ip <MACHINE>):8080/api/coffeeshops/
```

If you don't have cURL on your system, you can use your web browser to make a similar request. The output from the request should be familiar:

```
{
  "coffeeshops": []
}
```

Take time to experiment by scaling the coffee service up and down. Examine where Swarm schedules each container. When you've finished with the example, shut it down with `docker-compose stop` and remove the containers with `docker-compose rm -vf`.

Clustering an application is viable for some use cases in spite of this limitation, but the most common use cases are underserved. Server software typically requires multi-host distribution and service discovery. The community has built and adopted several new and existing tools to fill the absence of a solution integrated with Docker.

12.4.2 Ecosystem service discovery and stop-gap measures

The primary interface for network service discovery is DNS. Although software providing DNS has been around for some time, traditional DNS server software uses heavy caching, struggles to provide high-write throughput, and typically lacks membership monitoring. These systems fail to scale in systems with frequent deployments. Modern systems use distributed key-value databases that support high-write throughput, membership management, and even distributed locking facilities.

Examples of modern software include etcd, Consul, ZooKeeper, and Serf. These can be radically different in implementation, but they're all excellent service discovery

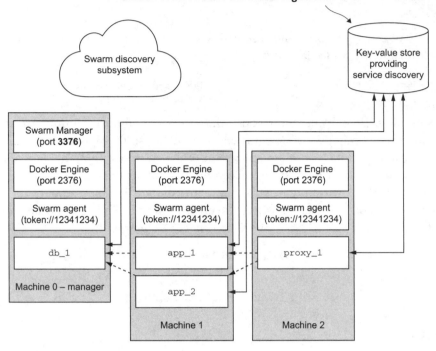

Service names are resolved by an external service discovery system that has been integrated through the DNS configuration of the containers. In these topologies containers are either left to register themselves with the external system, or a bystander watching individual daemon event streams will handle registration of new containers.

Figure 12.12   Containers on the fleet are responsible for registration and service discovery with an external tool like etcd, Consul, ZooKeeper, or Serf.

providers. Each tool has nuances, advantages, and disadvantages that are beyond the scope of this book. Figure 12.12 illustrates how containers integrate directly with an external service discovery tool over DNS or another protocol like HTTP.

These ecosystem tools are well understood and battle-tested, but integrating this infrastructure concern at the container layer leaks implementation details that should remain hidden by some basic abstraction. Integrating an application inside a container with a specific service-discovery mechanism diminishes the portability of that application. The ideal solution would integrate service registration and discovery at the clustering or network layer provided by Docker Engine and Docker Swarm. With multi-host, networking-enabled Docker Engine and an overlay network technology integrated with a pluggable key-value store, that can become a reality.

12.4.3   *Looking forward to multi-host networking*

The experimental branch of Docker Engine has abstracted networking facilities behind a pluggable interface. That interface is implemented by a number of drivers

Docker engine creates an overlay network and abstracts the service discovery mechanism from
the containers running on any one host. While the underlying mechanics of service discovery and
registration are the same, the abstraction requires less specialization of individual containers.
A Swarm cluster with multi-host networking enabled acts like a single machine.

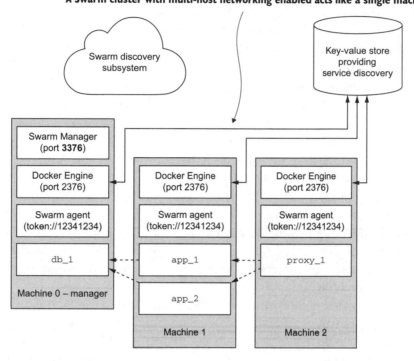

Figure 12.13 Swarm on top of Docker Engine with multi-host networking enables a cluster to
behave as a single machine and containers to act as equal members of a network.

including bridge, host, and overlay. The bridge and host drivers implement the
single-host networking features you're already familiar with. The overlay driver implements an overlay network with IP encapsulation or VXLAN. The overlay network provides routable IP addresses for every container managed by a Docker machine
configured to use the same key-value store. Figure 12.13 illustrates the interactions in
building such a network.

With an overlay network in place, each container gets a unique IP address that's
routable from any other container in the overlay network. The application can stop
doing work to identify or advertise its host IP address and map container ports to host
ports. All that work is performed in the infrastructure layer provided by Docker and
the integrated key-value store.

While we wait for multi-host networking to land in the release branch of Docker
Engine and multi-host Swarm node provisioning with Docker Machine, we can get by
with direct integrations to other ecosystem projects. When this does land, it will be a
major relief to developers and system architects alike.

12.5 *Summary*

Both Docker Machine and Docker Swarm provide functionality that enhances the applications for the Docker Engine. These and other related technologies will help you apply what you have learned in this book as you grow from using Docker on a single computer into managing fleets of containers distributed across many computers. It is important to have a thorough understanding of these points as you grow into this space:

- A user can use Docker Machine to create a local virtual machine or machine in the cloud with a single `create` command.
- The Docker Machine `env` and `config` subcommands can be used to configure Docker clients to work with remote Docker Engines that were provisioned with Docker Machine.
- Docker Swarm is a protocol that is backward-compatible with the Docker Remote API and provides clustering facilities over a set of member nodes.
- A Swarm manager program implements the Swarm API and handles container scheduling for the cluster.
- Docker Machine provides flags for provisioning both Swarm nodes and managers.
- Docker Swarm provides three different scheduling algorithms that can be tuned through the use of filters.
- Labels and other default attributes of a Docker Engine can be used as filtering criteria via container scheduling constraints.
- Container scheduling affinities can be used to place containers on the same host as other containers or images that match a provided pattern or expression.
- When any Docker client is configured to communicate with a Swarm endpoint, that client will interact with the entire Swarm as if it were a single Docker machine.
- Docker Swarm will schedule dependent containers on the same node until multi-host networking is released or you provide another service-discovery mechanism and disable the dependency Swarm filter.
- Multi-host networking will abstract container locality from the concerns of applications within Docker containers. Each container will be a host on the overlay network.

index